The Author

Malcolm Archibald, one of Scotland's most prolific ⸱ ꞏied to write *Dundee at a Glance*. He has a deep ' ⸱ts people. His first degree, in history, wa⸱ was his master's, also in history, and McDonald prize. There is in addition a ⸱ ⸱ city's fine university: his wife took her first d⸱ ⸱ꞏere, and his daughter too is a graduate. After leaving full ⸱ Malcolm Archibald worked for Dundee central post office as a p⸱ ꞏor the McManus museum as a researcher and taught history at Dundee College. This is his fifth book about the city, one of which, *Whales for the Wizard*, his debut novel, won the prestigious Dundee International book prize in 2005. His love for, and admiration of, Dundee and its good citizens is deep-rooted and genuine. As Archibald writes, 'I have found Dundonians to be the most tolerant people in Scotland: warm-hearted, open-handed, hardworking and always keen to talk about their home city.'

DUNDEE AT A GLANCE

Malcolm Archibald

Fort Publishing Ltd

First published in 2016 by Fort Publishing Ltd, Old Belmont House,
12 Robsland Avenue, Ayr, KA7 2RW

Cover design by Mark Blackadder

Photographs by Duncan I. McEwan

Typeset by 3btype.com

Printed by MBM Print SCS Ltd, Glasgow

Cover painting: *The Royal Arch, Dundee* by James Falconer.
Courtesy of Dundee City Council

Back-cover photograph: View from the Law, looking north

ISBN: 978-1-905769-52-0

Preface

Both my wife and I attended Dundee University and we lived and worked in Dundee for so many years that it feels like home. Our son was educated at Menzieshill high school and our younger daughter at the Harris, and both now live in the city. I have found Dundonians to be the most tolerant people in Scotland: warm-hearted, open-handed, hardworking and always keen to talk about their home city. In Dundee, the people matter more than the fabric of the city, but the city itself is worth a second glance.

Mention Dundee and many people immediately respond with the three 'j's' – jute, jam and journalism, three industries for which Dundee was justly renowned. However, this is a false image. The period when Dundee relied on this trio was limited and has long passed. Dundee is a city of many facets. In the course of writing this book I unearthed fact after fact of which I was either only dimly, or even completely, unaware. Some are fascinating, others verge on the incredible. For example, the first-known elephant dissection was carried out just outside Dundee by Dr Patrick Blair on 27 April 1706. The elephant belonged to a circus and was named Florentia. Not many cities can claim a distinction like that, but Dundee is unique in many ways. The city also has a claim to an early aircraft pioneer: Dundee man Preston Watson (1880–1915) was involved in flights from 1903 onward, with his first powered flight said to be in 1909.

This book follows a simple format: there is a general introduction to give a brief history of Dundee, followed by an alphabetical guide to more than six hundred streets of Dundee, with details of the street-name origin and some indication of events that have occurred there. Significant buildings, parks and monuments as well as themes important to Dundee have also been included. Finally, there is a brief conclusion to tie things up.

One last word: this book is not academic in any form. It is intended to be easily accessible for all, an introduction to the city for those who do not know it and a reminder for those who do. Any mistakes and omissions are entirely my own.

Welcome to Dundee.

I would like to thank the following people and institutions. Without their help this book would not have been written: Iain Flett, Dundee city archives; Dundee central library; Inverness College library; Beatrice Faulkner; James McCarroll, for his patient editing. And Cathy, my wife, to whom this book is dedicated, always.

Malcolm Archibald
October 2016

Introduction

From its focal points of the harbour and City Square, Dundee extends its arms east and west in an embrace that welcomes the world. From modest beginnings, the city has expanded along the north shore of the Firth of Tay to become the fourth largest urban centre in Scotland with a population of around 148,000 souls (2014 estimate). It is a fortunate place, blessed with one of the finest situations of any city in Europe.

To the north, the low ridge of the Sidlaw Hills acts as protection from the worst of the Scottish weather, while the ever-altering river Tay washes the city's face and creates some of the splendid views and reflected light she enjoys. Two bridges cross the river to link Dundee to Fife and the south, while roads and railways connect to Perth in the west, and Forfar, Arbroath and Aberdeen in the north. There is also a small airport with regular connections to London. However, despite these definite advantages, it is the sea that has made Dundee what it is.

Dundee is ancient. It was sufficiently important to be designated a burgh in the 1190s and the coat of arms has the motto *Dei Donum*, which means gift of God. That is only one of the possible meanings of the name Dundee, with other suggestions including *Dun Deagh*, Gaelic for fortress of Daigh or Deagh, whoever Daigh might have been, if indeed he ever existed. Whatever the origin of the name, Dundee was one of the most important urban centres of mediaeval Scotland, with its prosperity based around trade and shipping.

Situated seven miles from the North Sea on a navigable river, Dundee was a significant port. As much of its trade was conducted with the Baltic, it is hardly surprising that the town has a similar set-up to the urban centres on the coasts of that northern sea. The early builders knew their business: they gave the wynds between the town centre and the harbour gentle curves to baffle the east-coast wind and to allow easy access from the harbour to the town centre. Couttie's Wynd, the sole useable survivor of these mediaeval streets, gives a flavour of the shape and scale of the original burgh. Dundee was also home to a school that reputedly taught William Wallace, later to become Guardian of Scotland.

However, Dundee's importance had negatives as well as positives, in the shape of unwelcome attention from the English during the Wars of Independence. In 1296 Edward Plantagenet destroyed the church of St Mary's in his self-appointed task of turning Britain into a personal fiefdom. Repelled by the forces of Robert I, the English returned in the sixteenth century, grabbing Broughty castle and other strong points during the period of the 'Rough Wooing', and little more than a century later both the Marquis of Montrose and Cromwell's men, at different times, hammered at the town wall, bringing death and destruction in their wake.

These episodes harmed Dundee's prosperity, but the rugged spirit of the Dundonian dragged the town back from the nadir of wartime destruction to relative prosperity and then to the forefront of world trade. In 1772 the Welsh traveller Thomas Pennant thought Dundee 'a well-built town' with a 'very commodious' harbour and industries that included linen, shoes and saddlery while 'Broughtay' salmon were exported to Holland. A year later the famed Dr Johnson, creator of the dictionary and critic of Scotland, graced Dundee with his self-important presence and termed the town as 'nothing remarkable'. There is no record of what Dundonians thought of the good doctor.

We should also remember the similarly named Samuel Johnston, a scion of the town who could, had he so chosen, have been even more famous than the eminent lexicographer. Johnston was born in Dundee in December 1733 to a mother who was a Scrymgeour, an important family in Dundee history. Three years after his birth Johnston's parents emigrated to North Carolina, then a British colony with a strong thread of Scottish tartan. In time Johnston entered politics, became governor of North Carolina and supported the settlers' side in the War of Independence. He was elected as the new country's first president before George Washington was offered the post, but refused to serve. So there could have been a Dundonian as president of the United States: an intriguing thought. Could we imagine the world with a Dundee-American 'peh' rather than American hamburgers?

By the end of the nineteenth century Dundee was the world's jute capital, as well as Europe's leading whaling centre. Dundee shipbuilders constructed the finest Arctic vessels in the world, the engineering works were clattering with business and there was a spirit of enterprise and pride, mingled with crime and, reputedly, the richest square mile in the Empire at Broughty Ferry. Queen's College of St Andrews University had been founded in the Nethergate and learned professors moved to what was becoming known as Juteopolis. At the same time Mary Lily Walker and the Dundee Social Union strove to improve appalling living conditions and child mortality. Dundee was indeed a city of contrasts.

In 1889, Dundee officially became a city and five years later it became 'county of a city', one of only three in Scotland, the others being Edinburgh and Glasgow. The First World War shattered the pattern of constant growth with Dundee contributing tens of thousands of men to the front lines. The blood price demanded by industrial warfare, combined with new economic realities, severely damaged the economy of the city. Despite the setbacks there was a real determination to improve the lot of the poor, although well-intentioned attempts at solving the housing problem were only partly successful. The great Scots poet, Hugh MacDiarmid, spoke of 1930s Dundee as a 'grim monument to man's inhumanity to man' but it was equally grim for the women who worked long shifts in the clattering mills. Decades of depression ended only with the

Second World War and once more men from Dundee marched to the sound of pipes and grumble of guns as they helped defend the world from evil.

In the post-1945 period the city was designated a development area and attracted a number of US companies, including Timex and NCR. The jute industry advertised for labour from abroad and new houses, some of them prefabricated, sprang up alongside council schemes that included Douglas and Angus, Ardler and Menzieshill.

Things looked good for a while and the population soared. But in the 1970s NCR crashed and the city lost thousands of jobs. The company stayed in Dundee, leaner and more resilient, much like the city itself. Timex was next; the 1980s was a disappointing decade for Scotland as a whole as the nation bled manufacturing jobs and Dundee's population fell. Dundee's reputation dipped further as the city was seen as a place of poor housing and low-paid work, or no work at all.

The housing boom of the Sixties had always been well intentioned but the houses not always well designed. Vast new housing schemes had brought light and air for the citizens, but often divorced them from the snug communities they had known and loved. The ancient closes of old Dundee were swept away in an uncompromising display of civic disregard for heritage, and replaced with concrete and plate glass. The new buildings did not last as grand dreams turned to bitter reality and the isolation of the peripheral schemes was augmented by damp conditions and continued unemployment. Dundee swayed with each blow that fate landed but always fought back.

The new schools brought fresh teaching methods; there was a vast new teaching hospital and the straight road bridge provided an easy link to Fife. In 1982 six areas of Dundee became an enterprise zone, in which private investors were encouraged to invest their money. Those struggling years led to a Dundee of the 1990s and thereafter based not on textiles and industry but instead on education, technological innovation, medical research and computer technology. There are ambitious plans for redevelopment of the waterfront and a sparkling new museum sitting by the silver waters of the Tay, and, to add icing to the cake, Dundee has also been designated a UNESCO city of design. Once again, the city is surging forward.

Dundee, then, is a city with a lively history with her street names a microcosm of the people and their interests. The names exist in their own dimension, contextualised by the fabric of the city whose story they project. They exist in concentric groupings, with the oldest names in the mediaeval core, surrounded by a ring created by the Industrial Revolution, with twentieth, and now twenty-first, century housing estates as the outer guard.

In the older, central part of Dundee the names often chose themselves, deriving from tradition and habit, with the names of prominent inhabitants often used to denote the street in which they lived. A good example is Argylegait, where a member of the Campbell of Argyll family had his town house; it later became the Overgait, altered in time to Overgate. The name 'gait' merely meant a way or passage, so Overgait was the upper way into Dundee while Nethergait was the lower way.

The industrial grouping is characterised by the names of mills and workplaces, speckled with the memories of the large houses of the elite, now mostly gone but remembered by street names. By the second decade of the nineteenth century it was obvious that the town required better managing so from 1824 a police commission was created to manage and improve the burgh. The commission was composed of a mixture of elected officers and the standing magistrates. To perform their work, the police commission created a number of committees, including the paving committee, which was chaired by the provost and was responsible for creating and naming new streets as well as paving the streets.

Dundee council, through the offices of the paving committee, had taken on the role of town planner, regulating the width of the streets, the sanitary arrangements, and the height of the housing. Despite the power of the paving committee, there were occasions when private landowners chose names without permission or consultation. Such an event occurred in May 1867 when a clutch of new streets was created in the Dudhope and Hospital Park areas of west Dundee with the names being decided before plans were submitted to the paving commissioners. The names included Kinnaird Street, Mortimer Street, Albany Terrace and Airlie Terrace.

When the paving committee found out about the unauthorised names, one of its members, a Mr Stewart, posed the question:

'Can we approve these streets?'

The provost could not give him an answer.

'I don't know,' he admitted.

Stewart continued. 'It is in our public capacity to allow these to be permanent names. The [Police] Act says the commissioners shall name the streets.'

Another councillor, Mr Brownlee, thought they were 'very nice names' but the provost ended the debate by concluding that the committee could change them if they thought fit. So, many of Dundee's street names were not organic, but the result either of momentary consideration by the committee or the whim of a landowner. The council groused about landowners having this power and in December 1872 the police commissioners stated that only they should have the power to name streets.

The names could commemorate many things: famous people, not-so-famous people and people who would have liked to be famous; events with a Dundee connection; folklore, industries, the spectacular and the mundane. There are politicians with or without a Dundee connection, the names of estates that town expansion swallowed up, soldiers and admirals, industrialists and seamen, battles and triumphs, royalty, literary figures including, arguably, the worst poet in the world. Other streets commemorate long-gone farms; it is often forgotten just how close the city was to agricultural land, and how close in time the industrial workers were to the soil that held generations of their ancestors in thrall. In the twentieth century some areas of Dundee had streets named for a specific theme; for instance, Menzieshill in the west of the city has streets named after Scottish rivers while, in the north, Ardler's streets echo famous golf courses.

There are many streets that reflect the Gaelic or Pictish people who lived here or in the surrounding areas. Others hint at the industrial past of factories or mills, the maritime past of trading links or whaling fleets or the political past when radicals challenged the status quo. There are a number of street and area names that end in *town* or *ton*: that ending could mean a group of houses that was a farming community or perhaps an estate named after a landowner, while Kirkton was the community based around the kirk. Names that end in *field* point to the rural background of much of Dundee as the town expanded into the neighbouring countryside. Rural connections are also indicated in names that end in *shade*, such as Chapelshade, meaning a larger parcel of land, while the word *croft*, as in Blackscroft, is well known in Scotland, a Gaelic word that has crept into everyday usage.

There are areas that end in *bank,* indicating the steep nature of Dundee. A walk in this city can provide the very healthy exercise of slogging up and down some fairly precipitous slopes. Other streets and areas have the prefix *bal*, which has nothing to do with the Middle Eastern god Baal but everything to do with the Gaelic background of much of Scotland. The word *bal* derives from the Gaelic *baile*, a small settlement, and either Dundee absorbed the original settlement or just used the name of a nearby farm or hamlet. Equally Celtic is the preface *pit*, which is often taken to be a sign of an original Pictish presence.

As Dundee expanded it swallowed up surrounding villages, such as Broughty Ferry and Lochee. There were streets in these new urban additions that shared their names with those in Dundee, so, in 1907, the council changed many of the duplicate names to avoid confusion. One such street was Albert Street in Lochee, named after Queen Victoria's husband, Prince Albert; that became Atholl Street. Other street names vanished during demolition while more have been added, such as Bash Street, a reminder of the comics that have been read by generations of children.

With the exciting development of Dundee's waterfront, a number of new streets and public spaces were created. The council asked the public to suggest suitable names and appointed a panel to select the best entries: Lord Provost Bob Duncan, city archivist Iain Flett, the chairman of partnership group DD One, Jon Walton, and city development director Mike Galloway.

Most suggestions hinted at Dundee's past but some revealed the city's humour. There were names such as Margaret Thatcher Piazza – and that from a city long radical and now strongly Scottish Nationalist. Tongue in cheek, perhaps? The Square of Eternal Suffering was also thought suitable, for whatever reason. Some bright spark wanted to honour a controversial television presenter with the Jeremy Clarkson Cycle Path, no doubt tongue-in-cheek given Clarkson's love of cars. Lorraine Kelly's Trail was, it is to be hoped, linked to that lady's connection to Dundee University, while Yes Plaza and Salmond Way were blatantly topical in the year of the independence referendum.

But Dundee is much more than streets. Dundee has a plethora of significant buildings, parks and statues, not to mention historic ships and street art. Each of these has its own story and character, from the statue to Admiral Duncan – the Dundonian who won the battle of Camperdown – to the monument that commemorates those lost when the first Tay bridge collapsed, taking an entire train and all its passengers into the wintry Tay. Sport too is prominent. Dundee has two major football teams, ice hockey, yachting, cycling, sports centres and, in 1824, Scotland's first ever steeplechase horse race from the Law to Kinpurnie castle.

However, although the past may be written in street names, statues and architecture, the future, as always, is in the hearts and minds of the people.

Abbotsford Place/Street

Named after Abbotsford, the magnificent house built by Sir Walter Scott (1771–1832) in the Borders, which is now a major tourist attraction. Scott, arguably our greatest novelist, portrayed Scotland as a place of wild scenery and dashing heroes. He was the most significant figure in the reinvention of Scotland after the loss of national confidence that followed in the wake of the 1707 Union with England and the failure of the Jacobite risings. His vision undoubtedly romanticised Scotland, but that was better than no image at all. The novels also created a cult of Scott-isms that much of the western world embraced, and which enchanted Queen Victoria. Streets, pubs, houses and estates across three continents were named after his characters and novels.

Abercromby Street, Broughty Ferry

Commemorates the Honourable Montague Abercromby (1807–53). She was married to Fox Maule Ramsay (1801–74) the 11th Earl of Dalhousie, who was a major landowner in the Dundee area. He was known as Lord Panmure until 1860, at which time he succeeded to the earldom of Dalhousie in Midlothian. Dalhousie was the Minister for War in the latter period of the Crimean War (1854–6) and a supporter of the Free Church of Scotland at a time when the Free Church had split from the Church of Scotland. The Honourable Montague was born on 25 May 1807, the daughter of George Abercromby and Montague Dundas. She married Fox in 1831, and died in November 1853, leaving no children.

Aberdour Place, Barnhill

Named after the small but historic village on the south coast of Fife. The *aber* prefix was chosen by the council to maintain consistency with the previously named Abercromby Street. The name means 'confluence of the dour'.

Aberfoyle Gardens, Broughty Ferry

Derived from the picturesque village of Aberfoyle in the Trossachs. The name is said to mean 'mouth of the muddy pool'.

Aberlady Crescent

This name has no local connection but refers to a coastal village in East Lothian, a few miles to the east of Edinburgh. The streets hereabouts follow a pattern of being named after towns and villages in Lothian and the Borders. The historian Nigel Tranter said that the name meant 'river mouth at a flat place', which describes the situation of the village perfectly, although it also mingles two languages, English and Gaelic.

Abernethy Road, Barnhill

There are two communities from which the name could derive. One is the Perthshire Abernethy, whose origin is thought to be Obair Nechtan, or Nechtan's work, after a Pictish king named Nechtan who founded a monastery. Abernethy was once capital of a Pictish nation. There is also an Abernethy in the Highlands, with the name meaning 'confluence of the Nethy river'. As noted above, the 'aber' prefix names were chosen to maintain continuity.

Abertay Street, Broughty Ferry

Named after the mansion of Abertay that was owned by James Pattullo, a prominent nineteenth-century solicitor who worked with some of the most important people in the Dundee area.

Abertay University, Bell Street

Abertay University, Bell Street

The word *aber* means 'confluence of' so Abertay would mean the confluence of the Tay. Right in the centre of the city, this university is fast rising in reputation particularly in the area of computer arts and computer-games technology. It was the first university in the world to offer degrees in computer games.

In a previous life the university was the technical institute, which opened in Small's Wynd in October 1888 and later became the Institute of Art and Technology. The Baxter family, textile giants, provided the funding for the institute, as they did for the University of Dundee. In 1911 the institute moved to Bell Street and larger premises, with the oldest part of the Bell Street building designed by the prominent architect J. H. Langlands. It prospered and, in so doing, spread along much of the street.

In 1946, the University of London recognised the quality of the institute's work and six years later began to award external degrees to the institute's graduates in various disciplines, including civil engineering and pharmacy. By 1955 the institute also offered British Institute of Management courses in commerce and management. Twenty years later it was recognised as one of the best institutes of higher education in Scotland outside of the universities. Innovation was important and the institute was the first in Scotland to have a science-based degree in nursing, and, as early as 1980, a higher diploma in computing. In 1994 the institute took a giant leap forward when it became the University of Abertay.

At the Bell Street entrance there is a blue plaque, one of twenty-five placed throughout Dundee. Each plaque highlights the achievements of one of Dundee's most eminent women. In this case the woman is Victoria Drummond, a Perthshire-born relative of Queen Victoria. After being trained at the technical institute, Drummond became a motor mechanic and eventually a ship's engineer. She sailed the world's oceans, including through the Second World War, becoming the world's first female engineer in her field.

Abertay University library

Abertay University Library

This building is one of the most distinctive in Dundee and is situated to the west of the main campus of the university. It is also known as the Bernard King library after Professor Bernard King, who was the first principal of the university as well as vice chancellor. It is open most of the time and provides group-study rooms as well as over five hundred individual study spaces, many with networked personal computers and wireless facilities. There are plasma screens and more than 126,000 books, with access to 32,000 electronic journals and 175,000 e-books.

The building itself won many awards for its innovative style including a RIBA award in 1998. Ingenium Archial were the architects and it includes

3

circular lecture spaces, service areas and open-plan library decks behind a curved glazed wall that allows splendid views to the west.

Accordion Way
Set beside John Huband Drive. As John Huband (1942–2000) was a famous accordion player, it is obvious that the street honours his memory.

Addison Road, Broughty Ferry
Honours James Addison Kidd, a local councillor, who worked as a butcher and sang in the choir of St Mary's Episcopal church. In 1887 when a professional troupe, the J. W. Turner Company, was touring Scotland, Kidd volunteered to take the place of their sick baritone. He was also convenor of public works in Broughty Ferry.

Adelaide Place
Situated on the upper slope of the Law, this street is a terrace of nineteenth-century cottages with an unmade road. In the nineteenth century royalty worship was rife and this street honours the queen consort of William IV, Adelaide of Saxe-Meinengen (1792–1849). As such it shares its name with Adelaide in South Australia. Adelaide was born in Meiningen, Germany and lived in Hanover immediately after marrying William, who was twenty-seven years her senior. Their two daughters died in infancy.

Affleck Castle
Also known as Auchenleck castle, Affleck sits at Monikie in Angus, a few miles north of Dundee. In 1296 the owner of a previous building on this site was Mathew de Naper de Aghelek, a name that time corrupted to Affleck. The present building is an L-shaped tower house of the late fifteenth century, which is in surprisingly good condition for its age. At one time mariners sailing up the Tay were said to use the castle as a mark to check their navigation. The Reids of Affleck supported the Jacobite cause so the government forfeited the estate after the last Jacobite rising of 1746. The lady of the house promptly stripped Affleck of all she could carry and fled to France, where her husband was waiting. Thereafter the Yeamans, a prominent Dundee family, became owners but seem to have preferred city life as the castle was empty by 1760.

Agnes Square, Broughty Ferry
This development of white houses was built in the mid-1970s. It was created for the Isabella Agnes Smith housing association. Isabella Agnes Smith (1876–1965) left money to house elderly single ladies.

Airlie Place

Built in 1846 and sits in the heart of the university area. The 1821 map of Dundee shows a house named Airly Lodge in the vicinity and the name was transferred. The university gradually bought it over and now dominates what is a most attractive street with the student union at the head and a fine view over the Tay at the foot.

Albany Road, Broughty Ferry

Celebrates Prince Leopold, Duke of Albany, Earl of Clarence and Baron Arklow (1853–84), the youngest son of Queen Victoria. Albany Road boasts the splendid house of Balnacraig, built in 1863, which has echoes of Osborne house in the Isle of Wight. Balnacraig has a three-storey Italianate tower, which must give far-reaching views over the Ferry. There is also the mansion of Claremont at no. 61, in which William Boyd, of Keillers marmalade fame, lived during the 1920s.

Albany Terrace

The street was set out by the landowner, Richard Gardner of Dudhope. Albany refers to the royal dukedom of that name. The Victorians treated royalty and the aristocracy to the same fascinated scrutiny as the twenty-first century views film or sporting personalities. The architecture mirrors that interest, with an Italianate tower at nos. 10 and 11 an interesting feature.

The Duke of Albany was a title occasionally given to the younger sons of Scottish, and later British, royalty. Robert III created the title in 1398, with Albany referring to Scotland north of the Forth. In 1881 Queen Victoria granted it to her fourth son, Prince Leopold, but when his son, Prince Charles Edward, Duke of Saxe Coburg and Gotha, fought against Britain in the First World War, his title of Duke of Albany was revoked.

Albert Institute

When Prince Albert, the consort of Queen Victoria, died in 1861, the nation mourned. Albert streets and Albert monuments sprang up the length and breadth of the land, including in Dundee. As the city was short of money at the time, it fell to a private company to fund the building, with the Baxter family, as so often, the leading light. For two years from 1865, the area that is now Albert Square was a building site as Dundee created the largest provincial memorial to Prince Albert.

Sir George Gilbert Scott, one of Britain's leading architects, worked tirelessly to create what he fondly said was a 'new Scottish style' as the building rose. It was originally intended to be a reading room for the working man but evolved into one of the finest examples of a Victorian museum and art gallery. The

Albert Institute, Albert Square

museum is now known as the McManus galleries, named after a former lord provost, Maurice McManus (1968–1970).

In 2010 the area was further enhanced by a multi-million-pound upgrade and it is worth a few hours of anybody's time. Even the surroundings have been pedestrianised, while the café is light and airy and the bookshop has many interesting local volumes. The interior is a cornucopia of Victoriana with some collections of national interest, including the whaling collection, while the Orchar collection of Scottish art is a delight.

At the entrance of the institute is another of the blue plaques that highlight the achievements of notable Dundee women. This commemorates the life of Katharine (sometimes Catherine, or Katherine) Read, the daughter of a Jacobite who had to flee Dundee after the 1745 rising. Read became a prominent portrait painter and was 'painter to the queen' at a time when few, if any, women achieved high status in that profession.

Albert Road, Broughty Ferry

This street honours Prince Albert, the consort of Queen Victoria. There was quite a cult of monarch-worship when Victoria was on the throne, and, when her husband died, communities rushed to prove their loyalty by building memorials and naming streets in his memory.

Albert Square

This also honours Prince Albert. The area was once meadowland, but in 1799

Albert Institute and Square

was enclosed with stone dykes and drained for use as a bleaching green. The land remained marshy, however, and when in the 1860s the Albert institute was begun as a memorial to the recently deceased prince, laying the foundations created major problems. The square has been recently pedestrianised and updated and is therefore a beautiful island in the heart of bustling Dundee, with the Albert institute as a magnificent centrepiece.

On a new building at no. 25 there is another of the twenty-five blue plaques commemorating prominent Dundee women. This is for Frances Horsburgh, Dundee's first female MP, the first female Conservative cabinet minister and the first female Privy Councillor. Edinburgh-born, Horsburgh was elected to the House of Commons as a Unionist when she was 41. The property at 25 Albert Square was the site of the Unionist party headquarters while she was in Parliament.

In the Peace Gardens in the square there is also a plaque to the memory of the sixteen Dundee men who joined the international brigade in the Spanish civil war and died fighting the fascists. The area is enhanced by statues of various eminent people, including Robert Burns and George Kinloch, who have been recorded separately.

Alexander Street, Maxwelltown

According to A. H. Millar in *Glimpses of Old and New Dundee*, around 1780, David Maxwell of Tealing, Lord Dean of Guild, bought this land. When the feuing (street) plan was created he insisted that the streets were named after members of his family. This street carries the name of one of his male relatives.

Alexandra Fountain, Riverside Drive

The fountain commemorates Queen Alexandra, who sailed from Dundee to her homeland of Denmark in 1907. It also marks the Dundee terminal of the Tay ferry to Fife. Princess Alexandra (1844–1925) married Albert Edward, the son of Queen Victoria, in 1863. That same year her father succeeded to the throne of Denmark and her brother to the throne of Greece, so she was a well-connected lady. Alexandra was Princess of Wales from 1863 until 1901 when her husband ascended to the throne as Edward VII. She opposed the 1890 agreement by which Britain handed Heligoland to Germany in exchange for Zanzibar and quite understandably distrusted German foreign policy.

Alliance Trust headquarters, West Marketgate

Alliance Trust Headquarters

RMJM Architects designed this highly glazed and distinctive building, which was completed in 2009. Alliance Trust is an investment and savings business with a fascinating history, particularly in relation to Dundonian investment in the Old West.

Its history stretches back to the 1870s when jute was king and factory smoke filled the streets of Dundee. The businessmen of the town were experienced in international trading and flush with money, and turned to investments in overseas markets. In 1873 they founded the Oregon & Washington Trust Co Ltd to lend money to the pioneers who were opening up the American north-west. Three years later the Dundee Mortgage and Trust Company Ltd also looked to United States farmers as a potential source of investment, but added Canada and other imperial possessions to their remit. In 1878 the Dundee Land Investment Company Ltd completed Dundee's trio of overseas investment companies. Dundee Land concentrated on purchasing land near North America's growing railway network to profit from the inevitable increase in value. Within a year the latter two companies merged, with Robert Fleming one of the directors.

In 1880 a new player entered the financial circus, with 170 Dundonian investors among the 218 of the Hawaiian Investment & Agency Company Ltd. Seventeen of the investors were from Hawaii, including the Hawaiian king, and within a few years the company expanded to the American mainland. There was a period of restructuring to take advantage of local laws and toward the end of the century the original three Dundee companies merged to form the Alliance Trust.

In 1895 the Trust became involved in the half-million-acre Goodnight ranch, home of Charles Goodnight, reputed to be the inspiration behind John Ford's 1956 epic film *The Searchers*, starring John Wayne. As the company entered the twentieth century the value of the investments multiplied and in 1918 the Alliance took over the management of the Western & Hawaiian Investment Company. The value of the investments increased throughout the century, although with the occasional blip. Many US assets were sold during the Second World War, but by 1994 assets had increased to a billion pounds. In 2006 the Alliance Trust fully merged with the Western & Hawaiian, by then known as the Second Alliance, creating the largest generalist investment trust in Britain – and based in Dundee. Assets increased to £3 billion by 2008.

The Alliance Trust continues to prosper and is one of Dundee's unsung success stories.

Alloway Terrace
Named after the village of Alloway, south of Ayr, birthplace of Robert Burns.

Al-Maktoum College of Higher Education

Al-Maktoum College of Higher Education

Established in 2001, this college has a professed aim of bridging the 'possible gap between the Muslim and western worlds by focusing on intelligent debate and scientific understanding of Islam and the role of Muslims in the contemporary world'. It has an international group of students and is a place of higher education rather than a religious college.

The college is funded by HH Sheikh Hamdan Bin Rashid Al-Maktoum, deputy ruler of Dubai and minister of finance of the United Arab Emirates. It is openly multicultural, with lecturers and students from a variety of nations and religions. It not only teaches Islam-related subjects, but also its website claims it has 'ties with local and national communities'.

Ambrose Street, Broughty Ferry
Smack in the centre of Broughty Ferry's conservation area it recalls a local landowner and stonemason, Thomas Ambrose, who erected some of the houses. The coastguard custom house was at no. 2.

Americanmuir Road, by Downfield
According to the council, this was the road to Meric Muir but when Dundee expanded in the nineteenth century the city took it over and popular usage altered the name. However, the Ainslie map of 1794 suggests there was an American Moor just west of Kirkton and the street name Mericmuir Place did not arrive until much later. The name may mean 'the moor of the Americans', but it would be fascinating to find out exactly what the American connection was. The original village buildings still existed as late as the 1950s, with single-storey cottages and cobbled streets.

Amond Gardens/Amond Way, Fintry
These were erected in the early years of the twenty-first century. They are on the site of part of the street that was originally named Grampian Gardens, but which was demolished due to inadequate foundations. The nomenclature honours the late PC Trevor Maurice Amond, the local policeman, who did a lot of hard work to make the community a success. He was involved in trying to ameliorate the problems of alcohol and drugs.

Anchor Lane, off Henderson's Wynd
The name of the lane does not seem to refer to any particular incident, but is a general reminder that for centuries Dundee was a major trading port. A. & J. Adie's South Anchor mill was nearby. That mill was badly damaged by a fire in 1869, with four hundred people losing their jobs. It later reopened but was affected by the great strike of 1875.

Ancrum Road

Before Ancrum Road was created, the land was owned by Harry Scott of Balgay. His father was Sir William Scott of Ancrum in the Borders, so the name was transported north to Dundee.

Ancrum Road school

This school of 1904 has some interesting architectural features. It was designed by Arbroath-born William Gillespie Lamond, who specialised in schools and other public buildings. It has a projecting staircase with slit windows for bored children to peer out at the freedom beyond.

Ann Street, Maxwelltown

Around 1780, David Maxwell of Tealing, the Lord Dean of Guild, bought this land and had it laid out for streets. He insisted that each street was named after a member of his family, with Ann Street named after a female relative.

Annan Terrace

There are two people that this now-vanished street could commemorate. The most obvious is Annan the stonemason, who had the street built, but the more interesting character was his son.

Robert Annan (1834–67) was an evangelical preacher from the Hilltown who died saving a boy from drowning in the Tay. He was a keen swimmer who often had to break the ice in the Tay before he jumped in; his local nickname being 'the water dog'. Unfortunately, Annan was also a wild youth who got into trouble with the police. He emigrated to the United States, survived a shipwreck en-route and continued with his drunken, violent life. Returning home, he enlisted in the army, deserted, wandered the streets and lanes of Britain, joined the marines and gave himself up as a deserter. Eventually, he returned to Dundee, found God and handed out religious tracts in the Hilltown. He preached in Couttie's Wynd and saved eleven people from drowning in the Tay, including a suicidal prostitute and his own brother. On the last day of July 1867 he saved a boy aged eleven but, tragically, was drowned himself. He is buried in the eastern necropolis.

The street was demolished in the 1970s and a school built in its place but the story, and the character, are too good to waste.

Annandale Avenue

References the broad valley in south-west Scotland. Annandale featured in Scott's *Minstrelsy of the Scottish Borders* and was once owned by Robert the Bruce when he was lord of Annandale.

Annfield house

Annfield House, Annfield Street

This fine town house was completed in 1793, when Edinburgh's famous New Town was in the process of being built, and it would grace that area or indeed any other. The three-bay central bow looks down on Dundee with faded glory. It is a Grade-B listed building with vague links to a ghost known as the Black Lady of Logie.

Annfield Road/Street

Named after Annfield house. In the 1840s a gentleman by the name of Urquhart had a market garden in this area.

Anstruther Road

Derives from Anstruther, the erstwhile fishing town in the East Neuk of Fife, which shares a whaling heritage with Dundee. Men from Anstruther and its neighbour, Cellardyke, regularly sailed in Dundee whaling vessels.

Anton Drive, Broughty Ferry

Recalls the Anton family, who owned the mansion then known as Forthill house and now as Anton house. The family gave their home to the Scottish Orthopaedic Council as a residential training centre for girls with disabilities. Charles Edward Anton was the son of a London corn merchant and joined the Jardine Matheson trading house in 1884, rising to be the *taipan*, or head, of the company. Jardine Matheson has an amazing history that includes drug smuggling on a commercial scale, helping to found Hong Kong and allegedly being instrumental in starting the First Opium War with China. Anton was not, however, involved in such interesting endeavours as he joined the company later, dying in Broughty in 1935. As well as Anton Drive, Dundee he has Anton Street in Wan Chai, Hong Kong named in his honour.

Applecross Gardens
There is an area of Highland Scotland called Applecross, which is on the mainland directly across from Skye.

Arabs
A term sometimes applied to Dundee United and its fans, but it predates the formation of the club. In the nineteenth century there were large numbers of destitute boys in Dundee. The product of broken homes, they were known as street Arabs, perhaps because of their nomadic habits. Strangely, destitute young girls were not termed Arabs. The street Arabs lived by stealing and slept in water closets or in doorways and public closes; sometimes they were taken in by adults and trained as thieves or abused in other ways. It is difficult to say when the term was coined but in January 1867 the chairman of Dundee Industrial School said the term 'wild Arab' was appropriate for such boys.

Arbroath Road
Named after its destination, Arbroath, a fishing port, trading centre and industrial town. It is one of the major routes north and can be very busy, but once outside Dundee the sea views are well worth experiencing. Try driving in the early morning to catch the sun rising from the North Sea and the thin pencil of Bell Rock lighthouse just visible on the horizon. Night times are also interesting, when the flash of the Bell Rock reminds those on land of the perils of life at sea.

Archer Street, Broughty Ferry
Recognises the achievements of James Bell Archer, the housing convener of Broughty, and a builder, stonemason and Conservative councillor. He lived in Church Street and became deputy lieutenant of the county of the city of Dundee in June 1927.

Ardestie Place/Street
The source is Mains of Ardestie farm, which, in the 1850s, was home to a progressive farmer named William Fullerton. He was known for his cattle breeding and was keen to improve the homes of agricultural labourers. When provost Anderson of Broughty worked the land Mains of Ardestie was one of the first in Scotland to try Patrick Bell's new reaping machine. The farm was one of the many properties of Lord Panmure and was sometimes the target of poachers.

Ardler

Ardler Complex, Turnberry Avenue

This housing scheme in the north-west of Dundee shares its name with a small village a few miles to the north in Perth and Kinross. The meaning of the name is uncertain, but on maps of the eighteenth century there was a settlement named Airdlaw here, which might mean a hill belonging to a man or family named Aird. However, the *Concise Scots Dictionary* gives the meaning of *erd* as earth, which suggests the hill of earth. David Dorward, an expert on Scottish place names, suggests an original name of *aird dal*, meaning 'ploughland height'. The Victorians believed the name came from two Gaelic terms: *aird*, a point, and *lar*, ground – therefore ground point. Dorward's meaning makes most sense.

With old Dundee still overcrowded after the Second World War, the council cast around for land on which to build more houses. They procured Downfield golf course and handed the course a different home. Because of the location, the council chose to name the streets of Ardler after famous golf courses. What was, in effect, a new town was built, with multi-storey blocks, 'courtyards' (bungalows with an enclosed courtyard) maisonettes and walk-ups. In the tradition of Dundee, most houses were small with only two bedrooms. When it was at its peak, Ardler had 3,254 houses, all ultra-modern for the time. The people who came from the overcrowded tenements of the town centre with shared toilets thought they were in heaven. When the scheme was first built, six 17-storey multis dominated Ardler.

The scheme had the usual social problems associated with housing of this type: the lack of larger housing for growing families; lifts that often malfunctioned; vandalism and graffiti. As was common at the time, the design and materials were not always suitable for the Scottish climate.

For a while Ardler had a bad reputation but it has been the beneficiary of a massive regeneration programme that upgraded houses, demolished the multis and altered public perceptions of the area. Locals were heavily involved the regeneration process through the Ardler village trust and helped create the new Ardler, a place of light and hope with a strong community.

Ardminish Place
In common with other streets in the area, the name has no local connection. There is an Ardminish on the island of Gigha, one of the Inner Hebrides. The name means 'the headland of the narrow point'.

Argylegait
An old name recently reinvented. Although Argylegait was the early name for the Overgate, the name now refers to a stretch of road between Lidl's supermarket and the West Port roundabout. The original Argylegait was so named because a prominent house there was owned by one of the Campbells of Argyll.

Arklay Street
Commemorates local landowner David Arklay of Easter Clepington, who died in 1822. Many Dundee streets were named after landowners or mill owners. In August 1890 a patch of open ground at the top of Arklay Street was the venue for the fifth exhibition of the Clepington working men's horticultural society. Lord Provost Hunter opened the exhibition, which was staged in a large marquee. William Briggs was president of the society, which had 106 members.

Arnhall Drive
This street in the west end boasts some art nouveau railings designed by the famous W. W. Friskin. The name comes from the mansion of Arnhall that stood here.

Arnhall Gardens
This is a lovely street made lovelier by the 1936 white-walled house designed by Lowe and Barrie, with flat roof and cutaway corner. The architecture is unusual for Dundee and all the better for its originality.

Arthurstone Terrace
Another street that remembers a prominent person. Peter Carmichael of Arthurstone (1809–91) was the superintendent of Dens mill and a senior partner in Baxter Brothers & Co. From 1869 he owned the estate of Arthurstone, until his death in 1891. This was a mixed residential and industrial street with Malcolm Ogilvie & Co. owning a two-storey factory here. The factory is long gone and the street is mainly residential. There is also St Patrick's RC church, an 1897 structure by T. M. Capon, with an unusual octagonal belfry.

The paving committee gave this street its name, shortly after the Dundee Clipper Line barque *Arthurstone* arrived safely in Britain after an epic voyage that saw her hit an iceberg and limp home, a journey of thousands of miles, with a badly damaged stem. Arthurstone derives from a standing stone in Perthshire, after which the estate was named. The stone was the centre of a persistent legend that linked King Arthur with the area. It was destroyed in 1792. Guinevere is also mentioned locally, with connections to Meigle where a mound is said to mark her grave.

Arthurstone community library is a red-sandstone building of 1903 and one of Dundee's Carnegie libraries, which means that Andrew Carnegie (1835–1919), the Scottish-born American tycoon, funded its construction.

Ashbank Road
Part of the Logie development, this 1919 scheme was arguably the most successful housing in the post First World War building programme. The street name reflects the garden-city ideals of Logie, with its idea of a more rural life than normal in the centre of the city.

Ashkirk Gardens/Place
In common with other streets in the area, the name has no local connection. Ashkirk is a village in the Scottish Borders.

Ashludie Mews/Terrace, Monifieth
Derived from the mansion house of Ashludie. The original name seems to have been Asludie, when, in 1591 it was the property of William Durham. The mansion was built in 1866 by a flax manufacturer from Arbroath named Alexander Gordon. In 1913 Dundee corporation bought the house and forty-eight acres for £7,500 and made it into a hospital, which is now (2016) closed.

Auchterhouse
A few miles north of Dundee in the Angus countryside, Auchterhouse is on the southern flanks of the Sidlaw hills. According to David Dorward the name is Gaelic, from *uachdar*, or 'upland place'. Today it is a peaceful village and a favourite home for commuters to Dundee but in the early nineteenth century Auchterhouse was a major player in the whisky-smuggling trade. Whisky was distilled in the Highland glens and sent by packhorse to the main urban centres without paying the high rates of duty. Naturally, the government was somewhat displeased with this arrangement and did everything in its power to control the smuggling. There were many pitched battles between revenue men and the smugglers. Old Whisky Road in Auchterhouse commemorates these spirited days.

Auchterhouse also has a seventeenth-century mansion with older roots; this building was known as Auchterhouse castle.

Old Whisky Road, Auchterhouse

Backhill Road

The term 'back' means the side facing away from the sun, so this street takes its name from the north side of a hill, ridge or slope.

Backmuir Drive

There is a Backmuir wood just outside Muirhead, after which this street may be called. The wood is 140 acres in extent and open for all, with varied wildlife and beautiful views. Backmuir means the north side of the moor, the side away from the sun.

Bader Square, Broughty Ferry

This square held a hospital specialising in prosthetics, opened by Douglas Bader (1910–82) in September 1965. London-born Bader lost both legs in an air accident in 1931 but still flew with the RAF during the Second World War, becoming a squadron leader. After notching twenty confirmed kills he was shot down and held in the notorious Colditz prison camp.

Baffin Street

This street was completed in 1830 and recalls Dundee's connection with Baffin Bay in Arctic Canada. Dundee's whaling fleet worked either in the Greenland Sea east of Greenland and around Spitsbergen, or in Davis Straits. Baffin Island and Bay are off Davis Straits and were well known to the Dundee whaling men. Interestingly, Baffin, which is within the Arctic Archipelago in the Canadian territory of Nunavut, is the largest island in Canada and the fifth largest in the

Baffin Street

world, extending to more than half a million square kilometres, much of which is permanently covered in ice. It is the wintering ground for narwhal, walrus, beluga and bowhead whales, which is no doubt why it was so attractive to hunters. The ships that set sail from Dundee were by no means the first visitors to its spectacular shores and there is evidence that the Vikings landed here in the eleventh century.

Balbeggie Place/Street
Many of the streets in the Douglas and Angus area were chosen because of the prefix *bal* whether or not they had a Dundee connection. *Bal* is from the Gaelic *baile* and means place, farm or village. Balbeggie is a small village about seven miles north of Perth.

Balcairn Place
There is a Balcairn farm near Blairgowrie. Balcairn could mean farmstead of the cairn, with a cairn being a pile of stones.

Balcarres Terrace
Balcarres is an estate in the East Neuk of Fife.

Baldovan house, Old Glamis Road
The Scrymgeours were a major name in Dundee throughout the Middle Ages. Baldovan house was one of the Scrymgeour properties until it passed to the Nairnes in the late seventeenth century, followed by the Wedderburns, who sold it to a returned nabob who bought both the estate of Baldovan and Balgay. His

name was Dr Walter Tullideph. For a few years in the early eighteenth century the estate was known as The Bank. The Ogilvies then took over. The name is from the Gaelic *baile domhain* and could mean 'farm in the glen or hollow'. The present house dates from the middle of the eighteenth century, with nineteenth-century additions.

Baldovan industrial school

Dundee architect James Maclaren designed this impressive Gothic building, which stands in Baldovan Road. It was opened in January 1855 with Sir John and Lady Ogilvie of Baldovan as major patrons and Queen Victoria chipping in with £100. Originally intended for 'imbecile and idiot children', it was extended to give accommodation to adults with special needs. Later it became a List D school and today it is the Strathmartine hospital.

Baldovan Road

This name derives from an estate and village that was situated outside the town. The village was developed from the 1830s, at a time that Dundee was expanding northwards. Baldovan Road runs from Downfield to Strathmartine. The Ogilvies of Inverquharity owned Baldovan village. Lady Jane and Sir John Ogilvy gave part of their land at Baldovan house and helped fund an 'asylum for imbecilic children' and held bazaars to raise money for the cause.

Baldovie house, Broughty Ferry

This two-storey, L-plan house of 1734 has typical Scottish corbie-stepped gables and is a C-listed building. It is enhanced with a heraldic panel 'God Give Grace' and an interior inscription '1734 RSH', which refers to the owner, Richard Holden, who was involved in improving linen processing. At the time of writing Michelin athletic club occupies the house, whose name means a low-lying farmstead.

Baldragon View

The name comes from the dragon stone – named Martin's Stone – at Strathmartine. (The tale is related under 'Dragon', below.)

Balerno Place/Street

Balerno is a small town outside Edinburgh and a stepping-off point for the Pentland hills. The name is Gaelic: *baile airneach*, 'town, or farm, of the hawthorns'.

Balfield Road

Relates to the farm of Balfield, which was another possession of the Cox dynasty. The name is a mixture of Gaelic and English, 'the settlement of the field', or perhaps 'the field that belongs to the village'.

Balfour Street

Opened in 1828, Balfour Street pays tribute to Alexander Balfour (1765–1855) who was not only provost of Dundee but also a cofounder of Bell & Balfour, flax spinners. Many of Dundee's most prominent local politicians came from an industrial background. Fife-born Balfour became a burgess of Dundee after serving his apprenticeship to Bailie John Thoms, who was also a merchant. In 1780 Balfour partnered Thomas Bell. He became a town councillor in 1793 and was dean of guild five times and provost in 1826, 1827 and 1830.

Balgarthno Place/Road/Street

The farm of Balgarthno was part of the Invergowrie estate. The name may mean 'farm of corn'.

Balgarthno stone circle, off Myrekirk Road

Balgarthno Stone Circle

As always with ancient monuments, its purpose and usage can only be guessed at, although experts think it may have been a type of judgement centre. It now sits in splendid isolation, but seems to have been part of a series of such monuments, the survivors of which include a circle at Mylnfield and the 'Druid temple' in Campderdown park, of which only a single standing stone remains. Apparently, there were once stories of an underground cave on the site but this seems to have been apocryphal. The circle is officially recognised and has an explanatory sign board.

Balgavies Avenue/Place
Balgavies is a farm and loch in Angus.

Balgay house
Now part of the Royal Victoria hospital beside Balgay hill and built around 1760. Balgay is derived from the Gaelic *baile gaoithe* – windy place.

Balgay park

Balgay Park

One of the finest parks in a city of fine parks and centred around Balgay hill, which rises on the north-west of Dundee. At one time it was the custom for the youth of the town to ascend Balgay hill to wash their faces with dew on the first of May but that tradition appears to have died out.

The park boasts the city observatory, a plethora of mature trees, semi-rural walks in the heart of the city, squirrels, the occasional fox, bird life and lovely views. At the western side, between the park and the cemetery, is a beautiful avenue once known as Windy Glack, which was used by smugglers bringing whisky from the Angus glens into Dundee. On a dark night the atmosphere in this cutting is interesting, with thick woodland on one side, and a cemetery on the other, and so it is easy to imagine the smugglers passing through here with their pack horses and illicit whisky. There is a graceful bridge overhead that does not detract from the atmosphere but rather, in daylight, adds to the picturesque appearance.

The park was opened to the public in 1871 at a time when the Victorians were desperately attempting to improve the health and morals of the people in crowded urban areas.

Balgay Street

The council's paving committee gave the street this name in July 1866, describing it as, 'that street formed the first connecting link between Dundee and Lochee'. The area was part of the Balgay estate and is dominated by Balgay hill.

Balgillo hill

This name is from the Gaelic *baile gille-each*, which means 'horse servant's steading'. There was a fort here in the Dark Ages, and possibly before, but the hill came into prominence in the sixteenth century during the Rough Wooing. Scotland suffered from periodic English invasion and interference for much of her nine hundred years of independent existence, but the wars of the mid-sixteenth century were amongst the ugliest of them all. Both sides were guilty of atrocities as Henry VIII of England attempted to force Scotland to wed her infant queen to his equally youthful son. His attempt to win Mary's heart included the mass slaughter of men, women and children, while the Scots retaliated by using English prisoners for target practice. The English captured Broughty castle and built a temporary fort on Balgillo, until a combined Scots-French force eradicated them.

Balgillo housing estate, Broughty Ferry

This is a housing estate built in the Sixties and Seventies with nothing to distinguish it bar the friendliness of the inhabitants. The streets in this estate have a theme of Scottish lochs although the estate was named after the lands of Balgillo that in the nineteenth century were owned by Hunter of Burnside.

Balgillo Road

There was a Balgillo landed estate in the mediaeval period, which stretched around the eastern side of Dundee and encompassed most of Broughty Ferry. The house of Balgillo was where Claypotts Road is now.

Balgowan

An area in the north of Dundee. The name comes from Gaelic: *baile ghobhainn* means 'blacksmith's steading'. Balgowan estate was in Perthshire and in the 1840s was owned by the Napoleonic war hero, Thomas Graham, Lord Lynedoch (1748–1843). When Lynedoch died, William Thomson bought it for £43,000. Thomson had recently returned from China.

Balgray Place/Street

Named for the farms of East and West Balgray that stood here. James Bell, who farmed Balgray, was a Church of Scotland elder in 1844 while, in 1850, George Webster was foolish enough to be caught after committing an assault at Balgray farm in Mains and Strathmartine parish and was jailed for ten months.

Ballantrae Gardens/Place/Terrace

Many of the streets in the Douglas and Angus area were chosen because of the prefix 'bal', whether or not they had a Dundee connection. Ballantrae is a small seaside town in Ayrshire, once noted for smuggling. Robert Louis Stevenson used the name in his book, *The Master of Ballantrae*. The name means 'the place by the beach'.

Ballater Place

Ballater is a small town in Aberdeenshire and a centre for hill walking. The town has royal connections and is said to be the most picturesque Victorian village in Royal Deeside. The name could mean 'place at the hillside'.

Ballinard Gardens, Broughty Ferry

Named after the villa and grounds of the same name. The house had been owned by James Smith, a jute merchant of Henry Smith & Co. When he died in 1884 his estate, including property in Dundee, was worth £109,000. At a later date the whisky distiller John Jabzy Watson (1846–1924) owned the house. The mansion of Ballinard is now used as a hotel.

Ballindean Crescent/Place/Road/Terrace

The name's origin is Ballindean in the Sidlaw hills, near Inchture. The name *balle* could be from the Gaelic *baile*, a place or town, but dean is confusing, as there is no record of a religious dean here, or an ancient dun. Dorward suggests *baile an fan*, 'place of the slope', which would make sense. There is also a definite Dundee connection as Sir John Wedderburn of Blackness owned the estate. He supported the Jacobites in the 1745, marching with the Airlie regiment, but when the fighting ended he moved to America and then to Jamaica. He was a surgeon there, returned to Scotland and purchased Ballindean estate.

Another Wedderburn owner was Sir John Wedderburn of Ballindean (1775–1858), MP for Perth Burghs. Wedderburn of Ballindean was a London merchant and a politician who opposed the abolition of slavery; he was Scotland's postmaster general from 1823 to 1831. The house was sold out of the family but in the middle of the twentieth century it was bought by Walter Campbell, interestingly another Dundee surgeon.

Balloch Place

The name is Gaelic, 'from the grazing land', or 'a mountain pass' but in this case would be chosen because of the 'bal' prefix, which fits in with the local street naming. There are many Ballochs in Scotland including one in Fife, one near Inverness and one at Loch Lomond.

Ballochmyle

The address of this interesting house is 3 Norwood Crescent. It was built for, and by, John Murray Robertson and completed in 1880. The house is distinguished by its flattened stone tower.

Ballochmyle Drive
Ballochmyle is in Ayrshire and has a famous railway viaduct and a golf course. The name corresponds to the Ayrshire nomenclature of the area.

Ballumbie Braes/Drive/Meadows/Road
Ballumbie castle is close by.

Ballumbie castle

Ballumbie Castle

With *baile* being Gaelic for a settlement, and Lumbie being a person's name, this is Lumbie's settlement or place or farmstead of Lumbie. Although the castle was built in the fourteenth century, the most famous, or infamous, inhabitant was Henry Lovell, who, in the late sixteenth century terrorised his neighbour, James Durham, the laird of Pitkerro. Lovell was so persistent that Durham told Queen Mary of his 'manifold oppression', which was so bad that he 'dare nocht resort' home 'neither by day nor nicht'. Lovell also looted from Durham's son and burned down the manse of the minister of Monifieth. It was not only the rich he attacked: 'several poor tenants of West Ferry and Monifieth' approached the Privy Council to complain that the laird of Ballumbie had savagely evicted them.

That was a wild period in Scottish history, with clan warfare endemic in the Highlands and Borders, so Lovell was simply following a contemporary trend. It is possible that a mini ice age had caused years of bad weather leading to crop failures, which necessitated a raid on one's neighbour in order to make up the shortfall.

The castle is now a ruin, with only a curtain wall and a pair of rounded towers to remind one of past excitement.

Ballumbie castle golf course
A parkland course situated on the outskirts of Dundee, Ballumbiue castle has a resident professional, a fine restaurant, choice of tees and a par of 70.

Ballumbie house
Once a Victorian mansion, the house was altered to a hotel but burned down in 1982. It was recently rebuilt and converted to flats, with houses built in the grounds.

Balmedie Drive
Balmedie is a village and country park in Aberdeenshire, north of Aberdeen.

Balmerino Place/Road
Balmerino is in Fife, across the Tay from Dundee. There is a small village and a ruined mediaeval abbey. The name may derive from 'dairy farm' or from *bal* – farm – of Merinach, a Celtic saint who was associated with St Regulus of St Andrews.

Balmoral Avenue/Gardens/Place/Terrace
Balmoral is the Queen's Highland home, conceived as an extravagance of tartan and romantic fantasy by Queen Victoria and Prince Albert.

Balmore Street
The name is Gaelic for large farm or large settlement and in 1891 the *Dundee Courier* termed houses in this street as 'magnificent blocks of shops and dwelling houses'.

Balmossie Avenue/Braes/North Balmossie Street/South Balmossie Street
Relates to the small estate of Balmossie, which contained a farm, mill and bleachlands. In 1846 Robert Collier of Balmossie was created a justice of the peace. He was also a judge at local ploughing matches, while his wife regularly donated items to the industrial school. In spring 1882 children playing with matches were blamed for a fire at the farmhouse.

Balmuir Place/Road
The name comes from the farm and area of that name north of the Dighty water and south of Bridgefoot. It means 'the settlement on the muir'. There was also a Balmuir house and a number of mills along the river and in the 1880s the area was used for bleaching.

Balmullo Place/Square
Two more streets in the Douglas and Angus area whose names were chosen because of the prefix 'bal'. The name Balmullo is from the Gaelic *baile* and *mullaich*, which means 'village top'. It comes from a village in Fife near St Andrews.

Balmyle Road, Broughty Ferry
This street commemorates local landowner James Nicoll Constable of Balmyle.

Balshando Place
Takes its name from the farm of Balshando, a property on the estate of the Earl of Camperdown. The name means 'farm of the old davoch'. A davoch, or davach, was a parcel of land, with the size differing throughout Scotland.

Baltic Chambers, Bell Street
Another reminder of the once vital linen trade with the Baltic ports, this is a C-listed, four-storey tenement of the mid-nineteenth century.

Baltic Street
This vanished street commemorated Dundee's long participation in the linen trade, when fleets of ships sailed from the Tay for flax. During wartime Dundee vessels joined the Baltic convoys, which were protected by the Royal Navy. It must have been a splendid sight to watch a score or so of vessels sail down the Tay, and an even better sight when they returned safely, with the threat of privateer or storm temporarily lifted.

Baltic Street was opened in 1840 as a connection between Wellgate and Meadowside. It survived as an important thoroughfare for over a century and even had its own ghost, which startled the local policeman in the Victorian era. Sadly, however, it was destroyed when the Wellgate centre was created in the late 1970s.

Today there is a short stump of a lane as a reminder of the days when great fleets left the Tay to sail to the Baltic to bring back flax for the linen trade.

Baltic Works, Annfield Road
This can also be ascribed to the old Baltic trade. The former mill and chimney is now a B-listed building. The chimney stack was built in 1864 and in design terms is considered second only to Cox's stack at a time when mills were designed for effect as well as function. It was one of the earliest octagonal stacks in the city. The interior of the works has Gothic cast-iron spans. When in use, this was a power-loom factory.

Balunie Avenue/Drive/Street/Gardens
Balunie was an estate in this area, owned by the Douglas family, after which the streets are named.

Baluniefield Road
Baluniefield is also named after the Douglas-owned Balunie estate.

Banchory Road
Takes its name from the town in Aberdeenshire, eighteen miles west of Aberdeen. A *banchor* was a religious college.

Bank Avenue, Downfield
There was no financial connection to this street. Rather it reflects the estate of Baldovan, which was known locally as 'the Bank' at the beginning of the eighteenth century.

Bank Street, central Dundee
This street was originally created to join Willison Street with Reform Street. The name came from the Bank of Scotland that stood at the junction with Reform Street. At one time, Sir John Leng – the newspaper magnate who owned and ran the *Dundee Advertiser* – worked in offices at nos. 7–9. The sign for the *Advertiser* is still visible on the exterior of the building although it merged with the *Courier* many years ago and the combined newspaper is published by the DC Thomson group.

Bank Street, Lochee
The original Bank Street in Lochee connected Lochee High Street to South Road and took its name from the Royal Bank that stood at the top corner. It was knocked down in the 1970s when Lochee was redeveloped. In 2014 a new Bank Street appeared, named after the original.

Bannatyne house, by Newtyle (eleven miles north of Dundee)
The home of George Bannatyne. He collected Scottish poetry, with the 800-page Bannatyne manuscript (held by the National Library of Scotland) one of the most important sources for Middle Scots literature. The house is Grade-B listed, sixteenth century, but was modernised in the late Victorian period.

Barnes Avenue
Commemorates Councillor Barnes, the first convenor of the housing-and-town-planning committee.

Barnhill rock gardens
The Barnhill rock garden is a public park extending to more than two hectares and is owned and maintained by Dundee City Council, with significant support from the Friends of Barnhill Rock Garden, whose members, as well as providing seeds, bulbs and plants, also assist with the many everyday gardening tasks. The

Barnhill Rock Gardens

Friends insist that although this help is greatly appreciated it is not a condition of membership! One of many of the city's welcoming green 'lungs', Barnhill sits on the site of a former nine-hole golf course, which was laid out at the same time the Dundee–Aberdeen railway line was built. Work on the garden began in 1955 when an area of volcanic rock was cleared, which at one time was the old shore line. Over the years it was extended eastwards, to areas that had once been sand dunes, and rock from Carmylie quarry was used to form a major part of the garden. In 2007 it won the Green Flag award, the first place in Dundee to be so recognised. With its wonderful views over the river Tay, the splendid water features that act as a haven for wildlife of every description and the beautiful flowers and fauna, it understandably has many ardent admirers and is well worth a visit.

Barns of Claverhouse
There was a farm of this name situated here. The term 'barns of' was not uncommon with farms in eastern Scotland. In the 1850s George Grieve of this farm was a consistent winner in ploughing competitions.

Barometer cottage, Bell's Lane, Broughty Ferry
In the nineteenth century the Scottish fishing industry exploded and thousands of men hunted herring and long-lined for white fish. In the early part of the century most boats were open and there were many disasters. After a storm in 1848 drowned scores of Scottish fishermen the government began to tackle the problem and safer, decked boats were introduced.

It was also thought that barometers could help fishermen tell whether or not they were safe to venture out to sea. Lord Duncan applied to the Admiralty for a barometer for Broughty Ferry and was successful in obtaining this 'friend to warn them when a storm is coming on'. The barometer was manufactured by Negretti and Zambra, which specialised in precision instruments. This valuable piece of equipment was housed outside the cottage from 1859, but unfortunately it has been stolen. It is said that, one day in October 1881, the local fishermen consulted the barometer, saw that it predicted bad weather and did not go to sea. The ensuing storm caused havoc along the east coast of Scotland with 189 fishermen drowned, most from Eyemouth, but none from the Ferry. For that incident alone, the barometer should be remembered.

Barrack Street

This short street at the western edge of the Howff holds the McManus collections unit, part of Dundee's museum service. However, the name Barrack Street is comparatively modern. The original name was Friar's Wynd or Friar's Vennel, as the street extended from the Kirk of the Blessed Virgin Mary – now renamed as St Mary's parish church – to the friary of the Grey Friars. There was also a port (a gateway) into Dundee here, for Barrack Street was outside the city. This port was known as Friar Wynd Port. It incorporated a lodge house, positioned directly above the arch, which was home to the town hangman. For that reason, local people gave the gateway the cheerful name of Hangman's Port.

With the Reformation, and the temporary demise of the Roman Catholic faith in Scotland, the religious usage died, and as Mary, Queen of Scots had given the friary burial ground to Dundee as a public burial ground the street became known as Burial Wynd. Perhaps not unnaturally, those who lived here were unhappy with the name and in 1807 asked the council to change it. Yet it was not until the 1830s that the council introduced the name Barrack Street, chosen because it was on the direct line of march from the barracks at Dudhope castle to the city.

On the front of Willison House in this street there is a blue plaque, one of twenty-five around the city commemorating eminent women. This plaque is for Mary Alcock, a shoemaker's daughter who became a highly successful business-woman in the early years of the nineteenth century. She was a genuine eccentric who, in retirement, instigated lawsuits against people who had offended her and in consequence was often seen carrying large bundles of legal papers. Finally, she became a Mormon but never fulfilled her dream of visiting that church's spiritual headquarters in Utah.

Barrack Street collections unit (also known as McManus collections unit)

McManus Collections Unit, Barrack Street

This fine building of 1911 is an annex of the McManus museum in the Albert Institute. It stands on Barrack Street overlooking the Howff and houses a major part of the collections of the McManus. Open on certain days every year for visitors, it also hosts talks and other events. The interior has extensive storage facilities for the many thousand exhibits that the museum holds, from Zulu spears to whaling harpoons and priceless silk. Members of staff are very friendly and always delighted to help.

Older citizens may remember when this building was a natural history museum and there was a beehive on the landing, with the skeleton of the Tay Whale also on display.

Bash Street

Bash Street

Believe it or not, the inspiration was the *Beano*'s comic characters, the Bash Street kids. It could only happen in Dundee! The original Bash Street kids were apparently based on the pupils of Dundee high school. The street is between West Marketgait and Brown Street, with the street sign illustrated by two of the comic's pupils, Plug and Wilfred, who are portrayed leaving messages for the teacher. It was named in February 2014 to commemorate the sixtieth anniversary of the first appearance of the Bash Street kids in the *Beano*.

Bath Street, Broughty Ferry
There are no baths in this street but the south end faced the public baths in Fisher Street, which might be the reason for the name.

Baxter park

Baxter Park Pavilion

Baxter Park

In the nineteenth century there was a movement to bring space and light into industrial cities by means of public parks. Sir David Baxter of Kilmaron donated the thirty-eight acres of this park to Dundee in 1863; it is the only formal Victorian park in Dundee. Sir David was a founder of Baxter Brothers & Co., one of the large textile companies that dominated Dundee. Designed by Sir Joseph Paxton, of Crystal Palace fame, the park boasts a beautiful area of ornamental garden as well as acres of grass for young and old, and their dogs, to play. At the centre is an Italianate pavilion designed by George Stokes, Paxton's son-in-law, within which a statue of Sir David was placed.

Earl Russell, the prime minister, graced the opening, with a crowd estimated at seventy thousand in attendance. Dundee also had a public holiday to mark the occasion. The park has seen some interesting sights but few as strange as an 1879 cricket match where one team was entirely composed of clowns from Watson's circus. The crowd unfortunately interrupted the game, which was replayed in Dudhope park under the guard of the Forfar Light Horse. There was a flurry of activity on 5 November 1940 when a German bomb landed in the park, but with no casualties.

Although a board of trustees originally cared for the garden, the city took over in 1903. The park and pavilion have been recently restored and as well as offering a great place for families to play, is a splendid site for a wedding.

Baxter park glebe
Takes its name from Baxter park. A glebe was the parcel of land owned by the parish minister.

Bayfield Road/Gardens, Broughty Ferry
These streets were named Bayfield, after the mansion house of John Guild, chairman of three financial companies. The house is gone but the name remains.

Beach Crescent, Broughty Ferry
The name gives away the location of this picturesque street, which runs parallel to the coast. This street has been distinguished by several interesting residents. The house at no. 31 was designed by the architect James Maclaren for the Stephen family. The Stephens were prominent shipbuilders and produced some of the finest Arctic whaling and exploration vessels. The house later became the Orchar art gallery, with the collection of provost Orchar now in McManus gallery. There is an interesting lamp at the entrance while other lamps in the street carry the burgh coat-of-arms and are reminders of the days when Broughty was an independent town.

General Hunter lived in nos. 9–11, while Traquair house and Beach house, at nos. 41 and 47, have classical lines. At nos. 97–99, hard by the harbour and on the corner, is Red house or Broughty house, the 1801 home of Colonel Charles Hunter of Burnside, who designed the gridiron street pattern of Broughty Ferry and possibly encouraged others of the gentry to move to the area. This is a place to linger.

Beachtower
Designed by Dundee architect John Murray Robertson in 1874, this house graces the suburb of West Ferry. It was built from concrete heavily disguised by stucco, with added classical touches. West Ferry was formerly one of the most affluent suburbs in Europe.

Beaumont Crescent/Terrace, Broughty Ferry
Commemorates the early-seventeenth-century English playwright, Sir Francis Beaumont.

Beechwood estate
The name is taken from Beechwood house, one of the properties owned by the Cox dynasty, Dundee merchant princes. Beechwood is a council scheme that was built on the fringes of Lochee in the mid-1930s. It was planned with great care and was intended to be a model development with light, air and balconies, so there was quiet glee when it won a Saltire Society award for its architecture. However, Beechwood suffered because of the distance from services.

Beechwood park, Kingscross Road, Lochee
This stadium is the home of Lochee Harp, a prominent Junior football club in Dundee. Founded in 1904 to give the many locals of Irish Catholic descent a focus, the team still play in green and white. There was also another Lochee team named Lochee Emmett but they have long gone. The park is named after the Cox mansion of Beechwood house.

Bell's Lane, Broughty Ferry
Commemorates Thomas Bell who bought land here in 1807. The barometer in Barometer cottage in this street saved the fishing fleet from the great storm of October 1881.

Bell Street
Opened in 1828, Bell Street honours a provost, Thomas Bell, a cofounder of the flax-spinning company of Bell and Balfour. Bell played a small part in the famous incident on 1793 when the Friends of Liberty ripped a young tree from Belmont house in Perth Road, decorated it and hauled it to the Mercat cross in High Street. There they danced around it as a tree of liberty. Bell's part was

passive; he owned Belmont house, and therefore the tree, which was later returned to his garden.

Bell Street became the centre of justice in Dundee, with the Sheriff Court, police headquarters and jail all in a handy clump. The jail has long gone but the police station and court remain. For the more gruesome minded, murderers were hanged within the precincts of the prison and it was to the precursor of this prison that Richard Leggat came the day he murdered his wife in nearby John Street. He was a whaling mariner but on the long voyage to the Arctic he convinced himself that his wife was having an affair. When he returned home he shot her and then tried to commit suicide by throwing himself into Dundee docks. He failed in that so gave himself up at Bell Street police station. Better known is William Henry Bury, and was hanged here on 25 April 1889. There are suspicions that he was Jack the Ripper.

Today Bell Street is better known for the University of Abertay, which takes up much of the street.

Bellfield Street, off Hawkhill
The name means 'beautiful field'. This was a western suburb of Dundee, with villas moving into rural surroundings.

Bell Rock Square, Broughty Ferry
Named after the Bell Rock lighthouse, which stands north and east of Dundee in the North Sea. The rock is submerged at high tide and was a notable hazard to shipping for centuries before the lighthouse was erected in the early nineteenth century. The lighthouse can be seen on a clear day as a pencil-thin white building on the horizon and at night its signal is a reassuring beacon. In June 1848, during the Danish–Prussian war, a Danish frigate used this area as a hunting ground and is said to have captured a Prussian vessel off the Rock. For security reasons the light was darkened during both world wars except when a British convoy was passing.

The square was designed by James Parr & Partners and opened in 1973. There are sixteen houses, designed for the Tay Valley Housing Society, all looking out over the Tay. As is proper in the Ferry, the houses echo a fishing tradition, with walls harled to protect them from the Scottish weather.

Belmont halls, University of Dundee
Also known as Belmont flats, this building of the early 1960s was designed by Dundee architects Gauldie, Hardie, Wright & Needham and has Danish influences. It is situated off the Hawkhill and is used for student accommodation. The name comes from the mansion house of Belmont that once stood here.

Belsize Place/Road, Broughty Ferry
References Belsize house, which was built for merchant George Weinberg. His wife, Paula, was from Belsize Park in London.

Benholm Place
The name relates to Benholm, a parish near Montrose that holds an ancient water-powered mill.

Benvie farmhouse
This building is near Fowlis Easter, north of Dundee. At first sight this farmhouse appears to be a perfect example of one of the 'improved' houses of the early eighteenth century. At that time the lowland clearances, or improvements, were ongoing at which time landowners merged their small farms together. Many of the poorer tenants were forced to move and fine new farmhouses were built. However, appearances can be deceptive. This is indeed an early-eighteenth-century farmhouse but it was gutted by fire in the twentieth century and rebuilt.

Benvie Road
Named after the parish of Benvie in Angus; the name is from the Gaelic *banbhaidh*, meaning 'pig burn'.

Benvie well, Angus, north-west of Dundee
The White Lady of Benvie was a local ghost, who told people of the magical properties of this well. She was the spirit of a woman who haunted the Fowlis burn after dying of the plague and had been buried in un-consecrated ground. When the local minster asked her why she was so unsettled, she told him she would disappear if she was properly interred in the kirkyard. Even better, if she was buried, a spring would rise that would cure people of the plague. According to local legend, this was how the Benvie well was founded.

Berwick Drive
This name has no Dundee connection, but refers to Berwick-upon-Tweed, once Scottish, but now, after changing hands on numerous occasions, the most northerly town in England. The massacre of Berwick in 1296 marked the first act of the First War of Independence (1296–1328) that brought the great Scottish warrior William Wallace, formerly of Dundee High School, to international prominence.

Bingham Terrace
The Arts and Craft architect Edward Tough designed these neo-American houses with the timber balconies and other additions. Tough was educated at Dundee technical college but ended his career in the United States. The Church

of Latter Day Saints of Jesus Christ (the Mormons) has a place of worship in this street. Also worthy of note here is the Anchorage, a villa designed by the Dundee architectural firm, C. & L. Ower, in 1895. It has a nautical theme to match the name, with an outlook tower to act as a crow's nest, plus fine Corinthian columns in the hall to add grandeur.

Birchwood Place
Part of the 1919 Logie scheme that was arguably the most successful housing scheme in Dundee's post-First World War building programme. The name was chosen to reflect the garden-city theme of the estate. Birch trees are among the most beautiful of Scotland's trees, with the silver birch particularly attractive with its year-round, silver-coloured bark.

Birkdale Place
On the north boundary of Ardler, the name relates to Royal Birkdale golf course in Lancashire. Many streets in the area are named after famous golf courses.

Birkhill
The name means hill of the birch trees, but in this case the small village of Birkhill takes its name from Fife. The Wedderburn family, who were very prominent in Dundee, also owned the Birkhill estate near Balmerino in Fife and in 1829 the name came to Dundee.

Birnam Place
Relates to the village of Birnam in Perthshire, which features in Shakespeare's *Macbeth*. It may be significant that Lord Panmure – a local landlord and a noted beneficiary of many charities, including the infirmary – had a shooting lodge named Birnam cottage in Strathbraan, which could have influenced the choice of name.

Black Street, off Benvie Road
In 1892 a gentleman named Daniel Black had a house and shop here and the name may have been taken from him.

Blackness
The word 'ness' means a headland, such as in Caithness at the very north of the Scottish mainland. In Dundee, Blackness was an estate named after a point of black basaltic rock that thrust out into the Tay. Before Dundee expanded during the Industrial Revolution, great landowners owned the lands all around with the Hunter family owning Blackness and the Wedderburns close by. At that time this area, west of Dundee, elevated and with beautiful southern views over the river to Fife, was in great demand by the wealthy and there are some magnificent villas here.

Blackness Avenue

Blackness Avenue

Sweeping up in a graceful curve from Perth Road to Blackness Road, it was originally the approach to Blackness house. The avenue is a mixture of detached and semi-detached houses and rare Dundee examples of middle-class tenements complete with bay windows and decorative carvings. At the upper end of the street the houses, and even the passing pedestrian, can enjoy magnificent views over the Tay to Fife.

Blackness library

This 1904 Carnegie library stands on the corner of Blackness Avenue and Perth

Blackness Library

Road, a junction known as Sinderins. Frank Thomson was the designer and the two storeys of red stone watch over shoppers in Perth Road. A beautiful elliptical staircase enhances the interior.

Blackness Road
An interesting street of mixed detached houses, shops and tenements, this street is airy and, in the main, pleasant. It is enhanced by having Victoria park and Balgay hill as a neighbour to the north and views over the Tay to the south.

Blackscroft
This name has been in use since 1581. It comes from George, or Patrick, Black, who feued part of the Craigie estate, a croft being a parcel of land.

Blackshade
Due to the acute housing shortage in the wake of the Second World War, the government created thousands of prefabricated houses (prefabs) as a temporary measure. A prefab was a house built in a factory and pieced together on location. Many were placed in the area of Blackshade, which lies to the south of where Ardler is today. It was unfortunate that the Blackshade prefabs were first occupied in 1947, the worst winter since the 1880s. But they always seemed cold to residents. Pat Black, a local, spent much of her life in a prefab and said they were 'definitely cold in winter'. The prefabs were intended as a short-term solution but they lasted for decades and were generally popular with the people who lived in them. By the 1960s there were few people living in the prefabs, so the press termed this 'Deadwood city'.

Black Watch
Until the new waterfront development there was neither a street nor a building in Dundee named after the Black Watch, but to leave them out of a book on Dundee would be a travesty. Now designated as the 3rd battalion, the Royal Regiment of Scotland, and with their regimental museum close at hand in Perth, the Black Watch is integral to the history of the city. Many thousands of Dundonians marched to war wearing the famous red hackle and the battlefields of France, Flanders, Burma, Crete, North Africa, the Netherlands and Germany are salted with Dundee men. In the First World War the fourth battalion was known as 'Dundee's ain'. They left their barracks at Dudhope castle in February 1915 and fought in the battles of Neuve Chapelle, Aubers Ridge and Loos that summer. Fewer than half were still alive in the September. That is the reality behind the romance of the swinging kilt and the pipe music.

Since 1954 the Black Watch have enjoyed the freedom of the city, so they have the right to march through the streets carrying fixed bayonets, beating drums and bearing their regimental and national flag; nobody deserves the honour more. Today, A company, 51 Highland Division, 7th battalion the Royal Regiment of Scotland, has its headquarters in Dundee. The Black Watch still wear the red hackle and have recently served with great distinction in Iraq and Afghanistan.

Of course Dundee soldiers have served in many other regiments. Corporal Roy fought with the 24th Foot at the defence of Rorke's Drift against the Zulus; the battle made famous by the film *Zulu*, starring Michael Caine. Corporal Roy had been in hospital but managed to do his bit, after taking some of the sick and wounded to Helpmakaar. The McManus collection unit in Barrack Street has artefacts from that war, including Zulu assegais.

Black Watch memorial
Just outside Fintry, on the main road to Forfar and at the foot of Powrie Brae, stands the statue of a Black Watch soldier. The bronze memorial is to the 440 men from Dundee and Angus who died in the Second World War while serving in the 4th and 5th battalions of the Black Watch. Scott Sutherland was the sculptor; he also created the commando monument at Spean bridge.

Black Watch Parade
With the new development at the riverside, there are a number of new streets being formed. The public was asked to give suggestions and the best were chosen. Black Watch Parade will be the name of the footpath along the river.

Blairfield Road/Terrace, Birkhill
These streets took the name of the farm of Blairfield, part of the Camperdown estate. In the 1880s David Myles was the farmer and was also a Kirk elder and a member of the Liff school board. His brother was the local author James Myles, who wrote *Rambles in Forfarshire* and *Chapters in the Life of a Dundee Factory Boy*.

Blinshall Street
Named after the Revd Dr James Blinshall, minister of St Paul's church from 1764 to 1803. Educated at Aberdeen, he was minister at Biggar before moving to Amsterdam and thence to Dundee. In 1791 he petitioned for an infirmary in the town and died in 1803. In his will he left £25 to the infirmary.

Bonar hall, University of Dundee
This building commemorates George Bonar, who was prominent in the jute trade. He was managing director of Bonar & Low when the firm was founded in 1902. In 1924 the company took over Baxter Brothers & Co., one of the original jute giants. As the jute trade was declining rapidly in Dundee due to competition with India, Bonar & Law diversified into polypropylene production and engineering, becoming a major player in the former.

George Bonar founded the school of economics in Bell Street, originally intended to be part of the then Queen's College, but at first controlled by Dundee education department. In 1955 Queen's College did take control and in 1975 an economics building was erected in Park Place. The architects were Gilllespie, Kidd & Coia. The building itself is multi-functional with a low-key frontage that disguises the internal depth.

Bonar house, Meadowside
Built in 1928, George Bonar gave this building to Dundee as a school of economics.

Boniface Gardens/Place/Road, Invergowrie
Remembers the Saxon saint Boniface, who, it is said, built the church here. This was despite interference from the Devil, who stood in Fife and hurled stones at him. As Boniface spent most of his life spreading Christianity in what is now Germany, it is unlikely that he was here in person.

Bonnethill Court/Gardens, Hilltown
At one time Hilltown was known as Bonnet-hill because it was a centre of bonnet makers who sat outside their houses in the street and worked. That must have been an interesting sight on a fine day, but it has been known to rain even in Sunny Dunny so, presumably, on those rare occasions they worked indoors.

Bonnet makers were the fifth of the nine trades of Dundee and might have been instituted in 1529. By the nineteenth century the bonnet-making trade was a shadow of its former self and the last worker died in 1848 aged 99.

Bonnybank Road
The estate of Bonnybank stood here. The name speaks for itself as a bonny place but sadly that term could scarcely be used with the industrial expansion of the nineteenth century.

Bonspiel Gardens, Broughty Ferry
This street takes its name from the bonspiel, a major curling tournament, which takes place outdoors in Scotland when weather permits, and indoors when there is no suitably frozen loch. The street was built on the site of two curling rinks that opened in 1871, at a time that curling was a major and expanding sport in Scotland and many communities boasted their own outdoor rinks.

The Boreen, 6 West Grove Avenue
This B-listed, rubble-built house would be at home in the Lake District but instead enhances Dundee. It was built in 1911 when the Arts and Crafts style was in vogue. The name is Gaelic for a little road: *boithrin*.

Botanic Garden

Botanic Garden

Operated by the University of Dundee, the botanical garden occupies an elevated site off Burnaby Street in the west end of the city. The south-facing garden spreads its nine-and-a-half hectares around spacious buildings of 1973 and 1982. It holds both indigenous plants and many from other climes. There are glass houses and a small cafeteria as well as plant sales, access for the disabled and teaching resources. A splendid oasis.

Bowbridge Court/Place
Takes its name from the mill.

Bowbridge Works, Dens Road
Built in 1857, this impressive jute mill once employed three thousand people. The Grimond family were the owners, and marked their ownership with an ornate arched gate topped by a sculpted camel, with an Arab leaning against it. Why the camel? It was the family emblem of the Grimond family, although the less respectful of the workforce claimed that the Arab was an 'early Grimond'. The camel, like the factory and calendar, has gone; the stables and warehouses still stand. Joseph Grimond also built Carbet castle in Broughty Ferry.

The merchant princes of Dundee could do virtually as they pleased when it came to architecture but the Grimonds also cared for their workers with modern machinery and such comforts as a dining room and lavatories – state-of-the-art facilities for the time.

Bower Mill Lane

The Bower mill was situated at the junction of Lochee Road and Blinshall Street, with a frontage onto Douglas Street. It was owned by John Sharp, built in 1866, and employed over three hundred people. In 1869 there was a huge fire that virtually destroyed the mill and caused around £12,000 of damage. The building was of brick, unusual in Dundee; it survived the fire and continued to be productive.

Bowman's Lane, Broughty Ferry

Nothing to do with wandering archers, this street recalls Alexander Bowman, a local newsagent and stationer, whose printing facility was nearby.

Boyd Lane/Place, Broughty Ferry:

Commemorates John Boyd (1874–1926), director of Keillers, whose company gave Dundee the second j (jam) in the famous three j's.

Brackenbrae, Broughty Ferry

Linen merchant, Henry Smith (1816–74) owned this house. His wife employed a gardener named David Mathers who came to prominence when he won prizes in the 1876 international flower show in Dundee and the 1877 Dundee flower show. He continued with his prizewinning ways, becoming a judge of local competitions and writing on horticultural matters. The name of the house indicates it was built on a slope once infested with bracken, that pestilential, yet picturesque, fronded vegetation that can be the curse of Scottish fields and gardens if not controlled.

Brackens Road

A farm, the Brackens, stood here. It was part of St Mary's estate, along with the farm of St Mary's, and part of the lands of South Auchray, with a number of pendicles (smallholdings). In February 1873 James Dachers, a bleacher of East Brackens, was found guilty of breaching the peace at Baldovan bleachfield and fined twenty shillings.

Bradbury Street

This street is in Downfield. It honours Mrs Catherine Bradbury who took over the Strathmartine estate in 1872. Her maiden name was Laird and she was the daughter of Colonel David Laird. Laird Street is also named after her as both streets were created when she was the landowner. Mrs Bradbury was also patroness of the Strathmartine curling club. She died in 1887 and Thomas Cox of Maulsden, a scion of the famous Cox textile dynasty, bought the property.

Brewery Lane, Lochee

This street led to the Park and Pleasance brewery. The brewery was owned by Hugh Balingall, lord provost of Dundee, whose brother owned a wine-and-spirit merchant in Dock Street. The alternative name of the brewery was Balingall's brewery and bottle factory. At one time there was also a Hop Street, which has long gone. There was also a Brewery mill at Lower Pleasance, where, in July 1859, John Davidson, a young boy employed as gatekeeper of the mill, drowned in the mill pond. He had gone in to cool down on a hot day.

Bridgefoot

Originally known as Kirkton of Strathmartine, which is a much more evocative name. The bridge in question spans the Dighty water and was built in 1795. The village is best known for the stone a mile or so to the north where, according to legend, a dragon was killed.

Bright Street, Lochee

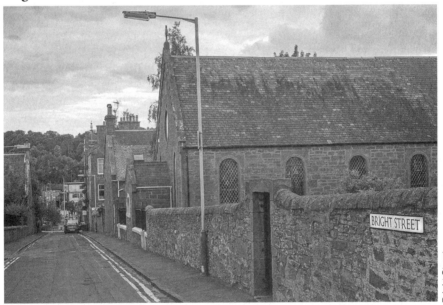

Bright Street

John Bright (1811–89) was a Radical politician who opposed the Crimean War with Russia and campaigned against Britain joining the American Civil War on the side of the South. He supported free trade, was instrumental in ending the Corn Laws (which kept the price of bread artificially high), opposed the rule of the landed aristocracy in Ireland and supported trade unionism. Before 1907 this street was named Union Street but the name was altered to avoid confusion with a street of the same name in Dundee.

Brook Street, Broughty Ferry

This street is one of the main thoroughfares in this delightful suburb of Dundee. It was named after a small stream that is now piped under the street and was the parish boundary between Monifieth and Broughty.

Brook Street should not be missed thanks to the many buildings of interest. These include the Eagle coaching inn, which has a fine carved eagle above the door. James Law, a carver of ship figureheads, was the artist. In the nineteenth century the stagecoach from Dundee – which was then a separate town – stopped here.

There are two interesting churches: St Stephen's, of 1871, has lovely stained-glass windows and a spire that was struck by lightning in 2011; across the street is the Congregational church of 1865, which has been converted to offices. There is also the Masonic hall at no. 152, designed by Frank Thomson, son of James Thomson the architect. Frank was helped by his brother in this instance. Mention must also be made of two other splendid structures: the burgh halls where the Broughty council met until the town became part of Dundee; and the Royal Arch tavern, which has nothing to do with Dundee's Royal Arch, but everything to do with the Masonic order.

Brook Street, Dundee

Was originally known as Scouring burn. The brook in question is now culverted and runs under the street.

Broomhall Gardens, Broughty Ferry

The name comes from Broomhall nurseries, which were named after Broomhall, the home of James Luke (1820–1903), jute lord of Pleasance works, Dundee.

Broughty castle

This castle may have been built on the site of the original *broch*, or fort, of the name. It is on the coast with easy visitor access but when it was a working castle defending the Tay from attack, it stood on a tidal rock, so at high tide the river formed a natural moat. The present structure dates to 1490 and was built by Andrew, second Lord Gray.

The English captured the castle in 1547 and battered Dundee with artillery rounds. The Scots took it back in 1550, but it was again fought over by Protestants and Catholics in the mid-sixteenth century. After these difficulties peace descended on Broughty, although by the latter half of the seventeenth century the castle was no longer a family home.

In 1846 it was acquired by the Edinburgh and Northern Railway, but when, in 1859, there was concern about war with France the government purchased the castle to help defend the Tay. Architect Rowand Anderson rendered it suitable for modern warfare, with artillery in position and local men recruited

Broughty Castle

to man the guns. It was still useful during both world wars, with powerful searchlights and heavy guns installed to defend the Tay against German incursions. There was also a seaward defence battery at Broughty Ferry on Castle Green.

Historic Scotland are the current owners, but it is run by the McManus gallery as a museum, with a children's play park outside and little memory of the day when Scots and English butchered each other for possession of these walls.

Broughty Ferry

Most often referred to as 'the Ferry' this is a very pleasant eastern suburb of

Broughty Ferry Harbour

Dundee but was once a substantial, and fiercely independent, town. It is an ancient settlement with an original meaning of *broch*, or fort, and perhaps linked to the freestanding *brochs* of northern Scotland. In this case the fort could have been on the same site as the present day Broughty castle that frowns up and down the Firth of Tay. A variation on the theme is that the name may derive from the Gaelic *bruach tatha*, Tay bank, or *broch* Tay.

The village was centred on the castle but by the nineteenth century was more geared to the sea. Many mariners were born or lived here, including David Blair, who was *Titanic*'s second officer during her sea trials. Broughty was also home to many of Dundee's merchant elite and was a notable fishing centre at a time when tens of thousands of Scots followed the herring.

Although the fishermen were all men, women were heavily involved in the industry as packers, gutters, salespeople and boat owners. From 1869 every fishing boat in the country had to be registered, with the owner being recorded. In the Dundee register, the first entry is *Matilda* of Broughty, a half-decked lugger with two masts and a crew of eight. She was owned by Barbara Ferrier, who later also owned *John and Davids*. Other Broughty fishing-boat owners included Elizabeth Gowans and Mrs Thomas Webster, who owned two vessels.

There was also salmon fishing here, and at the beginning of the nineteenth century Alexander and Thomas Boiter were employed to kill the seals that also depended on salmon for food. The Boiter brothers lived in a hut between the Ferry and Dundee and sailed a small boat to the sandbanks where the seals came ashore. Sprat fishing was seasonal but intense.

In addition, Broughty was a ferry port – hence the suffix – known as East Ferry, with West Ferry nearby and still retaining its name. The harbour, which was built for the railway, was Partan Craig from the Scots word *partan*, a crab. It had what was then called a 'flying bridge', but now would be termed a roll-on-roll-off ferry. Thomas Bouch – the then celebrated and now reviled designer of the first Tay bridge – also designed these ferries. The harbour is still the headquarters of an organisation known as the Amphibious Ancients, founded in 1889 as a swimming club. Its brave members enter the Tay on New Year's Day for a 'dook'.

During the nineteenth century Broughty became a haven for the wealthy keen to escape the smoke and congestion of Dundee. A grid pattern of streets was set out, coaches plied their trade and in 1838 the railway reached the town and things changed forever. There were some fifty palatial houses here, with the 1874 *Broughty Handbook* describing them thus: 'their exteriors being characterised by great architectural beauty, and higher in decorating the interiors, whilst in the beautifully laid out gardens adjoining, are greenhouses filled with rare exotica, fountains throwing up their tiny jets, and goldfish glittering in the water below'. It was a far cry from the desperate hard work and precarious existence of the fishing families only a few hundred yards away.

At the dawn of the twentieth century trams arrived, with some wild young Dundee lassies enjoying the freedom of taking over the top deck, lying on their back on the seats and scandalising the people on the streets by waving their feet and, shockingly, bare ankles and legs, at them. There was equally innocent fun along the beach as families from Dundee and further afield flocked to the sand and sun, as they still do today. The ground behind the coast rises, so the houses are elevated; many have secure stone walls and large gardens while most boast excellent views over the Firth of Tay to Fife.

This vibrant place has been home to shipping masters, whaling captains and fishermen, but arguably the inhabitant who made the biggest impact was Dudley Watkins, a religious man from a house named Winsterly. He was the creator of Desperate Dan among other famous cartoon characters from the *Dandy* and *Beano*. On 5 November 1913 the Ferry became officially part of Dundee, something not universally accepted even after a century. Broughty was also the birthplace of Lewis Spence (1874–1955), who was an authority on Central and South American folklore. Better known is his use of the Scots language in poetry, which patriotic interest continues with his being a founder member of the Nationalist Party of Scotland, which matured into the SNP.

Today Broughty is still popular to visit but there are no fishing boats drawn up on the sand and the greatest of the mansions built by the textile elite have gone. Yet it is still a lovely place with secluded and leafy streets facing the sparkling Firth of Tay.

Broughty Ferry railway station

This station is still in everyday use, although it was built in 1838, making it one of the oldest in the country. Look for the original old signal box on the southward platform.

Brown Constable Street

This street has nothing to do with police constables. It references Colonel Charles Brown-Constable, who succeeded to the Wallace-Craigie estate in 1852. Before that it was just plain Constable Street, named in honour of George Constable of Wallace Craigie who was a close friend of Walter Scott and said to be the original of Monkbarns in Scott's novel *The Antiquary*.

More recently, the marathon runner Jenny Wood-Allen MBE (1911–2010) was born as Jenny Wood Soutar in this street. She grew up in Blackness, took up cycling in the 1930s and became the unofficial women's Scottish road-race champion. Married, she brought up her children while her husband was fighting Hitler, and in the 1960s became the Scottish and British president of the International Toastmistress organisation. She was a Conservative councillor for West Ferry and helped organise the first Dundee marathon in 1983. After five months training she took part herself finishing in five and a half hours – at the age of 71. Two years later she set a new world record for a septuagenarian female of four hours, twenty-one minutes. Jenny took part in over fifty marathons in places as diverse as London, New York and Sydney, raising money for cancer research. In 2002, at the age of 90, she finished the London Marathon, earning a place in the *Guinness Book of World Records* for being the oldest woman to achieve that feat. As if that was not enough she was also a JP and was active in other areas such as the Good Neighbours scheme and helping women take up running.

Brown Street, Broughty Ferry
Captain Lawrence Brown commanded the customs cruiser *Princess Royal* at the turn of the eighteenth and nineteenth centuries when smuggling was rife and the seas were dangerous with French, Dutch and Danish privateers. He married Elizabeth Henry, the heiress to the Woodend estate in Perthshire.

Brown Street, Dundee
The 1809 *Dundee Directory* has a James Brown, yarn spinner, at nearby Witchknowe, so it is possible that this street was named after him. There was also a historic mill in nearby Guthrie Street owned by J. and W. Brown, for which William Brown left a detailed account. J. and W. Brown's South Mill was built in 1825, but the street had been known as Brown Street in the map of 1821 and existed without a stated name in the 1793 map. Overall, it is safe to claim that Brown Street was named after the firm of J. & W. Brown, which operated mills here.

Brown Street school

No longer a school – it is now a pub – it holds one of the twenty-five blue plaques that are scattered throughout the city commemorating prominent Dundee women. It highlights the career of Lila Clunas, who began her career as an elementary school teacher and later became a leading suffragette. She was very active in the Dundee suffragettes, ensuring that the movement represented every stratum of society, not just the middle class.

In 1908 Clunas was a member of a delegation that met Prime Minister Herbert Asquith but when she tried to thump him she was arrested and had the dubious honour of becoming the first Dundee suffragette to see the inside of a London jail. However, Clunas was not a passive

48

prisoner and went on hunger strike. It was many years later that she became a local councillor, but her memory is preserved in this building where she taught.

There was a fair bit of suffragette activity in Dundee or involving Dundee women. Around three hundred Dundee women took part in Scotland's first suffragette procession in Edinburgh in October 1907, with the jute and flax workers' union prominent.

In May 1908 Winston Churchill was chosen to be Liberal candidate for Dundee but he was unpopular with the women's movement, partly for his statement that 'women must be women first and suffragists second'. Suffragettes held meetings throughout Dundee, particularly outside jute factories; a suffragette interrupted Churchill's speeches by constantly ringing a bell and the women's movement received a massive boost by the publicity this small act engendered.

In the aftermath of Churchill's victory, the movement in Dundee became militant; they attacked a political meeting at Kinnaird hall and went on hunger strike when arrested. Others were arrested later. Unlike their colleagues in England, the humane Dundee authorities released suffragettes rather than resorting to force feeding. In 1913 suffragettes were blamed for burning down a mansion named Farington hall and there were plans to attack a trawler, the Old Steeple and various sporting venues. There was also a bomb found at the entrance to Dudhope castle, which was then a barracks.

Buckingham Point
Lord Buckingham was chairman of the railway committee of the House of Lords and was in power when the railway from Dundee to Perth was being laid. The point used to be called the Black Ness, after which the area of Blackness is named.

Bucklemaker Wynd (now Victoria Road)
The name originated from the number of skilled tradesmen here who made different types of buckles. The wynd was one of Dundee's most important streets but was cleared due to the Dundee Improvement Act of 1871 and the wider Victoria Road took its place.

Bughties Road, Broughty Ferry
Recalls Bughties house, built by Lord William Fergusson (1846–1923) in the 1880s. Fergusson was later honorary Captain, then Major, of the Royal Engineers Corps of Submarine Miners at Broughty castle. Mrs Fergusson was a charitable woman who allowed the girls from the industrial school to visit her house on various occasions and gave gifts to the convalescent home in Barnhill. In November 1893 a gale caused significant damage to the house.

Burns statue, Albert Square

Scotland's national bard sits outside the Albert Institute, quill in hand and eyes turned aloft for divine inspiration. His Dundee connections may be slight, but his statue looms as large as his words and ideas. Nowhere more than in Dundee is a man a man for a' that, and a woman equal to the best of them. The artist was John Steell and the statue is a replica of a statue that was sent to New York showing Burns writing a poem to Highland Mary. It was unveiled in October 1880 in front of a crowd estimated at 25,000 people with representatives of the Dundee trades.

Burnside Walk, Lochee

Near here stood Burnside mill, named after the burn beside which it stood. The Lochee burn is long, culverted and runs beneath the streets.

Butterburn Court and Square

Named after a burn, originally perhaps the Bitter burn, that rose on the slopes of the Law. There is an apocryphal story that in time of plague the burn marked a boundary between those segregated because they were affected and those healthy, who passed butter across the burn to help feed the sick. David Dorward – in his *Dundee, Names, People and Places* – suggests the name could be an alternative form of the Dens. Butterburn Court, a block of high-rise flats, was demolished in 2013.

Byron Street

A housing development of the mid 1920s, it did not meet the high standards of the Logie development of 1919. The name is presumably a reference to the half-Scottish romantic poet, as there are other poetically named streets nearby. George Gordon Byron, 6th Baron Byron (1788–1824), better known as Lord Byron, was said to be 'mad, bad and dangerous to know'. He was the son of 'Mad Jack' Byron and the grandson of 'foul-weather' Jack Byron. His father married twice, both times for money, his second wife being Catherine Gordon of Gight in Aberdeenshire. Byron's great uncle was the 5th Baron Byron, known as the 'wicked lord', or 'devil Byron', so all in all he had an interesting family. Byron had a number of love affairs, with women and men, and possibly even with his half-sister. He travelled across Europe and joined in the Greek War of Independence against Turkey. His daughter was Countess Ada Lovelace who was a founder of what is now known as computer science.

Caenlochan Place/Road, Broughty Ferry

From the area with that name at the head of Glen Isla.

Caird Avenue

James Key Caird (1837–1916) was a Dundee jute baron and philanthropist. He was also interested in Antarctic exploration and financed Shackleton's 1913 expedition there.

Caird was the son of Montrose-born Edward Caird, founder of the jute company Caird (Dundee), which started business with just twelve looms at Ashtown works in 1832. In 1870 James Caird took over the firm. He rebuilt and modernised Ashton works and in 1905 added Craigie works. Taken together they employed around two thousand people with Craigie supplying the yarn for Ashtown to weave. Caird had the reputation as a decent employer.

He married Sophy Gray and they had a daughter, Beatrix. Sadly, Sophy died in 1882, aged 38 and Beatrix followed her six years later. Caird did not remarry, spending his time and money on philanthropy, handing out an estimated £240,940. His bounty included largely financing the Caird hall that dominates City Square and contributing to Dundee Royal Infirmary for a cancer ward and to aid cancer research. He also gave money to the Royal Society for Physical Research and offered the University College in Dundee a physics laboratory.

Probably better known is his support for Sir Ernest Shackleton's Antarctic expedition of 1914–16. Indeed, Shackleton's famous eight-hundred-mile voyage from Elephant Island was in a small boat named *Sir James Caird*. Caird died at Belmont castle just outside Meigle, north of Dundee, two months before Shackleton reached Stromness in South Georgia. He is buried in Edinburgh's Dean cemetery.

Caird hall

This magnificent building takes up the entire southern side of City Square in

Caird Hall, City Square

the centre of Dundee. As Europe trembled on the brink of the First World War, the eponymous jute baron James Caird offered Dundee a new town house and concert hall as the original eighteenth-century town house was deemed no longer suitable for the needs of the much-expanded city. James Thomson, the city architect, designed most of the building, with Scott Morton drafting the concert hall. Caird donated £100,000 toward its cost.

The colonnade in front of the building was funded with a £75,000 donation by Mrs Emma Marryat (1849–1927), Caird's stepsister, and around these tall columns and on the steps, hundreds of new graduates gather each year as the university holds its graduation ceremony inside the building. There are also meetings, concerts, bands and gatherings of all kinds in this splendid building.

Included in the Caird hall complex is the 350-seat Marryat hall at the entrance to which there is a blue plaque, one of twenty-five scattered throughout the city. Each plaque highlights the contribution to Dundee of a prominent woman. This one is dedicated to Emma Caird, although the plaque itself reads 'Emma Caird (or Marryat)', presumably as some women dislike the concept of giving up their maiden names on marriage. She had a very interesting life, being well known in high society, attending the wedding of the Kaiser and travelling to Moscow, Vienna, the United States and even Japan.

She married Lieutenant Colonel Herbert Marryatt, but their daughter died, and then, in 1917, her husband also passed away, by which time Emma Marryatt had inherited her brother's wealth. As well as donating money to fund Marryatt hall, she gave to Dundee Royal Infirmary and handed over the Belmont estate, north of Dundee, as a home for injured soldiers. In return Dundee made her a burgess of the city. Her portrait sits inside the foyer of the Caird hall.

Caird park
Another prominent place related to jute baron James Caird, who donated it to the city. The park has Mains castle and the local beauty spot Den o' Mains within its confines as well as the Gelly burn and a 9-hole and 18-hole golf course. There are groves of oak trees and the watchful visitor may see red squirrels and kingfishers.

Caird park golf course
A parkland course in the north of Dundee, Caird park golf course is 6,280 yards long with a par of 72. It was opened in 1923, became one of the busiest courses in Europe in the 1980s and remains popular today. The course opens with a relatively easy few holes and then, having lifted the player's confidence, becomes stiffer as the round continues. Some of the greens will test any golfer. It is a picturesque course with fine views of the Sidlaw hills yet is within easy distance of the centre of Dundee. The park also includes an inexpensive nine-hole course, a practice net at the first tee and a golf simulator.

Caledon shipyard

Dundee's last shipyard, now sadly gone. W. B. Thomson, a Broughty Ferry man, established the Tay foundry in 1866 and W. B. Thomson Shipbuilding in 1874. His first vessel was a yacht, *Banshee*, for James Alexander, 4th Earl of Caledon (1846–98) and in 1896 the company was renamed the Caledon shipbuilding and engineering company. Within a few years Caledon was one of the largest ship builders in Dundee. The yard was renowned for the high-quality of its workmanship and, interestingly, built *California*, the ship that failed to respond to *Titanic*'s distress signal.

In 1914 Caledon had fifteen hundred workers, and, in common with other Scottish yards, was very busy during the First World War. When peace came the company relocated to Stannergate. The 1920s boomed but the depression of the Thirties hit hard until 1936 when business began to pick up, becoming hectic during the Second World War, with over a thousand vessels repaired. With so much work, and so many Dundee men away fighting, the yard employed women as welders and for other skilled work. Among the first work it was involved in during the war was repairing two Polish submarines that had escaped the German invasion. It also repaired and refitted other submarines from the Dundee submarine base, as well as building Castle and Loch-class frigates. The Caledon was the only Dundee yard to continue business well into the twentieth century, building all types of vessels including an aircraft carrier and in 1954 the 12,000-ton *Storeas,* the largest ship built on the east coast of Scotland. After merging with Henry Robb of Leith in 1966, the yard finally closed in 1981.

Caledon Street

Named after the shipyard.

Callender Gardens

Despite the different spelling, this street takes its name from a calender works, which was the finishing process in jute-making.

Camberwell Court

The Camberwell Beauty butterfly is Scandinavian and a summer visitor to these shores. All the courts in this part of Dundee are named after butterflies or moths.

Cambustay Gardens, Broughty Ferry

The mansion house of Cambustay was owned by Thomas Taylor (1828–86), a linen merchant and manufacturer. It is now a country pub and restaurant.

Camperdown

The name Camperdown is woven throughout Dundee. It commemorates a vital sea battle on 11 October 1797 when Dundee-born Admiral Adam Duncan (1731–1804) defeated a larger Dutch fleet that was sailing to take part in an invasion of Britain. The battle was fought opposite a Dutch village called Kaemperdoen and took place shortly after the Royal Navy had experienced a mutiny over pay and conditions.

Duncan led his fleet to a hard-fought victory over a brave enemy. He restored pride in the navy at a time that the army was not particularly efficient. The days of the Grand Old Duke of York marching his ten thousand men up and down hills were only a few years in the past, and the glories of Wellington still in the future; Duncan's morale-boosting win was badly needed.

Duncan was a real Dundee man, son of the provost, and born in Burnhead house on Castle hill. He joined the navy while young and his career was useful rather than spectacular until the great mutiny of 1796 when his crew remained loyal. With a mere three vessels, Duncan blockaded the Dutch in the Texel, signalling to the horizon to deceive the enemy there were more ships out at sea. After the battle of Camperdown, Duncan was created Viscount Duncan of Camperdown and Baron Lundie; he was also given an estate to the north west of Dundee, where the present day Camperdown house and park are situated.

Camperdown country park

Camperdown Country Park

Commemorates Admiral Duncan's naval victory over the Dutch. The park is on the outskirts of Dundee opposite Templeton woods and is a beautiful place to visit. There are not only over 190 different species of trees but also facilities for children and adults and in addition it plays host to Dundee flower show. At around four hundred acres this is the largest public park in the city.

Camperdown docks

Takes its name from the second Earl Camperdown, who was the grandson of Admiral Adam Duncan and a member of the harbour board. The docks were designed by Charles Ower in 1863–5 and together with Victoria dock and a fish dock are all that remain of what was once a vast network. The dock is a designated A-listed building, rectangular with a depth of eighteen feet and access to Victoria dock.

The quay was built of ashlar brought by lighter or raft from Kingoodie quarries, to the west of Dundee.

Camperdown golf course

Set within Camperdown country park, this 6,548-yard championship course has a par of 71 and was opened in 1959. It is a treat to play, with challenging fairways flanked by mature trees. There are no short cuts; the golfer must be on top form to master Camperdown, but the surroundings are beautiful and the course is only minutes from the city centre.

The player can hire golf trolleys, practise at the net and leave the children in the nearby play area in the park. There is also a pitch-and-putt course for those with limited time or experience.

Camperdown house

Camperdown House

Built in 1824, this neoclassical building is the architectural highlight of Camperdown country park. William Burn (1789–1870), one of the finest Scottish architects, designed the house for Robert Haldane-Duncan, the second

Earl Duncan. The building has an impressive portico on the eastern side. Inside there is a high-roofed hall with a stained-glass dome for a roof.

Camperdown wildlife centre

Situated within the confines of Camperdown country park, this is Dundee's zoo. There is a range of animals from Clydesdale horses to brown bears, golden eagles to white storks, plus a café, shop and educational tours. There is an admission charge for this year-round place of education and fascination.

Camperdown works, Lochee

Cox's Stack and Camperdown Works

In its late-nineteenth-century heyday this building was one of the most impressive examples of a mill in the country. Owned by the famous Cox family, and named after the nearby house and estate of Camperdown, around five thousand people worked here. With the demise of Dundee's textile industry in the twentieth century the mill fell into disrepair but the High, or Silver, mill was converted into seventy-four flats, with the clock tower and cupola as architectural features.

At its peak Camperdown works extended to around two hundred acres and contained schools, a stable, a foundry and even a railway. Thanks to an ambition that was never satisfied, the Cox family also invested in a line of clipper ships. In the early 1920s the mill was the scene of major industrial action when Cox, after a year of record profits, proposed reducing the workforce. Around thirty thousand jute workers came out on strike, with an estimated fifty thousand people meeting in Albert Square and the managers locking out the workers for eight starvation weeks. More often of course, this was the scene of hectic activity.

Camphill Road, Broughty Ferry

Runs from Queen Street to Abertay Street and takes its name from the supposed Roman camp that was on Balgillo hill rather than the much-later English fortification. Carbet castle, a palace of the jute barons, once dominated the street, which, before 1860, was known as Old Monifieth Road.

Campus green, University of Dundee

The campus green is between the Queen Mother building and the Students' Association, a green oasis that is the scene of various events including graduation garden parties and casual meetings. More often it is just a place to chill out, read a book or stroll through.

Candle Lane

Runs between Seagate and Dock Street. Joseph Sanderson set up a candle-making workshop here at the beginning of the nineteenth century and his widow, Elizabeth Smith, and their sons, continued the business. The workshop survived until 1844.

Canning Street

Runs between Strathmartine Road and Moncur Crescent in Coldside and recalls Irish-born Prime Minister George Canning (1770–1827). Canning's father was an impoverished barrister and his mother took to the stage. An uncle gave him a small Irish estate. He entered politics, married well but spent most of his wife's money on election expenses, paying debts and buying property. He was prime minister for a few months in 1827, supported Catholic emancipation and the abolition of the slave trade but opposed Parliamentary reform.

Candle Lane

Carbet castle, Camphill Road, Broughty Ferry

This 1998 block of flats is named after Carbet castle, which stood on the same site.

Carbet Castle Gatehouse

Carbet castle gatehouse, 7 Camphill Road, Broughty Ferry

When the textile princes ruled Dundee they built magnificent mansions in the West Ferry and Broughty Ferry area. One of the finest was Carbet castle, under the guard of a dragon weather vane and a camel.

The Grimond dynasty bought Kerbet house here, rebuilt it as a virtual palace and renamed it Carbet castle. Its splendour enhanced the magnificence of the Grimonds' reign. However, as the textile trade slid away from Dundee, so did the power of the princes. Dry rot blighted Carbet, which was demolished, leaving only fading pictures, memories, a painted ceiling that is now in storage and this opulent gatehouse as a reminder of the splendours of the past.

Cardean Street

The name is derived from a house and country estate in east Perthshire, north of Dundee. In 1840 there was a lint mill built at Cardean, on the banks of the Dean water, which employed about a hundred-and-fifty people. To venture even further back in time, in the first century AD the Romans chose this area to build a fort during one of their abortive attempts to extend their rule over what is now Scotland. The name could come from *Caer* or *Cathair* Dean – the fort or castle beside the Dean.

Cardross Place/Street

Named after the village between Dumbarton and Helensburgh.

Carlunie Road

Takes its name from Carlunie hill in the Sidlaw hills. Carlunie is 340 metres high and stands on the eastern edge of the range.

Carmichael Court/Gardens/Street

Commemorates the engineer, James Carmichael (*see entry below*).

Carmichael, James

There is a statue to this great engineer outside the museum in Albert Square. James Carmichael was a founder of James Carmichael & Co., an engineering works that became the Ward Road foundry. Together with his brother Charles he built a steam engine for the ferry between Dundee and Woodhaven, and from then on his reputation was assured. He invented the fan-blast system that improved the manufacture of iron and built the first locomotive on the Dundee–Newtyle railway, one of the earliest in Scotland.

James Carmichael

Carmyllie Place

The parish of Carmyllie is in Angus, inland from Arbroath. According to place-names expert David Dorward, the name is from Gaelic, *cathairamhilidh,* meaning 'warrior's fort', although the fort has long gone.

Carnegie building, University of Dundee (off Geddes Quadrangle)

This building hosts the research establishment, the centre for energy, petroleum and mineral law and policy (CEPMLP).

Carnegie Street, Maxwelltown

Originally Union Street it was renamed for Andrew Carnegie, the Dunfermline-

Carnegie Street

born steel magnate and philanthropist, who, in his lifetime, gave around $350 million to various good causes around the world. Among other things, he built the famous Carnegie hall in New York and created the Carnegie scholarships for Scottish universities. In Dundee he funded five libraries including Arthurstone, which he opened in person on 10 February 1905.

Carnelley building, University of Dundee

Celebrates Thomas Carnelley (1852–90), who was chair of the school of chemistry. This 1883 building was one of the first in Dundee to have electric lighting. Funded partly by a donation from Mary Ann Baxter, it was intended to house the first air-conditioned chemical laboratories in the world, but, unfortunately, the fans lacked power and there were also a number of faults in the system. The D'Arcy Thompson zoology museum is in the same building and is well worth a visit. At the time of writing (2016) the curator is one of the most enthusiastic anywhere while D'Arcy Thompson was the first professor of biology in the university.

Carolina house, Springhill

An Italianate building of 1870 with the usual paraphernalia of turrets and towers, Carolina house was built as an orphanage when there was nothing much here except a steep slope above the river.

The orphanage story began in 1815 when the Tay ferry *Nelson* sank, with seventeen people drowned and a number of orphans created. Ten days later there was a meeting of the Dundee orphan society in the city church and within a few months an orphanage in Paradise Road opened. The initial twenty-one children included a girl whose father had been killed at Waterloo. Dundee orphanage is said to be the oldest children's charity in Scotland with James Chalmers, who invented the adhesive postage stamp, among the founders.

In 1819 the problem of funds was solved by the governess when she raised money by organising a ball that included the new-fangled, and slightly scandalous, waltz. Church collections also helped while George IV gave his official blessing, allowing the name to become the Royal Dundee Orphan Institution. The orphanage soon moved to larger premises in Small's Wynd, where it remained for over fifty years, adding education to its caring function.

In 1859 Dundee was booming and the directors of the orphanage bought land for new and larger premises but it was not until 1870 that the improved Carolina house was completed. Numbers of orphans increased, many gaining apprenticeships while twelve died in the First World War. The Admiralty took over the building during the Second World War.

All this time the orphanage was supported by voluntary subscriptions. In the postwar period the orphanage changed its name to Carolina house as it was situated near Carolina Port. The orphanage later moved home, first to Strathmore Avenue and then to Roseangle. Although the location and methods of care have altered and updated, the idea of helping has never died.

Carradale Drive
The name of this street has no local connection, but, like others in the area, refers to a place in the west of Scotland. Carradale is a small fishing village on the east coast of the Kintyre peninsula in Argyll.

Castle Court
This passage extends from 27 Castle Street to City Square. The name relates to Dundee's long-gone mediaeval castle. At one time there was an inn known as Lion tavern here.

Castle Huntly

Castle Huntly

A few miles west of Dundee and on the fringe of Longforgan, the original castle was built by Lord Gray in the fifteenth century. The name changed to Huntly when a later Gray married into the family of Gordon of Huntly. The castle itself is not easy to view as it is now an open prison, but even when it was built it was formidable, being placed on a rock that protrudes from the flat floodplain of the Carse of Gowrie. It was originally an L-plan tower house but has been very extensively enlarged and modernised on various occasions.

One public scandal occurred in the 1880s when George Armitstead leased Castle Huntly. Armitstead was the local MP and was married to Jane Baxter of the renowned Baxter family. Unfortunately, he had a liaison with the daughter of Macpherson of Cluny. When Macpherson learned about the affair, he threw his daughter out. She ran to Armitstead at Castle Huntly and he took her in. Not surprisingly, Mrs Armitstead objected and apparently gave Armitstead an ultimatum: her or me. When Armitstead chose the Macpherson woman, Jane Baxter stormed out of the house in her nightgown and spent the night at the lodge.

Castle Huntly also has a couple of ghosts. One is of a young boy who was drowned in the Tay in 1939. The other is a White Lady who was said to have committed suicide by jumping from the battlements. She was a gentlewoman who had committed the terrible sin of dallying with a servant.

Castle Street, Dundee

Castle Street

The name refers to the mediaeval castle that stood on a small hill in this area. It was first mentioned in the late thirteenth century, and, in common with most Scottish castles, it changed hands a number of times during the Wars of Independence.

When Edward Plantagenet, King of England, demanded that Gilbert de Umphraville, Earl of Angus, hand over the keys of Dundee castle in 1296, the noble earl refused. However, the English took the castle and appointed Brian FitzAlan as custodian. William Wallace recaptured it the following year and in 1298 appointed Sir Alexander Scrymgeour as Constable. The English returned in 1303 but King Robert I finally captured and destroyed the castle in 1313.

Over time the road from the castle rock to the harbour was given various names. Originally Castle Wynd, it altered to Skirling's Wynd after a bailie of that name, and Tindal's Wynd after a local baker and councillor. By the late eighteenth century an expanding Dundee required better access to the harbour so, in 1795, Castle Street was thrust straight through the castle rock. The street is interesting for its own sake, with a Georgian house at no. 26 and a bust of Shakespeare in the building that was once the Theatre Royal. Designed by Samuel Bell, the theatre opened with high cultural pretensions but became little more than a music hall popular with sailors.

At the corner of Castle Street there is a blue plaque, one of twenty-five located throughout the city to honour prominent women. This plaque is for Janet Keiller who was the founder of the Keiller marmalade and confection business.

Together with her husband, John, Janet Keiller ran a confectioner's shop for years, but when she took delivery of a load of bitter oranges she boiled them into chip marmalade. In 1797, at the age of sixty, she went into business with her son James. When her son died, Janet and her daughter-in-law Margaret ran the business themselves, moving the shop to Castle Street. After their death the company continued, opening a factory off Albert Square in 1870, where it remained until 1972.

At 10 Castle Street was the book shop of James Chalmers, inventor of the adhesive postage stamp. The former Chalmers hall of residence at the top of the street was named after him.

Castle Street/Terrace, Broughty Ferry
Refers to Broughty castle. Colin MacDonald Gilray MC OBE (1885–1974) lived in Castle Terrace, the only man to play rugby for both Scotland (four caps) and New Zealand (one cap) before becoming headmaster of Scotch College in Melbourne. He won his Military Cross in the First World War and was a noted athlete, scholar and Christian. The terrace enjoys a beautiful situation with front gardens opposite a public park. This street was also the home of Captain Easson, who was a shipmaster for thirty years. Easson's son followed the family tradition and became master of *Arthurstone*, a ship of the Dundee Clipper Line.

Castlecary Gardens
Castlecary is a village near Cumbernauld; there is also a Castlecary in Ireland.

Castleroy Crescent/Road, Broughty Ferry
Commemorates the mansion of Castleroy, one of the most magnificent of the jute barons' mansions, built for the Gilroy family. It stood among twenty acres of grounds in Broughty Ferry. Now it is gone, but the Jacobean-style gatehouse sits in Queen Street, Broughty Ferry as a reminder of past glories. In April 1883 Sarah Annie Gilroy, only daughter of the Gilroys, married James Cox, the eldest son of George Cox of Beechwood and Invertrossachs, thus uniting two of the most

powerful textile families of Dundee. The bride wore white satin while the Cox works at Lochee were decorated with bunting and signs that declared: 'Long life and health to the happy pair.' The ships in harbour were also embellished with bunting. Bride and groom honeymooned with a tour of the Continent.

Cedar Grove/Road, Broughty Ferry
Occupy the site of a nursery where trees were grown.

Cedarwood Drive, Beechwood

Cedarwood Drive

As the estate was named after Beechwood house, many of the streets had the suffix 'wood' for the sake of continuity.

Chalk Hill Court
In common with other courts in this area, named after a butterfly or moth. The Chalk Hill blue butterfly is unlikely to be seen in Dundee as it lives on chalk downland.

Challum Crescent/Lane/Place/Walk
The council named these streets in 1984 to 'continue the naming strategy for the area, i.e. – names of Munros'. *Beinn Challuim* (or Ben Challum) is in the Loch Lomond and the Trossachs national park, near the village of Tyndrum.

Chalmers Street
Arbroath born James Chalmers (1782–1853) had a bookshop in Castle Street and invented the adhesive postage stamp, which he called a 'slip'. He was also a reform-minded councillor who campaigned for an end to the tax on newspapers.

Chapelshade

An area to the east of the original town of Dundee but now well within the city boundary. In the early nineteenth century it was a select suburb, but as industrialisation continued apace factories spread into the area and it became congested, busy and noisy. The name suggests there was a religious institution here, with the suffix 'shade' suggesting an extensive parcel of land around a chapel. There was an estate with this name from at least the sixteenth century.

Charles Bowman Avenue

Charles Bowman was born in 1924. He was a Labour councillor in Dundee and the director of a number of companies including the Claverhouse Group, Blackness Training Company, Dundee Enterprise Trust and the Tayside Council on Alcohol. He worked tirelessly to help the people of the city, especially those in difficult circumstances. He made an attempt to become the Labour MP for Dundee East in 1983 but lost to Gordon Wilson of the SNP.

Charleston Road

A street in the housing scheme of the same name in the north-west of the city. The original name suggests a settlement named after its proprietor, one Charles, but who he might have been is lost in the mists of time. Unfortunately, the scheme has nothing to do with Charleston in the USA, with whom Dundee had a thriving trade in linen. In the 1840s James Wilson ran Charleston farm, with William Wilson in charge by 1859. In 1954 the controversial politician George Galloway was born in this area.

Charlotte Street/Place

In 1740 shipowner and Caribbean sugar merchant Walter Tullideph bought the estate of Baldovan, then known as The Bank. He had two daughters, the elder being Charlotte. He gifted her The Bank as a wedding present and when she married the 5th Earl of Leven the estate name reverted to Baldovan. Charlotte Street is her memorial.

Cherryfield Lane

This lane was once the western boundary of a large nursery owned by James Urquhart. The name comes presumably from the cherry trees in the garden.

Cheviot Crescent, Fintry

Originally Fincraig Street. When the Fintry housing scheme was built in the 1940s the idea was for all the streets to begin with the prefix 'fin', presumably so they would be immediately recognisable as belonging to the 'Fin'-try area. However, Fincraig Street acquired a bad reputation so the name was changed to

Cheviot Crescent. The Cheviot hills form part of the border between Scotland and England. The late George McDonald Fraser, in his book *The Steel Bonnets*, termed them the 'most romantic hills in the world'.

Chirnside Place

In common with other streets in the area, the name has no local connection. Chirnside is a village in Berwickshire in the Scottish Borders.

Christian Road, Broughty Ferry

Takes its name from Christian Scott (c.1669–?) the mother of James, the first Baron Guthrie of Craigie (1698–1788). He was the third greatest (by value) landowner in Dundee.

Churches (town or city)

Smack in the middle of Dundee, this single ecclesiastical building hosts two congregations and is highlighted by the monumental Old Steeple, which is detailed elsewhere. Known as the town's or city's churches, the architectural quality of the original fifteenth-century buildings reveals the wealth and importance of Dundee. When built this was the largest parish church (as opposed to cathedrals) in the country. In common with most other buildings of this age in

City Churches, St Mary's Church

City Churches, Nethergate

Scotland, the church attracted unwanted attention, with the nave being burned by English invaders in the sixteenth century.

Never down for long, the townspeople of Dundee altered the choir and transepts into three distinct churches, with the town architect, Samuel Bell, rebuilding the nave into St Clement's church in 1787. In 1841 a massive fire devastated the building so the following year the architect William Burn began rebuilding work, which is the building that now sits proud outside the Overgate centre.

Church Street, Broughty Ferry
Before the Reformation, a chapel stood at the junction with this street and Fisher Street.

Churchill Place, Broughty Ferry
Does not refer to Sir Winston Churchill, but rather to his father, Randolph, the Conservative MP for Woodstock. The Cowan family, true-blue Conservatives, owned this street.

City chambers, City Square
Reputedly the greatest architect in Scotland, Sir John Burnet (1857–1938), designed this building in 1924, but James McLellan Brown (c.1886–1967), Dundee city engineer, altered the façade. It is uninspiring but functional.

At the entrance is a small blue plaque, one of twenty-five positioned throughout the city. Each one is dedicated to a prominent Dundee woman. This plaque is for Agnes Husband (1852–1929), a suffragette and a councillor who campaigned on behalf of the poor and for improvements in education. She was awarded the freedom of the city when she was 74 years old.

City Quay shopping centre

City Quay, Victoria Harbour

67

Situated beside Victoria dock, this atmospheric area is handy for *Unicorn* and the *North Carr* lightship as well as easy access to the Riverside with its splendid view of the Tay and over to Fife. The centre has a number of eating places but retail outlets are limited. There is modern housing and hotels nearby, and parking alongside, although pedestrian access is not always easy.

City Square

City Square Fountains

In the centre of Dundee, with the Caird hall as a backdrop and the elegant Reform Street leading off, City Square is exactly what it says: a public square in the heart of the city. This is a place to sit and relax after shopping, to enjoy Dundee's reputation as the sunniest city in Scotland, to admire the architecture or to listen to the soothing ripples of the fountains – with their standing-stone poems – designed by Lizzanne Kempsell and funded by the Dundee public-arts programme. From the square, the pedestrianised High Street leads to the Marketgate.

Clatto Gardens, Brackens
This street is named after the nearby Clatto reservoir.

Clatto park, Dalmahoy Drive
This country park is centred on an old twenty-four-acre reservoir that is no longer connected to Dundee's water system. It has a mixture of woodland, a play area for children and paths to explore. The water sports here do not seem to disturb the resident fish, ducks and other bird life while the paths probe into neighbouring Baldragon woods, Clatto moor and Admiral Duncan wood.

Claverhouse Cottages/Road

The rural estate of Claverhouse was once a few miles outside Dundee but the city has expanded so it is now on the outskirts. The name is best remembered as belonging to 'Bluidy Claverhouse', otherwise known as Bonnie Dundee, depending on which side of the religious or monarchical divide the speaker was. This military commander brightened – or darkened – the seventeenth century with his mercurial flame. He was a burgess of Dundee, the owner of Claypotts castle, and spent much time in his other property of Glen Ogilvie, although he also owned the lands and castle of Dudhope.

Clayhills Drive/Grove

Alexander Clayhills was the proprietor of Invergowrie estate in the middle of the nineteenth century. He was one of a long line of Clayhills of Baldovie and Invergowrie, so the streets were named after this local family of landowners.

Claypotts castle

Claypotts Castle

Place-name expert David Dorward suggests that the castle may have been named after an ancient clay pit that was in the area. It is a tower house with what Charles McKean terms 'heraldic gunloops' beside the entrance that were more ornamental than defensive.

Like most things in Dundee, Claypotts castle tends to hide its charms. Yet it is an interesting castle with a fascinating architectural style. The castle itself is built to the Z-plan, which was not unusual in Scotland. That means there is a rectangular central building, with rounded towers at diagonally opposite corners. In the case of Claypotts, the top storey has been attractively completed in a square form with corbie-stepped gables. The overall effect is most interesting.

Claypotts Court/Place/Road
Named after the castle.

Cleghorn Street

Cleghorn Street

This street celebrates William Cleghorn (1830–95), who owned Garden works as well as warehouses on Fleuchar Street. He was the tenant and eventual owner of Logie house, on whose lands Cleghorn Street and others now stand. Logie house was built sometime before 1660 and demolished in 1908. Cleghorn Street was built in the middle of the nineteenth century and is composed of two-storey terraced houses, with outside staircases to the flats on the upper level and a small garden at the front and back.

Clement Park
Sits in Harefield Road and is B-listed. This mansion was built for James Cox in 1854 and is said to be the largest surviving jute-baron mansion in Dundee. It is a building of various architectural styles that makes clear the importance of the Cox family, who owned Camperdown works in Lochee (photo on facing page).

Clement Park Place/Road/Terrace
Named after the mansion.

Clement Park

Clepington Road

This road originally connected the two estates of East and West Clepington. The name Clepington is a version of the original Clephane-toun, which was named after the Clephanes of Carslogie in east Fife, who owned the lands. The estates were north of Hilltown and were known as the 'heights of Clepington'. Clepington Road is the longest street in Dundee and at one time was home to the first trolley-bus service in Britain, commonly known as 'The Stoories' because the road was unmetalled and vehicles created a lot of dust.

In the nineteenth century, when the Clepington area was still rural, the local people had their own names for old areas, paths, buildings and rights of way. There was the 'Glower-ower' which was also 'the big land in Clepington Road'. There was 'Lady Wise's' and the 'Rashie Well', 'Corbie wood' and 'Hedgie wedgie', also known as 'Whinnie ditch' that led to the 'Cadger Road'. Progress has obliterated these colourful and descriptive names and Dundee is the poorer for it. Does anyone know these places now?

Clepington Street

This street was the scene of a major fire in February 1884 when the Clepington waste work was burned and four firemen lost their lives.

Clifden Blue Court

In common with other courts in this area named after a butterfly or moth.

Clinkerheel Drive
Takes its name from Clinkerheel quarry at Muirhead of Liff. 'Clinker' means broken pieces of rock, which would be perfect for a quarry.

Cloan Road
This short street is in Downfield. The name Cloan came from the estate, near Auchterarder, of Viscount Haldane, who was related to Robert Haldane, the landowner who created the street.

Clock tower, or harbour warehouse, Victoria dock
Built as a grain warehouse in 1877, the clock was visible to any vessel in the dock. This A-listed building has been converted for use as apartments.

Clovis Duveau Drive

Clovis Duveau Drive

Honours Monsieur Clovis Duveau, a gentleman from Orleans, Dundee's twin town in France. Duveau was a guide to parties of Dundee visitors to the French town. The story begins in the Second World War, when three Free French submarines were based in Dundee. The good people of the city created a club in the Nethergate for these French seamen, and a friendship grew. As the war drew to a close, Scottish towns and cities formed strong bonds with newly liberated French towns and Dundee bonded with Orleans. There were reciprocal visits and M. Duveau led the Orleans contingent for many years. In 1996 this street was named in his honour, and 96-year-old Clovis Duveau travelled to Scotland for the official opening.

Clyde Place, Menzieshill

Many of the streets in this area are named after Scottish rivers. This small street carries the name of arguably the greatest of them all, the river Clyde.

Cobden Street, Lochee

Named after Richard Cobden MP, a prominent campaigner for free trade in the nineteenth century. Prior to 1907 it was known as Union Place, but the name was changed in order to avoid confusion with streets of similar names within Dundee.

Coldside library, Strathmartine Road

Coldside library

Designed by James Thomson in 1908, the front is uniquely concave, the library itself is Y-shaped, with amazing gables that face onto Strathmartine Road and Strathmartine Avenue. This is one of Dundee's Carnegie libraries, financed by a grant from the Dunfermline-born steel magnate Andrew Carnegie. The land for the library was donated by a former Lord Provost, Sir Charles Barrie, whose house had been on the site. Barrie (1840–1912) was a shipowner, whose son became a Liberal MP and the first Baron Abertay.

Coldstream Drive

This name has no local connection but refers to the town on the border with England from which the crack regiment, the Coldstream guards, took its name.

Colin Gibson Drive, Monifieth

This is one of the few Monifieth streets in this book but Colin Gibson was well known in Dundee and beyond. Born in Arbroath in 1907 he taught art at Dundee High School for twelve years. He was the official artist to University College, Dundee, while his work is displayed in royal collections. He was also a writer with several books to his credit; however, he may be best remembered for his 'Nature Diary' column in the *Dundee Courier*.

Collace Crescent

The meaning of the name is ambiguous but David Dorward suggests that it could be from the Gaelic *cuil an eas*, 'nook of the bog'. Collace is a parish and village in Perthshire.

Collingwood Street, Broughty Ferry

Commemorates Admiral Cuthbert Collingwood. Northumberland-born, he fought alongside Nelson and was known for his friendship with the more famous admiral. Both men fought at Cape St Vincent, where Collingwood rescued Nelson from a tricky situation, and later Collingwood was second-in-command at Trafalgar. He was much moved by Nelson's death and died in 1810.

Commercial Street

Commercial Street

The eastern part of this street was designed to copy the architecture of Paris, with the name reflecting the economic aspects of the city. The street was designed in 1871 by the burgh engineer, William Mackison (1833–1906), as part of a major city improvement scheme that destroyed much of Dundee's mediaeval core. Today we may regret the loss of many ancient buildings, but retaining

Commercial Street, architectural detail

unhygienic and crowded wynds was not considered important when city pride, ease of transport and the health of the population was at stake.

Based at Mackay, Irons in Commercial Street, the Matador Land & Cattle Company clearly illustrates the commercial aptitude of Dundee as jute barons reached out to invest in the United States. The company was begun by Henry Campbell, a Texas cattleman and ex-Confederate soldier. The following year a man named Colonel Alfred Britton came to Dundee for financial help and a group of Dundee businessmen including Robert Fleming, George Halley and John Robertson invested heavily in the idea. In 1882 the Dundee businessmen bought the Matador Cattle Company of Texas for $1,250,000 – around £250,000 at the time.

Dundee jute barons were used to dealing with North American customers, having sold sandbags to both sides during the American civil war and covers for the wagons that carried settlers into the American West. At its height the Matador owned 100,000 acres but ran cattle over a further 1.5 million acres of open range. The most successful manager was Murdo Mackenzie from Easter Ross who based himself in Trinidad, Colorado and made the Matador 'the mother of British cattle companies in the United States'. Mackenzie rose to head the American National Livestock Association. Although he lived and worked in the US, Mackenzie kept his Scottish accent and clothes, befriended Theodore Roosevelt and kept the Matador profitable when other similar organisations failed.

Contrary to popular images of the West, Mackenzie did not allow his cowboys to gamble or drink when they were at work. However, one of his sons was killed in a bar-room fight and he used 'range detectives' to sort out rustlers and other troubles. The company remained in Dundee ownership until 1951.

Congregational church, Panmure Street
This B-listed building of 1855 was designed by David Bryce, one of Scotland's foremost architects of the nineteenth century. The central Gothic rose window is protected by flanking pointed towers. No longer a place of worship it is now called Trinity hall and Dundee High School uses it as a library.

Constable Lane, Broughty Ferry
This street remembers James Nicoll Constable of Balmyle in Strathardle, who also owned land here. Constable also bought the Perthshire estate of Soilzarie that had been once owned by Brigadier John Pennycuik, who was killed at the battle of Chillianwalla in the Second Sikh War. There are memorials to the Constable family in the Howff graveyard in Dundee.

Constitution Road

Constitution Road

A steep street that soars from Bell Street upwards to the Law. It could perhaps be called Education Road as it once housed the Watt Institution (to teach 'young tradesmen . . . arts and sciences'), the Constitution campus of Dundee college and is near to Abertay University. The name is obviously political.

Constitution Terrace
Planned by David Mackenzie in 1851, this compact horseshoe of lovely detached and semi-detached villas shelters behind well-kept gardens. It is a secret little street with a unique atmosphere.

Constitution Terrace

Corbie wood

Corbie is the Scots word for a crow. Bird names were very distinctive in Scots with, for example, a corbie being a crow, a yellow-yite or yorling being a yellowhammer, a mavis a thrush and the very evocative whaup being what is now more often called a curlew. On the 1857 map of Dundee, Corbiewood cottage stood here, at the end of a short drive from Clepington Road.

Corn Exchange hall

Later known as Kinnaird hall, in November 1859 this hall was visited by Lola Montez who lectured on the comic aspects of fashion. Irish-born, Montez was an actress and personality whose full title was Marie Dolores Eliza Rosanna Gilbert, Countess of Landsfeld. As well as acting she was a dancer and the mistress of King Ludwig I of Bavaria. The presence of such a famous celebrity showed that Dundee was no cultural backwater. The building became the Kinnaird Picture house and closed in the 1960s, shortly before it was demolished.

Cortachy Crescent

There is a Cortachy parish in Angus, which was part of the Airlie estate. The Earl of Airlie also owned Cortachy castle.

Cotton Road

In the eighteenth century David Wyse, the son of Alexander Wyse of Lunan near Montrose, erected a cotton mill in the area. His son, Thomas Wyse, became a doctor, emigrated to Jamaica where he made his fortune, returned to Dundee and bought Hillbank estate. Hillbank house stood on the top of the hill here.

Coupar Angus Road

It is fairly obvious that this is the road to Coupar Angus. There are two places named Cupar in Scotland, with the other being in Fife (different spelling, same pronounciation), so the suffix 'Angus' serves as a geographical identification. It is ironic, however, that boundary changes have placed Coupar Angus in Perthshire.

Courier building, Meadowside

Home to DC Thomson, the third 'J' in the Dundee litany of jute, jam and journalism. This red building stands opposite the Howff and is the source of such notable publications as the *Sunday Post*, the *People's Friend* and the *Beano* as well as local papers the *Courier* and *Evening Telegraph*, known as the *Telly*. Surprisingly for a city that is generally left leaning, the *Courier* tends to the right politically, but is still immensely popular, perhaps because of the consistently high quality of the journalism and its definitive reporting of local issues.

Courier Building, Meadowside Entrance

Courier Building

The building was erected in 1902 to the design of Niven and Wigglesworth of London. It has been called the most American-style building in the city, as Wigglesworth drew his inspiration from William Randolph Hearst, while David Barclay Niven, an Angus man, was more prosaic in his architectural styling. The external sculpture is by Albert Hodge and the overall effect extremely impressive. One of many talented journalists to work for the company was Jacqueline Wilson, the prolific children's author with over ten million book sales. The DC Thomson magazine, *Jackie*, was named after her.

Court Street

This street is often overlooked but it is one of the most interesting in the city as the houses were constructed of concrete, with a cement render covered in buff textured paint. The street was built in 1874–5 by the Concrete Building Co., so is an early example of concrete building in the city.

Couttie's Wynd

Couttie's Wynd

One of the most evocative survivors of old Dundee, Couttie's Wynd is a narrow, gently curving lane that extends from Whitehall Crescent to the Nethergate. This route is ancient; being used in the early Middle Ages by people moving from the town to the shore and vice versa. Duncan, Earl of Huntingdon had a mansion here at the beginning of the thirteenth century, enhancing the tradition that kings and noblemen used this route.

In the latter half of the fifteenth century the street was known as Spalding's Wynd after the politician David Spalding who lived here, but after 1521 it became Couttie's Wynd. One version of the name is that William Couttie was a local butcher who bought property in the wynd. A more colourful account claims that King James V gave the land to a drover named Couttie who had helped him drive off a band of robbers.

The wynd appears narrow now but was actually widened in 1769 to allow access to the harbour. By the early nineteenth century Couttie's Wynd was notorious for cheap lodging houses, brothels and sordid violence. Today it is quieter with no houses of ill repute.

Covenanters Pend, Fintry

There were two distinct phases of the Covenanters. The first relates to the early Covenanters, who signed both the National Covenant in 1639, and the Solemn League and Covenant in 1643. The former document states that the Church of Scotland recognised only God as its head and not the king. At that time, King Charles I was attempting to impose Episcopacy on Scotland. The Solemn League was a bond with Oliver Cromwell. The English Protector requested Scottish help in his war with the king, so the Scottish government hired out an army that held northern England in control and turned the tide at the Battle of Marston Moor. In return Cromwell promised to make England Presbyterian, a promise he broke.

The later Covenanters were dedicated Presbyterians at a time when the government was again forcing Episcopalian values onto the people. These Covenanters were persecuted, fined, tortured and hanged through a period of Scottish history known as the Killing Times.

As this street is near Claverhouse Road, it may refer to the latter period when John Grahame of Claverhouse was actively involved in the Covenanting wars. Claverhouse was known as either Bonnie Dundee or Bluidy Claverhouse, depending on the religious or political leaning of the speaker. He was a follower of King James and a noted persecutor of Covenanters.

Cowan Place

A small street that commemorates James Cowan (1822–93). He was a councillor and a salt merchant who advocated town improvements and proposed that Dundee should be a cattle port. He also supported district reading rooms in order that working people could spend leisure time away from pubs.

Cowgate, or Cow Gait

This was the gait, or 'way', down which cattle were driven to the city centre for market. In later years it was the crux of the linen area, the textile which Dundee traded before she turned to jute. This street was also the home of J. C. Bell, a flax merchant who was a patron of artists, including William McTaggart (1835–1910). There is an unassuming tenement on the Cowgate corner where the Grimond jute barons had their headquarters.

It is a short and less-than attractive street now, despite the historical connections, but has tremendous potential. (See photo on facing page).

Cox's stack

At 282-feet high, this amazing structure is one of the tallest free-standing chimneys in Great Britain. It was part of the huge Camperdown complex in Lochee, owned by the Cox family, which gave it the name of Cox's stack. The stack is of brick with an ornate pattern and was built by James Maclaren in 1865–6, to

Cowgate

highlight the importance of Cox's mills in a city of impressive industrial architecture.

David Cock was the first significant textile entrepreneur of the family, building up a weaving business of 280 looms. His son, James, further expanded the business and the family changed the name from Cock to Cox. By the time the Stack was built, Camperdown works had fifty-seven boilers, with the combined smoke gushing from the single, massive chimney. At that time mills and factories were viewed as buildings of civic pride with nothing of Blake's dark satanic mills negativity. Cox's Stack is an impressive landmark that can be seen for miles around, a testament to the grand vision of its creator.

Cox's stack

Cox Street, Downfield

Commemorates the Cox family that dominated Lochee and owned the largest jute factory in Britain, a string of mansions and a shipping line. The Cox in question, according to David Dorward, was Lord Provost James Cox (1808–85).

Craigard Gardens/Road

There is a Craigard house overlooking Campbeltown, and another on Barra. There was also a house called Craigard in Broughty Ferry but it is more likely that this name was chosen to fit in with the other 'craig' prefixes in the immediate area. *Craig* is a rock and 'ard' is from *aird*, 'high', so the name could mean a high rock.

Craigie garden suburb

Craigie garden suburb

The renowned town planner, Ebenezer Howard, was the inspiration for this 1919 suburb, designed by the busy city engineer, James Thomson (1851–1927). As in Howard's plan, a church is central to this part of Craigie, with the housing arranged in concentric circles around. The name comes from the estate of Wallace Craigie. The name Craigie comes from the word *craig*, Scots for a rock.

Craigie Street

In 1981 the city architect built this brightly coloured courtyard development, surrounded by five-storey housing. The name is from the Craigie estate.

Craigiebarn Road

Named for the Arts and Crafts house of Craigiebarn, which was nearby.

Craigowl Road/Street

The name is Gaelic: *creag gobhal*, forked hill. Craigowl is the highest of the Sidlaw hills and is easily distinguished by the television mast and radar station on top. It also affords fine views.

Crail Place, Barnhill
The streets in this part of Barnhill were named after places in Fife. Crail is a picturesque fishing village in the East Neuk.

Crawford Place, Broughty Ferry
This street was named in December 1938, perhaps after Crawford in Lanarkshire.

Crichton Street

Crichton Street

Legend holds that this street was named after Dr John Crichton, a local surgeon. However, as the street was begun in 1779, and Dr Crichton was born in 1772 and would therefire have been just seven years old, this is unlikely. In reality the Crichton family home stood squarely in the path of this street, which was planned to give easier access between the harbour and the Nethergate. There were some tricky negotiations before the family agreed to sell the house, with the stipulation that the street should be named after the Crichton family. Dr Crichton is not forgotten, however, as the McManus galleries has a picture of him!

Cricket
A major sport in Dundee in the nineteenth century with a number of clubs including Dundee Albion and Dundee Tay. These two clubs played each other on Magdalen green in June 1852 with Albion being victorious. There was also Dundee Lily, Dundee Angus, Maryfield and Dundee Thistle. Cricket was also played at Barrack park – now Dudhope park – and on the Fair muir.

Croom's Close, 66 High Street

Reaches to New Inn Entry and named after the eighteenth-century businessman, William Croom, who lived here. It is hard to access and dark to explore but for the persistent and curious there is an ancient well inside, long since closed off.

Curling

A major sport in the nineteenth century. With the Dundee curling club, the Camperdown and Lundie curling club, and other rinks that included Stobsmuir, Dundee was a vibrant place for sport in the Victorian winters. Sir John Ogilvy of Baldovan (1803–90), president of the Dundee curling club in the 1840s, was also the local MP.

Cuschieri skills centre, Ninewells hospital

Commemorates Maltese-born Sir Alfred Cuschieri, FRSE, professor of surgery, Ninewells hospital and medical school. Sir Alfred is a pioneer in minimal invasive surgery, known as keyhole surgery, and holds patents for fifty medical instruments. The Cuschieri centre opened in 1992 to provide specialised training for healthcare professionals, including staff at Ninewells. It is one of the most progressive training facilities in Europe.

Customs house

Old Customs House

This A-listed Greek revival building in South Marketgate was once one of the largest custom houses in Scotland, which reveals exactly how important Dundee's nineteenth-century docks were. Built in 1842–3 when Dundee docks were expanding and Dundee's trade routes stretched from the Arctic to the West Indies and the Orient. The building is three-storeys high with an impressive pediment on four ionic columns.

The Customs house was unused for some time but in 2014 Apex Hotels bought the building to develop as a luxury hotel.

Dalgleish Road

Dalgleish Road

Sir William Ogilvy Dalgleish (1832–1913) lived at Mayfield house, Arbroath Road, which was later used as accommodation for students at Dundee Training College. Dalgleish was an industrialist, associated with Baxter Brothers & Co. He was also generous to Dundee and spent much of his wealth in attempting to improve the lot of his fellow citizens. Dalgleish can also be thanked for the stained-glass windows in the Albert institute.

Dalhousie Road/Terrace, Broughty Ferry

Honours Fox Maule Ramsay (1801–74), 11th Earl of Dalhousie, who was a major benefactor to Dundee. He was known as Lord Panmure until 1860, at which time he succeeded to the Earldom of Dalhousie in Midlothian. He was at the War Office in the latter period of the Crimean War, Provincial Grand Master of Forfarshire and a supporter of the Free Church of Scotland. His father, the 10th Earl, gave Reres hill to Broughty.

Dallfield Court

The name comes from the small estate of Dallfield that the Scrymgeours of Dudhope owned. The Scrymgeours were one of Dundee's most notable families, with an early member of the clan being the standard bearer of Sir William Wallace the great Scottish patriot.

Dalmahoy Drive, Ardler

One of the Ardler streets that were named after famous golf courses. Dalmahoy is a course just outside Edinburgh.

Dargie church

Dargie Church, Invergowrie

Stands on a mound in Station Road in Invergowrie. The mound itself seems to be man-made and the church is ancient. The origins of Dargie are obscure but the legend that states it was founded by a pope named Bonifacius Queretinus, a descendant of St Andrew's sister, is probably apocryphal. There are other legends, including one that the devil himself threw rocks from Fife as he tried to knock down the church. Two landed in the Tay and became known as the Yowes o' Gowrie and the third passed overhead and landed in the grounds of a nearby hotel. Thomas the Rhymer is said to have made a prophecy that: 'when the Yowes of Gowrie come to land, the day o' judgement's near at hand'. That has not come true . . . so far.

Dargie Road, Invergowrie
Named after the nearby church.

David Lane/Street, Broughty Ferry
There are two Davids who may be honoured by this street. The first is David Ferrier, who was a fisherman and a member of the Royal Navy. He bought land here in 1813. On the other hand, it could be named after Captain David Webster (1801–47) who owned land in this area and who died when his schooner, *Tid*, sank on a voyage between the Baltic and Hull.

Davidson Street, Broughty Ferry
In the nineteenth century the fishing industry exploded in Scotland. Huge fleets

of Scottish fishing boats 'followed the herring' as the shoals swam around the coasts of Britain. While fishermen worked at sea, fisherwomen gutted and packed the catch. For most it was pure hard work but some made fortunes. One such was Peter Davidson of Broughty Ferry, who owned fish-curing businesses in Broughty Ferry, Wick and Ireland as well as being a shipowner. This street is his memorial.

Dawson park

One of the major recreational areas in the east of Dundee, Dawson park has facilities for football, tennis, basketball and bowling as well as a sunken garden and a beautiful cherry avenue. For the gardener there is the New Duntrune demonstration garden, which gives horticultural advice to those with small gardens.

The park was named after a spirit merchant named William Dawson (1853–1940), who left a bequest for 'the purpose of providing playing fields, sports grounds or other recreational facilities'. In 1949 the council bought the land from the Douglas and Angus estate and the park opened a few years later.

Dawson Place/Road, Broughty Ferry

References nearby Dawson park.

Dee Place/Gardens, Menzieshill

The river Dee rises in the Cairngorms and enters the sea at Aberdeen, the name of which city means 'confluence of the Dee'. This is one of many street names in Menzieshill that are inspired by Scottish rivers.

Deer

Shaped in cold cast resin, three impressively antlered deer leap over the fence at the border of Dundee technology park. These are just one example of the public art that is very much part of the city.

Denoon Terrace

Denoon Law in the Sidlaw hills is topped by a Pictish fort with three concentric ramparts, and must have been a formidable stronghold in its day. There is also Denoon Glen nearby; either of these places could be the origin of the street name. The name Denoon may come from *dun obhainn*, 'fort of the burn'.

Dens

A name that all of Scotland and perhaps further afield will always associate with Dundee, not least because it is the name of Dens park, home of Dundee Football Club. Not many people will know that Dens Road was also the location of Angus park where the Perseverance football club played in the 1880s. The name *den* is

Anglo-Saxon rather than Pictish or Gaelic, and shows the international mixture of Dundonian place names. It was originally spelled *dene* and means a valley.

In Dundee the name comes from the Dens burn, which has a short but very significant course through the city. The Dens was an early source of water for weavers even before large companies built the mills that propelled Dundee to the forefront of world textile production. The streets Dens Road and Dens Brae mark where this burn ran. The Dens burn also gave its name to the Dens works of the Baxter family, who were one of Dundee's premier industrial clans. As time passed the factories grew until they required more power than the Dens burn afforded, so it was culverted and the mills ran by steam power instead.

Dens Brae

Dens mill needed a constant supply of water, so the Baxters had a series of ponds, connected by dams. There was a new pond at the top of Dens Brae near Bucklemaker Wynd; it was 120 feet long by 60 broad, with a retaining wall five-feet thick. In June 1859 the dam burst and rushed into the lower mill, carrying trees and stones, injuring some of the workers and alarming the others. The torrent continued through Princes Street, flooded houses in Blackscroft and entered the Tay at the yard owed by the Narwhal whale fishing company. Fortunately, nobody was seriously injured.

Dens mills or works

There were two Dens mills, Upper and Lower, both owned by the mighty Baxter

Upper Dens Mills

brothers. The Baxters were originally from Angus but migrated to Dundee in the opening years of the nineteenth century, prospered, and became one of the most powerful textile dynasties in the country. The workers were said to be on poverty wages but the engineer Peter Carmichael said that Dens works was 'better than a gold mine' for the owners. Between 1860 and 1869 Sir David Baxter banked nearly £600,000; his lowest-paid workers would be very lucky to take home £200 in the same time period.

The Baxters were major employers in Dundee and also

funded, or helped fund, civic programmes such as Baxter park, the Albert institute and University college. They were one of the textile families who made nineteenth century Dundee what it was and whose legacy lives on. Their working headquarters were at the Dens mills, icons of industry with Egyptian-style-obelisk-chimney structures that soared skyward to proclaim Baxter's status in the world of linen. Baxters provided sails for both the United States and the Royal Navy. Nelson's flagship, *Victory*, had sails made by Baxter's of Dundee while the prairie schooners, the wagons that carried tens of thousands of emigrants across North America, also had covers made by Baxters of Dundee.

Dens mills were more than mere workplaces; they were like small towns within Dundee, with a workforce of some five thousand, schools and their own ethos and culture. The majority of mill workers were women and were justifiably proud of the skill with which they performed their work. The 40 per cent or so of the workforce who were male were mainly young. However, in the days before health-and-safety, there was always the possibility of an accident. For example, in December 1827, an 8-year-old boy named John Templeman fell backward into a carding machine and was 'shockingly mangled'. He died in the infirmary.

In common with many of Dundee's mills, the Upper Dens has been converted to housing so the fabric of the building survives as a reminder of the days when thousands of Dundonians lived in thrall of the clatter of factory machinery. It is still impressive with formidable mass and a cupola looking down on the surroundings.

Dens Park
The home of Dundee FC, one of Dundee's two senior clubs. The park is on

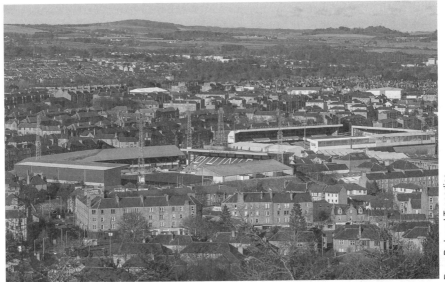

Dens Park and Tannadice

Sandeman Street, Dens Road, only a hundred yards or so from Tannadice, the home of city rivals Dundee United.

Today (2016) the ground capacity of Dens is 11,850 but the record crowd was over 43,000 for a game against Rangers in 1953. At that time there was little thought given to health and safety and the spectators were packed like sardines on the terracing. They also paid a lot less for the privilege.

In 1893 two teams, Our Boys and East End, merged to form Dundee football club. They played their early games at Our Boys' ground of West Craigie park, moved to Carolina Port but in 1899 relocated to their long-standing home at Dens park. Football players in those days were not quite so well paid as they are now, so when the East End club had an 'outing' with their 'lady friends' in April 1882 they travelled in open carriages to Blairgowrie in the rain and returned soaking-wet but happy.

The ground was improved in 1999 with the addition of two stands, named Bobby Cox and Bob Shankly in honour of the captain and manager who, in 1962, steered the club to the league title. Alas such heights have not been scaled since, although Dundee have an illustrious history, winning the Scottish Cup in 1909/10 and finishing as runners-up no less than four times, the most recent being in 2003/04. Dundee has also won the League Cup three times, including the 1995/96 season, and the League Challenge Cup in 1991 and 2010. Finally, and most gloriously, in season 1962/63, Dundee reached the semi-final of the European Cup. It is hard to imagine any provincial club even dreaming of such honours now, but Dundee is unique and should never be considered a mere provincial town.

The floodlights were recently upgraded and in 2005 undersoil heating was installed to help combat the winter frosts that can decimate sporting fixtures in Scotland. The team play in dark blue and are currently (season 2016/17) in the Scottish Premier League.

Dens Road

Another street that carries the name of the burn, Dens Road runs through the northern side of Dundee from Victoria Road. This long street has a primary school but unfortunately Dens road market, a fascinating confusion of everything under one roof, closed in 2013.

Dens Road was the home of the McTaggarts, a famous boxing family. In 1954 one McTaggart brother was the army boxing champion of the Middle East, another was the Navy boxing champion, and a third, Corporal 'Dandy Dick', was the RAF boxing champion (see Dick McTaggart regional gymnastic centre below).

Dental school, Park Place

Part of the university and a haven for those who have problems with their teeth.

With free treatment by students overseen by experts, this school was recently rated the best dental school in the UK. It is linked to the Franklin building that hosts the Dundee dental education centre.

Derby Street
Nothing to do with horse racing, this street commemorates a nineteenth-century statesman. Edward Stanley, Lord Derby (1799–1869), was leader of the Conservative party from 1846 to 1868 and prime minister three times. A decidedly aristocratic figure who loved racing and shooting, Derby was a politician of flair and dash but one who found the drudgery of everyday political life more than a little wearing.

Desperate Dan
There is a statue of this most forceful character from the *Dandy* in the centre of Dundee. He is large as life with his outthrust chin and prominent stomach. Minnie the Minx and Gnasher, the dog, are in the same group, with the dragon a few yards away, keeping well out of Dan's dangerous path.

Desperate Dan

Deveron Crescent and Terrace
In common with many in Menzieshill, these streets are named after Scottish rivers, in this case the Deveron in the north-east, which rises in the Grampians and reaches the sea between Macduff and Banff.

Devil's stone, off Myrekirk Road
Also known as the Paddock stone, or Paddock stane. An old legend claims that the devil stood in Fife and threw this stone in an attempt to destroy the church at Invergowrie.

Dick McTaggart regional gymnastics centre, Old Glamis Road
Commemorates Dick McTaggart MBE, the Dundee-born boxer, who won the gold medal in the lightweight division at the Melbourne Olympics in 1956 and

was further honoured by winning the coveted Val Barker trophy as the most stylish boxer at the games. 'Dandy' Dick's record was quite outstanding: he was also Commonwealth and European champion and the first British boxer to compete in three Olympiads, winning a bronze medal at the 1960 games in Rome. In all, he had 634 bouts, winning 610, in the process amassing thirty-two cups, fifty-seven plaques and forty-nine medals. To many aficionados, McTaggart is the finest amateur boxer Britain has ever produced. The centre named after him has a well-equipped sports hall. In 2014 a nine-foot-tall statue of the great man was unveiled at the St Francis amateur boxing club in King's Cross Road.

Dick Street, Broughty Ferry
Remembers Thomas Sturrock Dick (1852–1927), building contractor, councillor and alpine-plant collector.

Dighty Gardens/Place, Menzieshill
The name comes from the Dighty (pronounced Dichty) water. In Scotland, a water is somewhat larger than a burn but smaller than a river. The Dighty rises in the Sidlaw hills and eases around the north of Dundee to empty into the Firth of Tay at Monifieth. At one time the Dighty was the centre of an industrial landscape; as the industrial revolution cranked up in the eighteenth century, bleachfields and textile mills were established on the undoubtedly beautiful banks of the water. From the 1730s, Dundee interfered with the free flow of the Dighty by erecting dams to harness the water power and eventually there were sixty mills on the water.

Today the mills are all gone and the Dighty is no longer an industrial powerhouse, but a quiet length of water slowly recovering, albeit with stretches of urban growth along its banks.

Discovery
Built as an exploration vessel for Captain Robert Falcon Scott's 1901 expedition to the Antarctic. At that time Dundee was just beginning to slide from the height of her prestige; she was still the jute capital of Europe, and the whaling capital of Britain, although catches were diminishing. Her shipbuilding yards had built the best Arctic vessels in the world but *Terra Nova*, arguably the finest whaling ship of them all, was nearly two decades old. Then came the order for *Discovery*.

After a century-and-a-half of Arctic whaling and decades of building ships suitable for cold-weather sailoring, Dundee was the only place where *Discovery* could have been built. Hundreds of men laboured to create this wooden vessel, and she survived many years of adventures before finally returning to Dundee in

RRS *Discovery*

1986 and a new life as a tourist attraction on the Riverside, only a few hundred yards from the spot where she was launched.

She sits proud, three-masted, with her tall ochre funnel and a plethora of tales. The atmosphere around *Discovery* is tangible; it reeks of trips to Russia, exploration in the Antarctic and work with the Hudson's Bay Company. Yet of all her tales the most significant is one in which she was not the brave hero but a beleaguered heroine, trapped in a far-off castle of ice and hoping to be rescued by a knight in shining armour. In this case the knight spoke with a Dundee accent and his armour was another Dundee-built ship.

Captain Robert Falcon Scott sailed *Discovery* south to try and unlock some of the secrets of the Antarctic but he became stuck in the ice. Two ships were sent to relieve her; one was *Morning*, which later became a Dundee whaler, the other was the Dundee-built whaling ship, *Terra Nova*, commanded by Captain Harry McKay, Dundee born and bred.

Where Scott had tried ice-saws, McKay, more experienced in the ways of deep cold, used explosives and blasted *Discovery* free. Now *Discovery* can be admired with her 172 feet in length, her 1,570 tons and her eleven-inch hull. She is the pride of Dundee. Visitors sense the flavour of the Antarctic but should also listen for the ghosts: footsteps have been heard where no human walks and there is the sound of snoring in the cabin where Ernest Shackleton slept. Some people think the wardroom has an uncanny atmosphere as well, and there are stories of the suicide of a seaman. There is a lot to discover on *Discovery*.

Discovery Plaza

With the new development at the riverside, there are a number of new streets. The public were asked to give suggestions and the best were chosen. The space at the new railway station will be Discovery Plaza, named after the ship and the remarkable story of Dundee itself.

Discovery Point

Discovery Point

Where *Discovery* sits proud in the port that built her. There is an excellent visitor centre here, with exhibitions of Arctic and Antarctic life as well as the history of *Discovery*. The cafeteria and a book and gift shop are well worth visiting and there are facilities for many functions. Look for the penguins outside; a great place for children and adults to have their photographs taken.

Discovery Quay

Where the exploration ship *Discovery* now sits. This site was long known as Craig pier and was the Dundee terminus of the ferry to Fife. A craig is a crag or rock.

Dochart Terrace

Many streets in Menzieshill have names of Scottish rivers. The river Dochart is a tributary of Loch Tay, with the clan MacNab burial ground on a small island, Inchbuie, on the Falls of Dochart at Killin in Perthshire, while the chief of the clan's seat was at Kinnell on the banks of the Dochart.

Dock Street

Dock Street

Once this street was hard by the docks that provide the name. The spars of great three-masted ships overhung the road and a score of pubs roared with seamen returned from voyages to India, Greenland and half the world. Now there are vehicles and shoppers, but the bustle remains.

There are a number of notable buildings here. For example, at no. 20, was the headquarters of the Dundee, Perth & London shipping company and the Falkland Islands Company. The D. P. & L. was founded in 1826 when a trip by sailing smack to London could take up to two days, depending on the weather. The D. P. & L. moved to steam in 1830 and delighted in overtaking the slower vessels of rival companies on the east coast routes. One of their screw steamers, *London*, built by Gourlays of Dundee, remained in service for an astonishing fifty-three years, sailing not only to London but also to St Petersburg in Russia. By 1901 the company had a regular terminal at Limehouse in London.

During the First World War the Navy requisitioned many of the fleet for war service. One vessel, *Dundee*, attached to the tenth cruiser squadron, engaged a much more powerful German ship, *Leopard*, in March 1917 and kept her occupied for hours until HMS *Achilles* arrived to dispose of the enemy. The Admiralty also requisitioned vessels during the Second World War, and D. P. & L. ships were involved in convoy duty and support work for the 1944 Normandy landings. One vessel, *Gowrie,* was lost to enemy action.

Postwar expansion saw D. P. & L. ships sail as far as the Pacific, Libya and the West Indies, but times changed: the London passenger service ended, coastal shipping declined and the company altered its focus from shipping to other services. Its headquarters are now in the Dunsinane estate but the old building remains; it is distinctive with its Renaissance details and redolent of maritime history.

Docks

Dundee is a port situated on the Firth of Tay some eight miles from the sea. Throughout her early history, the town struggled with the actions of the Tay, which silted the harbour and created difficulties of access and anchorage. The Tay is tidal, with a fast current; the docks had various rocks near the entrance and the mouth of the river was complicated by sandbanks which, coupled with a fluky wind, caused many vessels to run aground. The question was: how did Dundee overcome these obstacles to become one of the most successful trading ports in the country in the nineteenth century?

The answer is by ingenuity and hard graft, two qualities that Dundee has in abundance.

Dundee possessed a harbour by the middle of the thirteenth century with ships trading to Flanders, but it was not large, which constrained growth. It expanded slowly through the Middle Ages, trading with European ports and especially the Baltic. By the sixteenth century at least one important Dundee family, the Wedderburns, had an agent living permanently in Elsinore (now Helsingor) in Denmark to ensure their cargoes travelled smoothly to Dundee.

The seventeenth century arrived with a destructive storm, continued with more trade and ravaging armies: first Montrose's Highlanders and then Cromwell's General Monck. Both wreaked havoc but it was Monck who allegedly looted Dundee and loaded the spoil onto his ships. Apparently, the entire fleet was destroyed in a sudden storm in the Tay. 1755 saw a tsunami in the wake of the Lisbon earthquake and Dundee harbour suffered accordingly.

All this time the harbour had been too small for the major port that Dundee struggled to become but then, in 1815, a commission took control of the docks, appointed Thomas Telford as consulting engineer and a period of major improvement began. A dry dock was added, then more docks for the expanding trade: King William IV dock, Earl Grey dock, Victoria dock, Camperdown dock.

In 1870 there were some 216 ships registered at Dundee including whaling vessels, Baltic traders and coasters. Forty years later the docks and harbour extended for 190 acres with three-and-a-half miles of quay. It was a major concern that provided the lifeblood of Dundee.

But things were not as rosy as they appeared. Ships were changing and improving at a speed that surpassed the modernisation of Dundee's docks. They were altering from sail to steam and then to diesel. They were larger and heavier, requiring deeper water in which to berth, and Dundee's docks could not accommodate the new type of vessels.

After the slumps of the twentieth century, only a rump remains of Dundee's once extensive docks. The frigate *Unicorn* and the lightship *North Carr* sit within Victoria dock as a reminder of past glories, while the City Quay shopping centre looks over the otherwise near empty waters of a dock that once saw jute vessels and whaling ships. Next door is the Camperdown dock; a sad reminder of better days. Dundee is still a port but a shadow of her Victorian zenith.

Donald Street, Lochee
Although Thomas Donald had a shop in this location, the street was named after James Donald who owned Pitalpen works nearby.

Dornoch Place, Broughty Ferry
This Bett brothers housing scheme from the 1960s is named after Dornoch in Sutherland. The name is derived from the Gaelic for 'pebbly place'.

Douglas Street
At one time the public slaughterhouse was situated here

Douglas Terrace, Broughty Ferry
Contains some lovely early-nineteenth-century semi-detached villas. It honours the Earl of Home of the Douglas-Home family, which produced a prime minister, Sir Alec Douglas-Home (1903–95).

Douglas and Angus
An area of east Dundee that is more often shortened to Douglas, a name that relates to the Douglas family, the local landowners. It is noteworthy for the Michelin factory that was the first in Britain to use wind energy to produce tyres. The wind turbines are a distinctive feature of the Dundee landscape. The indoor skate park is the largest in the area.

Douglasfield
There was a Douglasfield bleachfield works here in the nineteenth century, with a Mr Norrie as the proprietor and an annual fete held in July. The Douglas family were major landowners in the district.

Downfield
A small village of that name was founded in 1835. A legend states that the land was owned by John Wishart, a poultry farmer more modest than most. He refused to have the village named Wishartfield but toyed with calling it Featherfield, after the product of his birds, and settled on Downfield instead. Unfortunately, the reality is more prosaic: the name means 'lower field'. Downfield

was then deep in the country, and attracted the wealthier Dundonians who wished a rural retreat away from the bustle and smoke of the industrialising city.

Downfield golf club

Downfield golf club and clubhouse

Downfield originated as a nine-hole course named Baldovan in what was then the outlying village of Downfield, with a tramcar as clubhouse. In common with many courses, Downfield was closed during the First World War and the land used for agriculture, but, unlike many, it reverted to golf, reopening as a nine-hole course in 1932.

The course increased in popularity and extended to eighteen holes with Frederick Walker as the first professional, a position he held for thirty-nine years. His son, Bobby Walker, played golf for Scotland. The course was designed in its present form in 1964 after the housing scheme of Ardler occupied much of the original ground. Downfield has hosted the Scottish Open, the world seniors matchplay and the Scottish amateur championship and, among other events, was a qualifying venue when the Open was held at nearby Carnoustie in 1999 and 2007.

Downie Park Place/Road

Was the name of a grand house and estate near Kirriemuir. In the 1850s Mrs Rattray of Downie Park gave moneys to various Dundee charities. The estate also had yarn mills.

Dragon: the Strathmartine dragon

The dragon statue in the Murraygate was originally conceived by an artist named Alastair Smart but he died before his work was completed and instead one of his students, Tony Morrow, finished the creature, which was let loose on Dundee in 1993.

Strathmartine dragon

The legend comes from the dragon stone – named Martin's Stone – at Strathmartine a couple of miles north of Dundee. Protected by railings in the middle of a field, Martin's Stone is Pictish and could date from the seventh century. Carved on it is a strange beast, a serpent and two horsemen, and from this stone springs the legend of the Strathmartine dragon.

One version claims that the farmer of Pitempton – the prefix *pit* is said to signify a Pictish origin – had nine daughters. One day the farmer ordered the youngest to fetch water from the local well. When she failed to return he sent the next youngest, who also disappeared, so the farmer sent the others one by one until all were gone and he decided to search for them. He found his daughters, dead, at a place called Baldragon. They were in a great circle around a serpent, or dragon. Rather than tackle the beast himself he called for the help of Martin the blacksmith's son, who had been betrothed to one of the dead girls. Martin attacked the beast with his hammer and chased it toward the Kirkton of Strathmartine, now known as Bridgend. The dragon turned at bay and Martin smashed its head on a standing stone, now known as Martin's Stone. Martin's feat was commemorated in rhyme:

Tempted at Pitempton
Draigled at Baldragon
Stricken at Strathmartin
And kill'd at Martin's stane.

Even though this story is unlikely to be true it is a fine introduction to the dragon in the centre of Dundee.

Dronley Avenue

The name comes from the village and burn called Dronley in the nearby Sidlaw hills. The name means 'humped meadow', which could signify a field with a lump in the middle. The Dronley burn becomes the Dighty water at Bridgefoot on the outskirts of Dundee. The Duncan family owned the land around the village of Dronley while Dronley muir was a favoured area for poaching.

Drumgeith Road/Park

Takes its name from a farm that stood in this area. In 1852 the *Courier* mentioned that people from 'this rural district which forms a large part of the parish of Dundee' had raised £80 for a school. In the late 1850s, Mr Sibbald of Drumgeith was famous for his strawberries.

Drumlithie Place

The village of Drumlithie in the Mearns was mentioned in the classic book *Sunset Song*.

Drumlochie Gardens, Broughty Ferry

Named after an estate in Perthshire, near Auchterarder. There is also a ruined castle of that name.

Drumsturdy Road

Leads to the area and moor near Kingenny in Angus. Dorward suggests that it could come from a Gaelic term meaning 'vertigo ridge' or, alternatively, it could be related to the Scottish word *sturdy* – a brain disease in sheep, causing dizziness, hence the vertigo.

Dryburgh Crescent/Gardens/Place

There was a farm and estate called Dryburgh in this area.

Dudhope castle

Now used by Dundee City Council, Dudhope castle is one of the most interesting buildings in Dundee. It stands on the edge of Dudhope park, white and proud, but few people know of its ancient roots and heritage.

The suffix *hope* is common in Scotland and means a small valley, sometimes only open at one end, so Dudhope means the valley of Dudda, who lived so far back in time that he shall probably never be identified.

Dudhope castle was the seat of the Scrymgeours, the hereditary Constables of Dundee who carried Wallace's banner during the First War of Independence (1296–1328). Wallace, it may be remembered, was reputed to have attended Dundee High School. In his official capacity of governor of Scotland after his

Dudhope castle

victory over the English at Stirling Bridge, Wallace conferred the lands and castle of Dudhope to Alexander Scrymgeour. The Scrymgeour family remained as owners until 1668. They also remained loyal to the Scottish throne, fighting for Charles I at the Battle of Marston Moor (1644).

King James VI and I visited Dudhope in 1617, fourteen years after the Union of the Crowns of Scotland and England. Daniel Defoe – visiting Dundee in his role as English spy before the union of 1707 – said Dudhope was 'a noble and ancient pile'.

As well as the seat of famous families, Dudhope castle was a military barracks from 1796 to 1897, and had a very short life as a woollen factory. In 1837 the town council of Perth requested that Dundee send a military escort from the castle for the circuit court but the secretary of state decided that Dundee's 'large Manufacturing Population' necessitated the garrison remaining in place.

The original building was a simple oblong defensive tower, but wings were later added. Later it became more luxurious with a courtyard. After a period of decline, it is now beautifully restored as a jewel in Dundee's architectural crown.

Dudhope house

Boasts a massive conservatory and is on the site of an earlier classical building. Sitting on the slopes of the Law it is now the home of Dundee young people's unit and is part of the Tayside child and family psychiatry department.

Dudhope park

Dudhope park

It is around twenty-three acres in extent, a popular green oasis just to the north of the city centre and on the southern slope of Dundee Law. Although it was used by the people of Dundee for many years, it was not until 1893 that the park was obtained for the city from the Earl of Home. The park was originally known as Barrack park, after Dudhope barracks, but there was also a proposal to name it People's park, which the council rejected in favour of the present name.

In the 1880s the Dundee Celtic club held their annual games here, with donkey races, tugs of war between the Dundee Highland Volunteers and men of HMS *Unicorn*, athletics and a 'pedestrian race' with the competitors first running and then walking for fifteen minutes.

The park has relaxing walks with stunning views over the Tay as well as tennis courts and a skateboard park; there are also play areas for children. To keep park users safe, there is a cannon which faces over the Tay in mute defiance of any invasion from Fife.

On the gate opposite what was the Dundee Royal Infirmary there is a pair of blue plaques, two of twenty-five that are placed throughout the city. Each plaque highlights the life of a prominent Dundee woman. One of these plaques is to Margaret Fairlie, who was Arbroath-born but graduated at St Andrews and became a professor of midwifery and gynaecology. Fairlie was an innovator in the use of radium for treating cancer, pioneered the use of vaginal smears and pushed for a teaching hospital in Dundee.

The plaque on the gate post directly opposite commemorates Rebecca Strong, who was trained by Florence Nightingale at St Thomas's in London and vastly improved the training and working practices of nurses at Dundee Royal Infirmary. She was also credited with being a pioneer of the practice of taking a patient's temperature.

Dudhope Street
Adopted the name from the nearby castle.

Dudhope Terrace
George Angus was the architect responsible for the 1840 neo-classical villas in this street. This land had been agricultural but as the city industrialised, the middle classes looked outwards, and the lower slopes of the Law were utilised for better-quality housing. The house in this street named Fernbank was home to Margaret Harris, the Dundee-born sister of William Harris, who founded Harris academy. When William died, Margaret showed her true generosity by dismissing her rights to the rents of his estate, and instead ordered a school for girls in Dundee. This eventually became part of Dundee High School. She also left money to fund a chair of physics at the then University College, now the University of Dundee.

Dunalistair Gardens, Broughty Ferry
Named after General George Hunter's mansion house of Dunalistair. General Hunter (1784–1854) spent his career in the Honourable East India Company's

army. It is possible that the house was named after the 18,000-acre estate of Dunalistair near Loch Rannoch, once reckoned as one of the best sporting estates in Scotland.

Duncan, Adam statue
Erected in 1997 at the top of Castle Street where Adam Duncan was born, this statue shows the great admiral peering through a telescope into Dundee. The opening was marked by a ceremony in which members of the Royal Dutch Navy were present to commemorate their part in the epic battle.

Duncan mausoleum
Not in Dundee but in Lundie

Admiral Adam Duncan

churchyard, a few miles from the city. The original was designed for Lady Mary Tufton, the wife of Sir William Duncan, who had been physician to George II. It was built in 1789, nearly a decade before Admiral Duncan made his name at the Battle of Camperdown, and restored a century later.

Duncan of Jordanstone College of Art and Design

Duncan of Jordanstone College of Art

Part of the University of Dundee. The college building is slightly set back from Perth Road and the inside is undoubtedly more impressive than the exterior would suggest. This college began life as part of the technical institute that first opened in Small's Wynd in 1888 and by 1892 had a full-time art master named Thomas Delgaty Dunn.

It soon became apparent that the Small's Wynd site was too small so in 1911 the premises moved to a purpose-built site in Bell Street with the name of Dundee Technical College and School of Art. Two years previously James Duncan of Jordanstone had granted an impressive £60,000 toward a school dedicated entirely to art but it was not until the 1930s that plans were ready for a sparkling new art college on Perth Road. The idea was accepted but Hitler's war intervened so it was not until the early 1950s that the building was complete, with the neighbouring Matthew building added in 1974.

In 1975 the Dundee Institute of Art and Technology merged with Duncan of Jordanstone and became the Dundee College of Technology and Duncan of Jordanstone College of Art. There were further changes in 1994 when the institution became part of the University of Dundee. It is the largest college of art and design in Scotland and produces high-quality graduates.

The name Jordanstone comes from an estate north of Meigle.

Duncan Place/Street/Terrace

Take their names from the Duncan family of Lundie and Camperdown.

Duncarse

Duncarse Lodge

The name may come from the Gaelic *dun*, a castle, and the Carse of Gowrie – 'castle near the carse'. This mansion at the west end of Dundee is attractive in its setting overlooking the Tay, but is of interest mainly because of its first owner. Charles Wilson (1810–63) built it in 1858 for a gentleman named George Armitstead (1824–1915). Born in Riga, he was the second son of a Yorkshire jute merchant and moved to Dundee in 1843, where he began the George Armitstead linen and jute shipping business. He married Jane Baxter – sister of William Baxter MP (1825–90) of the famous Dundee Baxter clan – and shortly after became Liberal MP for Dundee, eventually becoming a justice of the peace and Deputy Lieutenant of Forfarshire. He separated from his wife after an affair, was a friend of William Ewart Gladstone, the prime minister, and left legacies for a number of good causes: to support the botanical garden in Dundee; for the Armitstead lectures; to fund the department of philosophy in the university; to fund a hospital bed. His company also built warehouses, including those used by the whaling companies on East Whale Lane and West Whale Lane.

Armitstead was interested in matters nautical and in April 1851 was present at the launching of a ship whose building he had supervised. She was named *George and Lucy* and was for the Riga trade, with a carved figurehead of two children, said to be his nephew and niece. The figurehead was praised as being the best ever produced in Dundee and the carver was Hutton of Dundee. In

1906 he became the first and only Baron Armitstead of Castlehill. The house has now been split in two and the western half was up for sale in November 2015.

Duncarse Place in Charleston is presumably named after the house.

Duncraig Road
Shares its name with the mansion of Duncraig in West Newport, which was the home of Hugh Scott, of the firm of Hugh and Alexander Scott. He was the proprietor of Tayfield works in Seafield Lane, which made linen and canvas products. However, the name was chosen for the 'dun' prefix that conforms to the naming practice of adjacent streets. It means 'castle rock'.

Dundarroch Gardens, Broughty Ferry
Named after the house that stood here. The house was once named Yewbank but when Alexander Campbell Halley, of the textile mill Wallace Craigie, bought it he changed the name to Dundarroch. The name means 'oak castle'.

Dundas Street, Broughty Ferry
Commemorates Henry Dundas, MP, 1st Vicount Melville (1742–1811), treasurer of the Royal Navy at the time the street was named. He became Viscount Melville and was known as the uncrowned king of Scotland. He encouraged the Scottish enlightenment, opposed the abolition of slavery and was active in expanding the British Empire. His statue stands high on a splendid column in St Andrew Square in Edinburgh and there are a number of thoroughfares with the Dundas moniker throughout Scotland.

Dundee airport
Situated on the riverside about a mile-and-a-half from the centre of Dundee and within the city boundary, the airport is unarguably one of the most convenient in Scotland. However, it pays for its accessibility by its limited confines. It is relatively new, being opened in 1963, and has had a chequered commercial history, but currently (2016), operates flights to London Stansted and Amsterdam. The airport advertises itself as a gateway to the home of golf.

Dundee and Angus college
The result of a 2014 merger between Dundee and Angus colleges. Dundee college was formed in 1985 when the Dundee College of Commerce on Constitution Road merged with the Kingsway technical college on the Kingsway. By the beginning of the twenty-first century there were four campuses – Constitution, Kingsway, Melrose and Graham Street – with the latter two being former schools. Another at Gardyne Road, Broughty Ferry was added.

Following the merger with Angus college and a host of alterations, the college

Dundee and Angus College, Gardyne Campus

has campuses in Keptie Road, Arbroath, Gardyne Road, Broughty Ferry and the headquarters at Kingsway college at Old Glamis Road. It is a further- and higher-education college and has around 23,000 students, making it one of the largest in the country. The vast majority of students are aged 16 and above, but it also works with schools so that a number of younger students can follow vocational courses.

Dundee central library

Situated on the top floor of the Wellgate centre, this is the busiest public library in Scotland with a wealth of local-history material as well as a business section and general books. It has a comprehensive collection of early Scottish music and hosts concerts in the Wighton heritage centre. This centre also houses the internationally important Wighton collection of some 620 bound volumes of ancient music, many of them Scottish. The eponymous Andrew John Wighton (1804–66) owned a successful grocery business in Hilltown and became a member of Dundee town council. Outside of commerce and municipal affairs, Wighton's passion was collecting musical manuscripts and on his death the council agreed to become custodians of the collection.

Dundee was one of the first towns in Scotland to provide a free library service, which began in the Albert institute in 1869. At first there was a two-tier system with those who could afford it paying an annual fee and having brand new books, while the 'free' users had to wait for a year to use the then well-thumbed books. Now the service is free to everybody. As would be expected in Dundee, the staff is friendly and knowledgeable.

Dundee central mosque

Central Mosque

Near the centre of Dundee, the mosque offers a warm welcome to all Muslims. It incorporates a madrasa to teach the young how to read the Koran and the meaning of the Muslim holy scripts. To reach out to people of other faiths the mosque offers group visits and open days as well as free English-language copies of the Koran to people of any faith.

The Dundee Islamic society first met at Erskine Street in 1969. The society was so successful that it moved to larger premises at 112–114 Hilltown. It remained there for a number of years but as the Islamic community in Dundee grew, it became obvious that there was a need for a larger mosque. In 1995 the society bought land at 6 Milne Street/Brown Street, which is both central for the citizens of Dundee and accessible for the Muslim students of Dundee and Abertay universities.

The mosque is a beautiful addition to the architecture of Dundee, with its double storey and flanking towers. It holds up to a thousand worshippers at one time, with a car park adjacent.

Dundee Contemporary Arts, Nethergate

Known as the DCA this beautiful building in the Nethergate opened in 1999. Based partly on a restored warehouse it is one of the most popular places in the city to meet, eat or be entertained. The DCA not only hosts international and local talent on its five floors, but also boasts a print centre, a café and Dundee University's visual research centre. There is also a popular two-screen cinema that shows international films. The DCA is the largest modern-art gallery in the

Dundee Contemporary Arts, Nethergate

UK outside of London, and has a friendly welcome for everyone, whatever their artistic tastes.

Dundee house, North Lindsay Street

Dundee house, North Lindsay Street

Reiach and Hall created this new headquarters for Dundee Council in 2011. It is close to City Square and was built in a regeneration gap site on the site of the

Victorian West Ward calendar, where jute was flattened and polished. The modern design and the listed factory blend together in a fashion that encapsulates Dundee's own continual forward thrust on a base of one of the most historic settlements in Scotland.

Dundee Hurricanes

Dundee's American-football team. The sport came to Dundee in the 1980s when the Dundee Whalers were founded. Today the Hurricanes carry the US flag in Dundee and are based at Morgan rugby club, Alloway Place.

Dundee ice arena, Dayton Drive

This is the home of the Dundee CCS Stars ice-hockey club and also caters for curling and family skating. There are skating lessons and function rooms. This was a multi-million-pound development with an Olympic-size rink as well as a café, restaurant and even a bar. It holds an impressive 2,300 people and is the third largest ice arena in Scotland.

Dundee International Book Prize

An initiative administered jointly by the city of Dundee and the University of Dundee, this award for an unpublished novel carries a £10,000 cash prize plus a guarantee of publication. Since its inception in 1999 it has grown in size and stature. Get writing!

Dundee International Sports Centre, Mains Loan

Where the 1998 European hockey championships were played. This centre holds fitness classes and has facilities for a vast array of sports from basketball to zumba, dance to table tennis. A world-class facility.

Dundee International Women's Centre, Manhattan works

A multicultural centre that caters for disadvantaged and excluded women. It has educational, social and recreational activities as well as helping women to find employment. It has mother-and-toddler groups, ECDL, youth groups, English-language training, advice on benefits and it also celebrates events such as Burns night and Christmas. In Dundee, nobody need ever feel excluded.

Dundee Museum of Transport

At present (2016) this museum is in Market Mews off Broughty Ferry Road, but there are plans to open in new premises in 2017. The museum was created by a number of volunteer groups and individuals who met in February 2010 and pushed for charitable status. Years of patient work saw the museum open in April 2014. In November that year the museum secured the old Maryfield tram depot in Forfar Road, which is an excellent centre to showcase the history of transport in Dundee. The current site has displays, a tearoom, shop and toilets.

Dundee Repertory Company
Based in the Rep theatre in Tay Square, off South Tay Street, the company produces a variety of fine plays.

In the early-twentieth century Dundee boasted a number of theatres but all had closed by the mid-1930s, killed by the rise of the cinema. However, a gentleman named Robert Thornley, who managed a touring performance company, fought back. He merged his company with the amateur Dundee Dramatic Society and in May 1939 the Dundee Repertory Theatre was born. They played in a converted mill until 1963 when a fire devastated their home and they relocated to an abandoned church in Lochee Road.

That venue lasted until the late 1970s when the Scottish Arts Council and Dundee City Council decided the Rep should have a theatre of its own. The university provided land and, after the inevitable problems with funding, the Rep opened a brand new 450-seat theatre in Tay Square in 1982.

The building itself is worth seeing, with a civic commendation from the civic trust award in 1984 and the RIBA architectural award in 1986. It is rectangular with a glazed façade and a cantilevered staircase, and combines the interior and exterior to create a truly unique space.

Among the actors who have appeared at the Rep is Dundee's own Brian Cox. The youngest of five children, Cox went to St Mary's Forebank and St Michael's junior secondary, left school at 15 and worked at the Rep before attending the London School of Music and Dramatic Art. From there he went onto stage and film roles. He is now a household name, with parts in films such as *Troy*, *X-Men United* and *Braveheart*. Ricky Ross of Deacon Blue is another Dundee-born star who has worked at the Rep. He grew up in Claverhouse and lives in West Ferry, as does his guitarist Gregor Philip.

Dundee Royal Infirmary
The origins of the DRI stretch back to 1735, although the firm beginnings are in 1782 with the founding of a voluntary dispensary for outdoor relief. In 1798 a building for indoor patients was opened in King Street, with two physicians, Dr John Willison and Sir Alexander Douglas, plus seven surgeons. In 1819, George III granted it a royal charter so it became Dundee Royal Infirmary and Asylum; the asylum later split from the main building and moved to Albert Street.

Right from the start there was a public subscription to run the infirmary with local landowners, mill owners and even the cash-strapped workers of Dundee chipping in. In 1852 new building work for the infirmary started on the southern slopes of the Law, with the institution opening there in 1855. It was, and still is, an iconic building that could be seen from many parts of the town. It expanded in stages throughout the nineteenth century and in 1948 the new National Health Service took over. It closed in 1998 with the patients and work transferred to the modern Ninewells hospital. The building remains, converted into flats.

Dundee Technology Park

Discovery House, Dundee Technology Park

This modern, clean and vibrant area is set aside for industry and technology at the western fringe of Dundee, about four miles from the city centre. The park was created to attract modern business to Dundee and is set in a beautiful environment beside the approach road and the main road to Perth and Aberdeen, with easy access and plentiful parking. The local streets echo the ethos of discovery, with names such as Apollo Way and Gemini Crescent.

Dundee University

Mary Ann Baxter of Balgavies and John Boyd Baxter of the famous linen-spinning dynasty donated the money for the foundation of a university college in Dundee. This college was originally an offshoot of the University of St Andrews but in the 1960s became a university in its own right.

Mary Ann Baxter gave £120,000, which was an immense sum for the time, while John Boyd Baxter, her solicitor, provided another £5,000. Mary Ann was not finished yet, adding £10,000 at a later date. Before the college was properly established it was sometimes referred to as the Baxter college.

The original deed establishing the university stipulated that it would provide education for males and females. At a time when the majority of universities

Bonar Hall, University of Dundee

only catered for men this condition placed Dundee firmly at the forefront of educational sexual equality. The deed also states that the university would teach arts, science and literature but not religion; nobody would be asked to reveal his or her religious beliefs.

In 1954 University College, Dundee became Queen's College, and in 1967 a royal charter gave it independence as the University of Dundee. In 2001 the university merged with the Dundee Campus of Northern College and then created a Faculty of Education and Social Work.

Location and expansion

When the original college opened in October 1883 it was based on four detached houses in the Nethergate. From these pleasant but modest beginnings it expanded westward and northward from the Nethergate until it now takes up a sizeable chunk of land in the west of Dundee. In 1888 the Baxters provided funding for the technical college in Small's Wynd; that eventually split and the art school became part of the university. In the opening years of the twenty-first century the university underwent an amazing process of rebuilding and expansion that saw a proliferation of new buildings along the Hawkhill, so the campus is modern and vibrant. There is the Medical Sciences Institute that includes the Centre for Anatomy and Human Identification (CAHID) where the arts of human identification, forensic anthropology, cranio-facial reconstruction and the human body are studied. CAHID was awarded the Queen's Anniversary Prize for Higher Education in 2013. There is also the Centre for Forensic and

Medical Art that is famous for facial reconstruction that aids both forensic identification and archaeological investigation.

Medicine and dentistry

In 1897 a faculty of medicine was opened, with a dental hospital added in 1914. In 1996 the university took over two local nursing colleges and created a school of nursing and midwifery as part of the faculty of medicine and dentistry. The dental hospital is beside the university and is well used by the people of the city.

Students and lecturers

Heathfield Flats, University of Dundee

Dundee University has been consistently voted as having one of the best student associations in Britain and is renowned for its friendliness and accessibility as well as the high standard of teaching. Its professors have included Patrick Geddes, the father of town planning, D'Arcy Wentworth Thompson and, more recently, Professor Christopher Whatley the historian, Professor Charles McKean, the architectural historian, and Dr Sue Black OBE, the forensic anthropologist.

At the end of 2015 the *Sunday Times Good University Guide 2016* named it Scottish University of the Year; and no wonder.

Dundee University Centre for Anatomy and Human Identification, Dow Street

This cutting-edge research centre won a Queen's Award while Professor Sue Black and her staff frequently aid the police at home and abroad.

Dundee University library

Set within the campus of the university this library has a host of computers, private study space and over a million books.

Dundee University Student's Association, Airlie Place, University of Dundee

A building that holds a shop, bars and Dundee's largest nightclub, this is consistently voted among the best student's associations in Scotland and best value in the UK.

Dundee waterworks, Clepington Road

Also known as Stobsmuir waterworks, this strange concrete building with castellated outer walls is actually a reservoir built in 1908.

Dunella, Broughty Ferry

Named after the mansion whose owner, Mr D. Luke of Dunella, was involved in the Dundee ornithological club in the 1880s. The house was later owned by Mr McVeigh of the firm McVeigh, McIntyre & Co.

Dunmore Gardens

This small street near Perth Road takes its name from Dunmore house, which stood here. Dunmore is Gaelic for large castle.

Dunrobin Walk

Named after Dunrobin castle in Sutherland. Dunrobin is a poem of a building but is also remembered as the home of the Duke and Duchess of Sutherland at the time of the infamous Sutherland clearances. The name means Robin's castle and could have its origins with Robert, 6th Earl of Sutherland, who lived in the early-fifteenth century. The castle is the seat of the Earl of Sutherland and the headquarters of clan Sutherland.

Duns Crescent

In common with most streets in the area, this name has no local connection but refers to the small town of Duns in the Scottish Borders. Duns has its own slogan 'Duns dins a', which means that Duns is the best place to be; a saying that dwellers in Duns Crescent may wish to use.

Dunshelt Road

The derivation is Dunshalt near Auchtermuchty in Fife. Local folklore tells us the name comes from Dane's halt, a place some long-forgotten Danish army stopped. It may also be from Danes Hold, after a battle on Falkland moor where the Danes were defeated, or Inschalt, with insch being an island, so the area could have been dry land amidst a bog. However, Dr Simon Taylor of St Andrews University believes the name derives from the Gaelic *dun* or fort, and there are traces of a circular fort in a field nearby.

Dunsinane

There is a Dunsinane industrial estate and a Dunsinane Avenue in the same area. There is no mystery about the name, which is a hill in the Sidlaws only a few miles to the north of Dundee. Dunsinane, of course, features in Shakespeare's *Macbeth*, with the name from the Gaelic, *dun*, or hill-fort and *sinean*, which could mean breasts, 'fort of the breast or breasts'. Dorward suggests the name could also allude to a St Senan, a sixth century Irish holy man.

There is a legend that King Cinead (or Kenneth) II killed Finella's son in battle at Dunsinane, with Lady Finella being the daughter of the Pictish mormaer (ruler) of Angus. The hill itself is a pleasant climb with the legendary 'Macbeth's castle' on the summit to augment the fine views.

Duntrune house

Now a welcoming guest house, this 1826 mansion was built on much older foundations by the famous architect William Burn (1789–1870). It is situated five miles north of Dundee. Possibly the most interesting owner was Seagate-born Miss Clementina Graham (1782–1877) who wrote the book *Mystifications* and was an acquaintance of Sir Walter Scott. Less well known was her personal vaccination of three hundred children against smallpox. A descendant of Grahame of Claverhouse, she had known Admiral Adam Duncan in her youth. In 1875, at the aged of 95, she is said to have modelled for the figurehead of the Alexander Stephen-built clipper *Duntrune*, and also performed the launching ceremony.

Duntrune Terrace, Broughty Ferry

Takes its name from Duntrune house; William Adams (1837–90) a famous whaling captain, lived at no. 12, a house also known as Disco after the island of that name off western Greenland. Born in Dundee in 1837, Adams worked with the Dundee, Perth & London shipping line and then sailed on Baltic and Far Eastern voyages before venturing into the whaling trade. He commanded *Arctic* and *Arctic II*, took part in the search for survivors of the Tay Bridge disaster and helped in Arctic exploration.

Dunvegan Road

The derivation is the ancient castle on Skye, home of the MacLeods for the past eight hundred years and one of the most evocative castles in Scotland. The earliest-known written version of the name dates from 1498, 'Dunbegane', which could mean 'the fort of Began', a Norse chieftain.

Dura Street
Situated between Dens Road and Albert Street, Dura Street was named after the Dura works that have sadly long gone. The works were built in the mid-1830s by John Walker, who was born in Kemback, Fife. The Walker family were connected with the Blebo mills in the nearby Dura den but moved to Dundee, either because of the availability of labour or because Dundee was in the process of shifting from linen to jute. The name Dura is from the Celtic word *dubron*, meaning water.

Durris Loan
Named after the parish and famous nineteenth-century fair in Aberdeenshire. The name is from the Gaelic *dourus*, 'a door or an opening', which makes sense as Durris is at the mouth of a pass over the Mounth. A nearby street is Dores so the similarity of names creates some sense of continuity, if possibly confusing to the postman.

Dykehead Place
The literal meaning is obvious, the head of a dyke or a wall. As this was once all farmland, it is possible that this street is in the position of a one-time stone dyke between fields.

Dysart Place, Barnhill
The streets in this part of Barnhill were named for places in Fife. Dysart is a vibrant village close to Kirkcaldy. The name could be from Gaelic and mean 'height of God' or its derivation could be the Latin *deserta*, meaning 'the fasting place of a holy man'. The latter meaning would make sense if it referred to the legend that St Serf came to that part of Fife around 500 AD.

Earl Grey Place
One of the new streets being created by the waterfront development. It is named after a dock, built in 1834, which closed to make way for the Tay road bridge. The dock was named after Charles Grey, 2nd Earl Grey, prime minister from November 1830 until July 1834. Northumberland-born, he was a Whig and backed the 1832 Reform Act that transformed British politics and began the slow climb to democracy. Under his government, Britain also abolished slavery. He is also associated with Earl Grey tea.

Earlston Avenue

Like so many streets in the area, the name has no local connection but refers to a town in Berwickshire in the Scottish Borders. The name could simply mean 'earl's town', although the Borders town traces its name to *Arcioldun*, which means Prospect Fort, after a nearby hill fort.

Earn Crescent, Menzieshill

In common with many streets in the area, this is named after a Scottish river, in this case the river Earn, which rises in Loch Earn in Perthshire and flows into the Tay near Abernethy.

Eassie Terrace

Eassie is a parish in Angus, which combined with the neighbouring parish of Nevay in 1600. The name is Gaelic and means 'beside the waterfall'.

East Craigie Junior Football Club

Scotland's oldest junior football club, founded in 1880. They play at Craigie Park, Old Craigie Road and are known as 'the shipbuilders'.

East Home Street and Home Street, Broughty Ferry

Commemorates the Earl and Countess of Home. The Douglas family achived possession of Claypotts castle in the seventeenth century and the Douglas estate eventually passed to Jane Douglas. Her daughter Lucy married Cospatrick Alexander Home (1799–1881) 11th Earl, who took the name Douglas Home. Both the Homes and the Douglases were Border families.

East Whale Lane

Now a car park, this lane was home to some of the whaling companies that sent ships to the Arctic. Whale oil was used for lighting and heating and was important in softening raw jute before it was made into usable textiles. In its heyday the lane would be a very busy place as outward bound and returning seamen frequented the whaling offices to sign articles for a forthcoming voyage or to receive their wages for one just completed, while clerks and managers ran sundry errands and whaling masters consulted with owners.

Eastern necropolis, Old Craigie Road

During the Victorian period there was nearly a cult of the dead. Books often contained deathbed scenes, widows wore mourning black for years on end and it was common practice to spend a family Sunday afternoon strolling around a graveyard admiring the carved stones. Dundee was no exception, with the

Eastern Necropolis, entrance

eastern necropolis built in 1863. The gateway is an imposing gothic triple arch with curving traceried screen walls on either side.

It is more commonly referred to as the eastern cemetery and has trees, shrubs and winding paths.

Easton Lane, Brook Street, Broughty Ferry
Commemorates Thomas Easton, a councillor and slater, who died in 1897.

Eastwell Gardens/Road
In the days before piped water, there was a well in this area after which the street was named.

Eden Street/Terrace
The source is the small estate of Eden Bank that stood here. In the 1860s Mr Small of Eden Bank was chairman of the Dundee Chamber of Commerce, helped create the Albert institute and was involved in British–French commerce.

Edward Street
Commemorates A. & D. Edward & Co., which owned the nearby Logie works. In the 1840s and 1850s Alexander Edward was senior partner while James Edward of Balruddery died in 1878. The works include the sinister-sounding Coffin mill, which massive building is just across the road from Edward Street. The Royal Mail central sorting depot is at the back of this street.

Edzell Street, Broughty Ferry
Lord Dalhousie owned Edzell in Angus and there is a Dalhousie arch in the village. Because of Dalhousie's Angus estates and his many contributions to Dundee charities, the street was named in his honour.

Elie Avenue, Barnhill
The streets in this part of Barnhill were named after places in Fife. Elie is a historic seaside resort in the East Neuk. The name could be from *ealadh*, 'tomb'.

Eliza Street, Maxwelltown
Around 1780, David Maxwell of Tealing bought this land for Dundee. When the feuing – street – plan was created he insisted that the streets were named after members of his family, including Eliza.

Ellengowan Drive, off Broughty Ferry Road
Retains the name of the mansion house of Ellengowan that stood here. The name became popular when Walter Scott's novel *Guy Mannering* included a character named Harry Bertram, the Laird of Ellengowan, living at Ellengowan castle.

Scott's works were so well read that they started a cult of town, house and estate naming as well as highlighting the romance of history. For example, there is an Ellengowan in Queensland, Australia, in Ontario, Canada and in Pennsylvania, USA and the name is also used in Callander and Milngavie in Scotland. The most famous resident of Dundee's Ellengowan was Mary Ann Baxter, who was the major influence in founding Dundee University. In 1894 the property was sold to the council for £8,000.

Ellieslea Road, Broughty Ferry
The mansion house of Ellieslea was owned by the insurance broker and shipping agent Joseph Gibson (1831–1915) who was instrumental in the Dundee Antarctic expedition of 1892 and that same year became a justice of the peace. Mrs Gibson gave charitable donations of boots and tea cakes to the Dundee convalescent home.

Elm Street
A street in the Logie development. Reflects the garden-city theme, with elms being one of the most beautiful of all European trees (see photo on facing page).

Elmwood Drive/Road
Carries the name of millowner James Donald's mansion of Elmwood, which stood in this area. Elmwood was also the name of a Lochee cricket club in the

Elm Street

later nineteenth century, possibly made up from men who worked for Donald's company.

Emmock Place/Road
Emmock farm is the source.

Erskine Lane, Broughty Ferry
This lane is at the junction of Brook Street and Fort Street. It was named after Thomas Erskine (1788–1870), who owned Linlathen house and Linlathen estate north of Broughty. He was a theologian and a good landlord, who helped his tenants when times were hard.

Erskine Street
According to A. H. Miller in his *Glimpses of Old and New Dundee*, this street could either be named after Dr Thomas Erskine of Linlathen or James Erskine of Linlathen. Thomas Erskine inherited Linlathen estate in 1816. He was an advocate and a member of Edinburgh's literary society but his main interest was theology. In March 1867 Erskine was given the right to feu land 'east of the Fair Muir Toll'. He was friends with many leading theologians of his time and studied and wrote on the subject. His dying words were: 'Lord Jesus'.

James Erskine (1787–1816) was also of a religious persuasion; he was Episcopalian with a Jacobite mother.

Etive Gardens, Menzieshill

Named after the beautiful and wild river Etive in the west Highlands. The name 'Etive' is sometimes translated as 'little ugly one'.

Euclid Crescent

Situated beside Dundee High School, Euclid Crescent is a tribute to the Greek scholar who wrote the *Elements*, which remained a standard textbook for over two thousand years. As Dundee High School taught geometry and mathematics, both of which Euclid dealt with, the name suits very well.

Ewing building, University of Dundee

Dundee-born and Dundee High School-educated Sir James Alfred Ewing (1855–1935) graduated in engineering at Edinburgh University. He became a physicist and engineer, worked on the magnetic properties of metals and discovered hysteresis. He played a part in the modernisation of Japan, was involved in the foundation of Japanese seismology and helped develop the world's first modern seismograph. From 1883 he was University College, Dundee's first professor of engineering.

His return to Dundee awakened his social conscience when he compared the living conditions of Dundee's poor with the better housing in Japan. Ewing tried to alleviate the poor sanitary conditions and the terrible infant-mortality rate He later moved to the University of Cambridge, worked with Sir Charles Parsons on the first steam turbine and was the first director of naval education in Greenwich in 1903. During the First World War he managed the Admiralty cryptanalysis department, decoding the Zimmermann telegram in 1917, which hinted that Germany was seeking an alliance with Mexico to attack the USA. That telegram was supposedly instrumental in bringing the USA into the war as an ally of Great Britain and France.

He habitually wore a grey suit, mauve shirt and a bowtie and married twice, on the first occasion to a distant relative of George Washington, and, on the second, to the daughter of a friend.

The Ewing building was constructed in 1954 and named in his honour. On the wall of this building is a blue plaque, one of twenty-five throughout the city that highlight the lives of extraordinary Dundee women. This plaque is to Williamina Fleming, who emigrated to the United States with her husband when she was twenty years old. The marriage did not last and Williamina found work as a housekeeper with Edward Pickering, the director of Harvard College's observatory. Her life took a turn for the better when he realised that she was feisty and intelligent. Pickering gave her a more suitable position and she rose to be a head of department, classifying over ten thousand stars and becoming the most prominent female astronomer of her time.

Exchange coffee house

Exchange Coffee House, Shore Terrace

The name has altered with time but this neoclassical building at 15 Shore Terrace should be revered for its past. It was designed by George Smith (1793–1877), a major Scottish architect. As Pevsner, the doyen of architectural historians, points out, with its Ionic and Doric columns the Greek influences in this fine two-storey structure are clear. The interior is also exceptional and well-preserved, with the Greek theme extending to corridors with Doric columns. Given the quality of the design, and its central role in the commercial life of the city, the Exchange is now A-listed.

The building was used as a meeting place by Dundee's elite merchants. The first floor had a coffee house, assembly rooms and a library and reading room. In 1828, when the coffee house was built, it was hard beside the docks so that merchants could watch the movement of their ships while they sealed their deals.

Beneath the building there is a number of fascinating vaulted storage areas from a previous building on the same site. In December 1854 during the Crimean War the building was used as a sale house for Russian ships that had been captured by the British. Such vessels were known as prize ships. It is now the Shore Youth Venue, an alcohol-free location for under-eighteens.

Exchange Street

This street was named after the exchange that opened in 1807 and was built above an area known as Packhouse Square.

Explorer Road

Hillcrest Building, Dundee Technology Park

Leads from South Road to the Dundee technology park. The name refers to the Explorers programme, which is a NASA method of allowing scientists to travel in space. Other streets in the technology park follow the same theme of names from space exploration.

Fairfield Road, Broughty Ferry

The house at nos. 5–7 is the original Fairfield, from which the street takes its name. In the nineteenth century an engineer named William Gordon Thomson lived here. He was the Thomson of Thomson, Son & Co., of Douglas foundry, and also proprietor of the Clepington Spinning Company in Clepington Road. Before moving to the Ferry, Thomson lived in Prospect Place.

Fairmuir

A historical name that means exactly what is says; there was a fair held on the muir (moor) here. Fairs were popular events at which animals or produce were bought and sold, people met old friends and boys met girls. Dundee had its share of fairs, including one at Stobsmuir, known as Stobs fair. The authorities decided to move the fair to Strathmartine Road, a site that became known as Fairmuir.

In the 1840s the landowner of Fairmuir, Sir John Ogilvy (1803–90), created a cricket pitch on Fairmuir and the Dundee cricket club played matches here, including one against Edinburgh in 1845. The muir had other uses as, by the 1870s, the Forfar Light Horse held an annual drill here. Ogilvy handed the Fairmuir to Dundee as a public recreation ground in September 1884.

Falkland Crescent/Place, Barnhill

Take their name from Falkland in Fife, a small town famous for the royal palace that was often occupied by the Stuart kings.

Farington Gardens/Terrace

Refers to Farington hall, in whose former grounds the streets stand.

Farington hall

In 1853 the London architects Coe and Goodwin built Farington hall for the Edward family, who owned Logie works. According to the architectural historian, Charles McKean, it was a Gothic manor house built in Normandy Caen stone with crystal chandeliers and a tower that enjoyed extensive views of the Tay.

Regrettably, this mansion house is now gone. When the suffragettes were engaged in what was often a quite violent campaign one of their acts was the burning down, on 11 May 1913, of Farington hall. The day after the arson attack a copy of the *The Suffrage* newspaper was sent to Dundee's chief constable with a message on the front page: 'Farington Hall. A protest against British tyranny. Blame Asquith & Co.'

The attack may have been directed at Henry McGrady, a former Lord Provost of Dundee, who was about to take possession of Farington hall when the suffragettes struck.

Ferndale Drive

As the surrounding streets, Deepdale and Avondale, end in 'dale', the name was chosen to have the unity of a corresponding suffix. A search found no local name of Ferndale, either of house or farm. The literal meaning is a valley of ferns.

Ferries

Dundee from Newport on Tay

For centuries ferries travelled across the Tay to connect Dundee with Fife. In Dundee these vessels were known as the Fifies. There were services from Dundee to Newport, which carried passengers and vehicles, and Broughty Ferry to Tayport, with a train service opening in 1850.

The passage to Newport dates from the early Middle Ages, with a regular service starting around 1700. In 1715 a new pier and inn was built in Newport, funded by the guilds of Dundee, but an attempt to change the name of Newport to New Dundee did not take hold. Steam ferries were introduced in 1825, with the Scottish Central Railway later taking control of the service. The opening of the second Tay bridge saw a temporary drop in use of the ferry but as more vehicles used the road it increased in popularity again, with one crossing every half hour. In the 1960s the ferries carried around eighty-thousand vehicles a year; they continued until the Tay road bridge opened in 1966.

Fettercairn Drive, Broughty Ferry
The council chose this name possibly because Fettercairn was geographically close to Edzell, which was already a street name in the same area.

Finavon Street, Fintry
When the council estate of Fintry was built, it was decided to give the streets the same prefix of Fin, from the Gaelic word *fionn* for white. Finavon castle sits about five miles north east of Forfar in Angus. The name means white river.

Findale Street, Fintry
Many of the names in Fintry have the prefix 'Fin' which is from the Gaelic *fionn*, meaning white. Findale means white valley.

Findcastle Place/Street/Terrace, Fintry
The word 'fin' is from the Gaelic *fionn*, for white, but the addition of the letter 'd' negates that meaning, so the 'find' prefix appears to be merely a method of geographical identification with surrounding streets in Fintry, all with a similar prefix.

Findchapel Place, Fintry
The prefix 'Fin' is from the Pictish or Gaelic *fionn* for white. This name appears to be an attempt at geographically identifying the street with its neighbours, as all have a similar prefix.

Findhorn Street, Fintry
When the council scheme of Fintry was built, it was decided to give the streets the same prefix of Fin, from *fionn*, the Pictish or Gaelic word for white. Findhorn is a small village on the Moray coast.

Findowrie Street, Fintry
The prefix 'Fin' is from the Gaelic *fionn* for white. Findowrie is a small place near Brechin in Angus.

Finedon Terrace, Fintry
Although the prefix 'Fin' is from the Gaelic *fionn* for white, Finedon is a town in Northamptonshire, England.

Finella Gardens/Place, Fintry
When the council scheme of Fintry was built, it was decided to give the streets the same prefix of 'Fin', from *fionn*, the Gaelic word for white. Lady Finella of Angus was an interesting character. She murdered Kenneth II in 995 AD, near Fettercairn. It seems that the king had killed her son in battle. After the death of the king, Kenneth's men hunted Finella and she jumped off the lip of a waterfall near St Cyrus, a place since known as Den Finella.

Fingask Street
Takes its name from a castle in the Carse of Gowrie between Dundee and Perth. It was owned by the Bruces of Clackmannan then the Threiplands of Peeblesshire. Forfeited after the 1745 Jacobite rising, it was visited by Robert Burns and means 'white tail'.

Finlaggan Place/Terrace/Crescent, Fintry
Many of the names in Fintry have the prefix 'Fin'. In this case the name is from *Port an Eilean,* 'fort of the island'. Finlaggan was the ancient seat of the MacDonald Lord of the Isles. There are three islets within a loch on the island of Islay, and from here the Lord of the Isles ruled his lands that extended from the Butt of Lewis to the Mull of Kintyre.

Finlarig Terrace, Fintry
The prefix 'Fin' is from the Gaelic *fionn* for white. The street shares its name with Finlarig castle near Loch Tay, built by Black Duncan Campbell in 1629. The name is said to mean the 'white, or holy, pass'.

Finlathen park, Fintry Crescent
A delightful park. With the Dighty burn flowing through the grassy spaces and the added attractions of a skateboard park, football pitch with changing facilities and children's play parks, this open area is also near the Green Circular walking or cycling route. While Dundee has many beautiful parks, this is one that the locals keep quiet about, and no wonder.

Once there were mills here, while the Finlathen bridge built in the 1840s was used to carry the water pipe over the Dighty from Monickie to Dundee. At nearly five-hundred-feet-long, with thirteen arches, it now serves as a footbridge.

Finlow Terrace, Fintry
When the council scheme of Fintry was built, it was decided to give the streets the same prefix of 'Fin', from *fionn*, the Gaelic word for white. There is a Finlow Hill in Cheshire.

Finmore Place, Fintry
Many of the names in Fintry have the prefix 'Fin', which is from the Gaelic *fionn* for white. This street seems to mean 'large white place'.

Fintry
Is an ancient name that is said to come from the Gaelic name *fionn*, meaning white and *tref* for place or steading, so the name means 'white place'. When the residential housing scheme was built, a variety of names were chosen for street names, all of which included the prefix 'fin'.

Fintry, however, is not a local name but travelled to Dundee from Stirlingshire with the Graham family. The Grahams had long held the lands of Fintry near Stirling. Sir Robert Graham of Fintry married into the Scrymgeour of Dudhope family and brought the name Fintry to Dundee. Another branch of the family was called Claverhouse and gave Scotland the warrior named 'Bluidy Claverhouse' – also known as Bonnie Dundee, depending on the speaker's religion or politics.

Robert Graham of Fintry was provost of Dundee on four occasions in the fifteenth century. In 1493 he left one of his houses to support a chaplain at the church of St Mary. There was a Fintry's Wynd in old Dundee, now long gone.

Fintry has produced a number of prominent people including the footballers Derek Johnstone, Stephen Glass, Charlie Adam and Scott Robertson. Johnstone, a Dundee United fan, won the League Cup for Rangers with the winning goal against Celtic when he was only 16, and went on to play for Scotland. There was also Brian Molko, lead singer of Placebo, who spent part of his boyhood in Fintry Crescent.

Fintry Place, Broughty Ferry
The arrival of this name in Dundee is detailed under the entry for Fintry. The Graham family's lands of Fintry extended from the Dighty burn to where this street now stands.

Fish Dock Road

Led to the dock that housed Dundee's fishing fleet. In the early twentieth century the Scottish fishing industry employed tens of thousands of men and women. Dundee had only a small part of this industry and hoped to expand. Accordingly, the city built a new dock for fishing boats, complete with railway connections to ship the catch to the larger cities. Deputations were then sent to existing fishing ports, including Aberdeen, the largest trawler port in the country, to persuade fishing companies to relocate to Dundee. However, Dundee's geographical position tended to negate these efforts. The trawling fleet based in Dundee remained small and the city never challenged the major fishing ports of Aberdeen and Leith.

Today Kinnes Shipping Ltd is one of the companies located here. At one time Kinnes was the major player in the British whaling industry.

Fisher Street, Broughty Ferry

Fisher Street, Broughty Ferry

The name comes from the fishing community of the Ferry. By the nineteenth century fishing was well established with the open boats dragged up on the beach as well as in the harbour. The men would long line for white fish or follow the great herring shoals around the British coast while women baited the lines and sold fish. If history is not enough, this street also has a fine pub – the Ship inn.

Fleming Gardens, east, north, south and west

Fleming Gardens South

The origin of the word Fleming is obvious; a person who originated from Flanders. The Flemings came to Scotland in the Middle Ages for trade, and settled along the east coast.

Fleming Gardens harks back only to 1929 and relates to the financier Robert Fleming (1845–1933), born in Liff Road. He worked for Baxter Brothers but became a merchant banker and prospered. His descendant, Ian Fleming, created the world's most famous fictional spy, one James Bond.

There is a plaque on an ornamental parapet in Clepington Road that reads: 'Fleming Trust Housing Scheme; this parapet wall and panel have been erected to commemorate the munificent gift by Robert Fleming Esq LLD, a native of Dundee, of £155,000 for the purpose of improving the housing conditions of the city. A grateful community honours his name.'

Fleming gymnasium, University of Dundee

Was created by adapting the jute warehouses that had been built in the garden of Alexander Edward, who had owned the Logie works. His villa was one of the original four that made up the first university here. The name honours the financier Robert Fleming, a university benefactor.

Fleuchar Street

So named in July 1866 by the paving committee, after a large house and estate called Fleuchar Craig, a Craig being a crag or distinctive rock.

Foggyley Place, Lochee

Maintains the name of the Cox mansion of Foggyley that stood here. The Cox family had a virtual monopoly of this area, owning a string of mansion houses, as well as the huge Camperdown works, railways and a shipping line.

Forebank Road/Street/Terrace

The name is taken from the estate of Forebank on which the present streets are built. This was a rural area in the early nineteenth century, in which affluent Dundonians spent the summer.

Forfar Road

The eventual destination of this road is the county town of Forfar, an important administrative centre. Nos. 53 and 55 are sandstone art nouveau bungalows and worthy of a second look.

Fort Street, Broughty Ferry

Fisherman's Tavern, Fort Street, Broughty Ferry

Has a number of eighteenth- and nineteenth-century buildings, with the Fisherman's tavern at no. 10 a deservedly popular watering hole for locals and visitors and listed in the CAMRA beer guide. In 1827 it was the Buckie tavern, named after the buckies, or whelks, that were found on the beach. The street was originally named Fort Aboukir Street in honour of Admiral Nelson's victory in 1798, better known as the Battle of the Nile.

Forth Crescent/Place, Menzieshill

Named after the river Forth, which broadens to become the Firth of Forth at the Forth bridges, and used to be termed 'Scotswater' or the 'Scottish Sea'.

Forthill, or Balgillo, hill

The name 'Forthill' refers to events in 1547 when an English force fortified the hill during one of their periodic invasions of Scotland. Lord Gray had handed Broughty castle to the invaders, who remained to terrorise the area until 1550. They fortified Balgillo hill, with the Scots naming this spot Bragyng Trouwble, or 'bragging trouble'. The English found major difficulties in obtaining supplies from a hostile populace and, in February 1550, a combined Scots and French force reduced the fort and disposed of the garrison. In February 1851 workmen uncovered a number of objects at this site including a skull, axe and a firearm with whinstone balls, presumably from that period.

Foundry Lane

Dundee foundry was established in 1791 and operated throughout the nineteenth century. It built locomotives for the railways but in 1843 the owners, the shipbuilding Gourlay brothers, decided to concentrate on marine engines. Dundee foundry provided engines for *Discovery*, which sits at the Riverside. Gourlay's ended operations in 1908.

Fountainbleau Drive

The name originated in France in the Middle Ages, from Fontaine, a 'spring', and 'Blitzwald', a personal name, although of course Fountainebleau is best known as the location of a royal palace south of Paris. In the Dundee case, Fountainbleau was a bleachfield that Dundee took over in the 1850s. In the 1860s James Wallace of Fountainbleau took part in horticultural shows.

Friarfield house, opposite the Howff

This 1873 block was originally intended to be the administrative centre for Ward mills. The name 'friar' has echoes of the original religious function of this part of Dundee.

Gallacher retail park, East Dock Street

Consists of a number of high-profile retail outlets.

Gannochie Terrace

There was a house and farm of that name in Perthshire.

Garden Mill Place
Carries the name of Garden works, which was also known as Blyth Street mill.

Gardner's Lane
Commemorates the local landowner, Richard Gardner of Dudhope house. He was one of the last people to be buried in the Howff.

Gardyne's Land, Gray's Close, 70–73 High Street

Gardyne's Land

After decades of neglect, this splendid five-storey building is now used as a youth hostel. It caters for casual visitors, backpackers and couples, with some of the most atmospheric rooms anywhere in the city. Tayside Building Preservation and Dundee City Council carried out the restoration work to a very high standard.

It is the oldest residential building in Dundee – castles excepted – with the first occupier and owner being John Gardyne, who bought the land in 1560. Gardyne's sons, George and David, were implicated in Huntly's rebellion against James VI in the late sixteenth century when they came 'in apparel of war with flying standards against the king . . . at Aberdeen to the Bridge of Dee'. They were both pardoned in 1590. The Gardynes also owned Gardyne castle in Angus.

The close was also known as Alexander Kyd's Close after another resident, and then Bogmill's Close after David Maxwell of Bogmill. From 1810 it was Gray's Close after the then owner, James Gray.

At the entrance to the building is a blue plaque, one of twenty-five in the city that honours prominent women. This plaque is for Mariote Ker, a sixteenth-century woman whom the king requested be made a burgess of Dundee. It was to be another 350 years before the city had another female burgess.

Garland Place
A short street dating from 1867, with finely detailed and rather beautiful tenements.

Geddes Quadrangle

Geddes Quadrangle

One of the most peaceful and beautiful spots in the whole of Dundee, and named after father of town planning Patrick Geddes (1854–1932), who taught at Dundee University. The quadrangle is situated within the campus and has a number of benches for people to enjoy the surroundings.

Gellatly Street

Retains the name of Peter Gellatly who owned a number of properties in this area in the early nineteenth century. There were two ancient closes on this site, Mitchell's Close and Drummond's Close, but they were removed when Gellatly Street was built.

Gemini Crescent

Situated in Dundee technology park, the name references NASA's Gemini programme. All the street names in the area are space-related.

George Buckman Drive, Lochee

George Buckman was convenor of Tayside Regional Council. He died in 1997. This street is home to the headquarters of Robertson Construction Group.

George Pirie Way

Honours one of Dundee's lesser-known heroes, Dr George Pirie (1863–1929), who was heavily involved in the development of X-rays. His father, Dr George Clark Pirie, worked in Dundee Royal Infirmary. Dr George Pirie attended St Andrews University as well as Edinburgh University. He returned to the Dundee Royal Infirmary and worked on X-ray technology from 1896 until 1925 when

George Pirie Way

he was forced to retire through work-related radiation illness. He lost the use of his arms and one eye as a result of his experiments.

George Street, Maxwelltown

Around 1780, David Maxwell of Tealing bought this land. When the feuing – street – plan was created he insisted that the streets were named after members of his family. This street carries the name of one of his male relatives

Gilfillan Memorial Church, Whitehall Crescent

Gilfillan Memorial Church

Not all holy men are gentle ascetics. Dundee's Revd George Gilfillan was a fiery, feisty preacher. McGonagall praised him highly:

All hail to the Rev George Gilfillan of Dundee
He is the greatest preacher I ever did hear or see

Gilfillan was also a social reformer who supported working-class poetry. He preached at School Wynd, held weddings in his manse and was so popular that the people of Dundee termed him 'oor George'. He also published a two-volume work on the poetry of Robert Burns.

The church in Gilfillan's memory was designed by Glasgow architect Malcolm Stark and completed in 1887. Now it looks forlorn, hemmed in on both sides by tenements but when it was built it stood in splendid isolation, a gem of a building with a cupola (now gone) and a lively congregation.

Gillies Place/Terrace, Broughty Ferry
Commemorates Ferry native and Conservative councillor James Gillies who lived at Beach Crescent. He founded the firm of James Gillies & Son, was a Freemason, a member of the bowling club and opposed Dundee's annexation of Broughty Ferry.

Girvan Gardens
The name has no local connection but refers to the Ayrshire coastal town of the same name.

Glamis Drive
Named after Glamis castle in Angus, this west end street contains impressive houses well shielded by stout walls and sheltered amidst fine gardens. The name, according to David Dorward, could be from the Old English *cleofan*, 'to cut', arguably referring to the situation of Glamis in the Sidlaw hills. Glamis castle is well known as the childhood home of the late Queen Mother and is reputed to be haunted. The village of Glamis, with the Angus folk museum, is worth a visit.

Glamis Road
Refers to Glamis castle, with its royal connections. It does not lead to Glamis and never will. There is also a Glamis Terrace nearby and a Glamis Street in the Hilltown.

Glasite Chapel, King Street

The Rev John Glas (1695–1773) became minister of Tealing in 1719 but left the Church of Scotland in 1725, saying that the New Testament did not give a warrant for a national church. The Glasite chapel was built in 1777 in the shape of an octagon. This church was also known as the Kail church because the congregation were fed with cabbage soup. The chapel is now the hall of nearby St Andrew's church, and contains a monument to John Glas.

Glasite Chapel, King Street

Glass pavilion, Esplanade, Broughty Ferry

At its height the esplanade at Broughty beach had a bandstand and a fancy Swiss-style tearoom, as well as this art deco former bathing shelter, but the former two have been removed. Such is progress.

Glebe Street

Famous for the *Sunday Post* characters, 'The Broons', this street stood in the Stobswell area of Dundee, parallel to Baffin Street. It has since been demolished and the site is part of the playground of Glebelands primary school. A glebe was the land owned by the parish minister, adjoining his manse.

Glebelands school, Baffin Street

The glebe was the land owned by the minister of the parish so Glebelands would be his fields and garden.

Glenaffric Terrace

One of the streets of the Glens area at Kings Cross. Although most streets in the area are named after the glens of Angus, Glen Affric is some thirty miles west of Inverness.

Glenagnes Road

This street off the Blackness Road carries the name of a mansion house of the same name. Alas the obviously once-respected Agnes has been forgotten, although her name persists. In 1850 George Baxter of Glenagnes cottage died. In the 1880s David Grey, one-time seaman and carpenter and later a grocer and spirit dealer, lived in the cottage.

Gleneagles Road, Ardler
One of many streets in the area that was named after a famous golf course; few courses in the world are better known than Gleneagles in Perthshire.

Glenesk Avenue
Glenesk is the longest of the Angus glens and has some beautiful walks. It is the glen of the river North Esk; with Esk coming from the old Celtic word *Isca*, which simply means 'water'.

Glenmarkie Terrace
Glen Markie is in upper Glen Isla in the Angus glens. The name is from the Gaelic *marcaidh*, meaning 'horse stream'.

Glenmoy Avenue
This street is the Glens council-housing scheme of the 1920s. Situated in the Kings Cross area, it was built between the wars to help alleviate Dundee's terrible housing situation. All the streets were named after Scottish glens, with the early streets named after the glens of Angus and the later ones taken from further afield. Glen Moy is in the Angus glens north of Dundee. The name may be evolved from 'yellow stream' meaning it carries a large amount of mud while in spate.

Glenogil Avenue
Glen Ogil is the glen of the Ogil water in Angus.

Glenprosen Terrace
Glen Prosen is in Angus, north of Dundee.

Glentruim Terrace
Glentruim Terrace takes its name from Glentruim which is in Badenoch, many miles north of Dundee near Newtonmore in the Highlands.

Gnasher
This famous dog has appeared in the *Beano* comic since 1968. Now the statue growls at passers-by from the fringe of City Square.

Godfrey Street, Broughty Ferry
Commemorates Councillor Clement Godfrey (1852–1925). He came from Dudley in England but had the good fortune to move to Dundee, where he became a merchant and councillor as well as a member of St Margaret's church.

Golspie Terrace, Broughty Ferry
Part of a scheme built by Bett brothers in the 1960s, with the streets named after Highland villages. Golspie is in Sutherland with the name meaning 'gully village'.

Gordon Street, Broughty Ferry
Commemorates Patricia Heron Gordon (c.1774–1821). She married William Maule-Ramsay, 1st Baron Panmure, and was the mother of Fox Maule Ramsay, 2nd Lord Panmure and 11th Earl Dalhousie. She had eight other children.

Gotterstone Avenue/Drive
The name comes from a farm in the area. The name Gothrasone was recorded in Coupar Angus in 1446 and may be a corruption of Guthrie's Town, the farm or dwelling of Guthrie.

Gourdie Crescent/Place/Road/Street
Named after the farm steadings of Gourdie Town and West Gourdie. Gourdie could mean trapped water or something heavy or dull.

Gowrie Court/Place/Street
Take their name from the area of Gowrie that stretches westward from Dundee towards Perth. The origin of the name is ancient and is reputed to be from the Cenel nGabrain, the people of Gabrain, an early royal house of Dalriada, the Gaelic kingdom that merged with the Picts to become Scotland.

Gowrie Park
This is a private residential area in the west of Dundee. The streets are all named after areas of the west Highlands so none have a local connection. This is a pleasant area through which the green circular cycle path passes as it follows the line of the old Lochee railway.

The name Gowrie comes from the Carse of Gowrie, which is the fertile, low-lying land between Dundee and Perth. Two authorities, Alex Woolf and William Watson, claim the name is from the Cenel nGabrain, the people of Gabrain, an early royal house of Dalriada, which was the Dark Ages Gaelic kingdom that much later merged with the Picts to become Scotland.

Graham Street
The 1938 chapel by W. W. Friskin is worth seeing. Until recently, Graham Street school was one of the campuses of Dundee college. It started life as St Michael's secondary school and had Brian Cox as a pupil. It was demolished in 2012 and new houses were built on the site. The name Graham is originally from 'grey house'.

Grampian Gardens, Fintry

When the housing scheme of Fintry was built in the 1940s it was intended that all the streets should begin with the prefix 'fin'. However, when Fingarth Street acquired a poor reputation in the 1970s the council altered the name to Grampian Gardens in order to attract better tenants. Some of the houses had to be demolished as they had been built with inadequate foundations, so higher-quality housing was erected in their place. The street was named after the Grampian mountains.

Gray, house of

Was built in 1716 for the 12th Lord Gray. It is near Liff but is currently (2015) abandoned and on the Buildings at Risk register.

Gray Street, Broughty Ferry

Distinctive because it contains a large railway tower complete with Victorian cast iron. Railways arrived at Broughty in 1848. The street was named after the Gray family, who owned Broughty castle.

Grayburn, on the Benvie Road

This 1905 Arts and Crafts house was designed by Patrick Thoms (c.1874–1946).

Green circular cycle route

A cycling and walking route that stretches for twenty-seven miles around the

Street art, Riverside

city. There is helpful signage along the way, pointing out the many places of interest and things to see, for example Camperdown wildlife centre and Discovery Point. The council also publishes a map on an annual basis showing the best routes around the city and the map is updated to reflect changes. Part of the green cycle route is close to the Riverside and so it has splendid views of the Tay and Fife; the observant cyclist may therefore see a seal sunning itself on a sandbank. After that the route keeps mainly to quiet roads as it links parks and green spaces around the city. All in all, a great way to see Dundee while at the same time keeping fit.

Greenbank Place

This street seems to be named after a geographical feature, a green or grassy banking. The alternative is the house of Greenbank at Arbroath, which seems unlikely although there was a Dundee connection as David Duncan of Greenbank owned shares in the Dundee Seal & Whale Fishing Company.

Greendykes Road

Takes its name from Greendykes farm, which was part of the estate of Craigie. The name means green walls, which suggests that there were drystane dykes perhaps overgrown or covered with moss or perhaps a hedge rather than the usual stone.

Greenfield Place, between Roseangle and Perth Road

Carries echoes of the area before Dundee was built up by industry and housing. At that time this area was all rural, then came a scattering of quality houses amidst rural surroundings as Dundee spread to the east. The industrial city followed after.

Greenmarket

The original Greenmarket was Dundee's largest marketplace, hence the name. The markets were held in the Nethergate but in the nineteenth century the location shifted to the Shore, in a place that had been known as Lime Tree Walk. The Greenmarket became the location for the herb market, sundry fairs, the circus that Victorians loved and a plethora of stalls and hangers-on. The modern name is merely a replica for there is no market. The present Greenmarket is north of Riverside.

Grey Lodge settlement

Grey Lodge settlement

Founded by Mary Lily Walker (1863–1913), one of the first students at Dundee University. The Grey Lodge is in South George Street, Hilltown, and is a youth-and-community-based charity that supports people of all ages.

At the entrance to the Grey Lodge settlement is a blue plaque to Mary Lily Walker. There are twenty-five such plaques distributed throughout Dundee. Each plaque highlights the achievements of a notable Dundee woman. Mary Lily Walker was the daughter of a Dundee solicitor and the first superintendent of the Dundee Social Union, a University-centred group that was determined to help the poor.

Walker founded the Grey Lodge to improve social welfare and was also involved in founding the women's hospital. In addition, Walker introduced health visitors and baby clinics to teach new mothers how to care for their young and brought in school dinners.

Greystane house, now known as the Double Tree hotel

This B-listed building has a two-ton boulder in the garden known as the Paddock stone or Devil's stone. The original name of the house possibly came from this grey stone, which is a scheduled monument. Legend says that when the devil saw St Boniface building a church at Invergowrie he tried to halt operations by throwing a large stone but this missed and landed where it is now.

Greystane Road/Terrace, Invergowrie

Takes its name from Greystane house.

Greywalls, Perth Road

Patrick Thoms (c.1873–1946) built this Arts and Crafts house for himself. It is built of stone, and Charles McKean, in his *Dundee an Illustrated Introduction*, suggests that the stone came from the area of Dundee known as the Vault, which was being torn down at the time.

Grimond Lane, Ardler

One of a series of streets named after old Dundee mills or mill owners. The Grimonds were major jute barons in the nineteenth century.

Grove Road, Broughty Ferry

Takes its name from a grove of trees that grew here. The Dundee whaling master and harbourmaster, Charles Yule, lived at Braeside in this street and survived to see his hundredth year.

Gullane Avenue/Terrace/Place/Road

This collection of Gullanes is in Ardler, among many streets that are named after famous Scottish golf courses. Gullane is on the East Lothian coast.

Guthrie Street

The first mill in this street may have been water-driven, using the Scouring burn for power, but in the 1790s a Boulton & Watt steam engine drove the east mill. This would make Guthrie Street the location of the earliest steam-powered mill in Dundee and one of the earliest in the world. The mill was originally used for cotton but was converted to flax spinning in 1799. It was owned by George Wilkie and then J. & W. Brown, whose surviving account of the mill's day-to-day operations is a fascinating piece of industrial history.

The mill stopped working in 1884 and was used as a pattern store, but the building still stands.

Guthrie Terrace, Broughty Ferry

Commemorates Colonel David Guthrie (1813–83) of the Angus Rifle Brigade, one of the many Scottish volunteer and militia units that were created in the nineteenth century. The French invasion scare of 1859 boosted the numbers of such units but part-time soldiers proved their worth during the Boer War of 1899–1902 when they augmented the regular army.

Haddington Place

No local connection, but refers to the East Lothian town of Haddington.

Haldane Lane, Broughty Ferry

Honours Robert and James Haldane, who were nephews of Admiral Adam Duncan. They initially followed in their uncle's footsteps by joining the navy but both were converted to evangelical Christianity. Robert Haldane retired from the sea aged 22 and commissioned Robert Adam to build a new castle on his estate at Airthrey. He built a hermitage on his estate and advertised for a full-time hermit to live there. He later sold the estate and became a preacher, with a church in Edinburgh and perhaps other places. Airthrey castle is now part of the University of Stirling.

Haldane Street

Robert Haldane was the early-nineteenth-century landowner who planned this street.

Halley Place/Terrace

William Halley was a flax manufacturer who became part owner of Wallace Craigie works spinning mill. The firm of William Halley & Sons Ltd was a major player in the Dundee jute trade in its later period and deserves at least one street as a reminder.

Hamilton Street/Terrace, Broughty Ferry

Commemorates Lady Mary Hamilton (1799–1864), the sister of local land-owner Fox Maule Ramsay, Lord Panmure.

Hansford Land and Cattle company

A nineteenth century, Dundee-based company that owned land and cattle in the western states of the USA. The company was founded in Hansford county, Texas by Scotsman James M. Coburn.

Haparanda café

Now gone, this establishment opened in 1957 and quickly became a major organiser of dances in the new, more leisure-conscious Dundee. These were the 'Hap dances', which up to six hundred people attended.

Harecraig, West Ferry

A villa built in 1835 and extended at the beginning of the twentieth century. In 1862 John Ogilvie of Harecraig gave money to help the people of Lancashire who were in distress due to the American Civil War.

Harefield Avenue/Court/Grove/Mews/Road, Lochee

Named after the Cox mansion of Harefield, one of a series of Cox-owned properties in the area.

Harestanes Crescent/Grove/Place/Road/Terrace

Take their name from Harestanes mill and bleachfield that stood hereabouts, with 'harestanes' meaning a boundary or memorial stone.

Harley Street, Broughty Ferry

Unfortunately, there is no connection with famous doctors. This street was named after Louis Harley (1857–1902) who owned Camperdown nursery and was a fruiterer, florist and seedsman.

Harris academy

Founder William Harris (1806–83) was a successful Dundee bailie, baker and miller. The original school was where Bonar hall now stands in Park Place, but was relocated in 1926 westward along the Perth Road and rebuilt. It is again being modernised and rebuilt. The Harris has a high reputation in Dundee.

Harris building

This fine building in the Geddes quadrangle, University of Dundee, was erected in 1909 for engineering but later changed its use to teach physics.

Harry Ogilvy's Close, 29 High Street to 17 Crichton Street

Sometimes known as Scott's close. It appears that this close was named after the keeper of an inn that stood at the Crichton Street entrance.

Hastings Place, Clepington

In 1886 there was an economic depression and high unemployment. Dundee council created a number of new streets to provide building work. The paving committee named this street Hastings Place, possible after George Hastings, a Liberal politician of the period, or, less likely, Warren Hastings, a former governor general of India.

Hatton castle

A few miles south of Dundee, near the planned village of Newtyle, Hatton castle sits on the slopes of the Sidlaw hills. It is an L-plan castle of 1575 built in the traditional Scottish fashion with the main hall on the first floor. The name means hall-toun or hall farm, the main farm of the estate.

Hatton Place

Takes its name from Hatton castle in the Sidlaws, Dundee's guardian range of hills. Hatton means hall-toun and is also the name of the hill on which the castle stands.

Hawick Drive

In common with many streets in the area, the name has no local connection. Hawick is a town in the Scottish Borders.

Hawkhill

The name says it all. This area was outside the town and was frequented by people who hunted with hawks. Hard to imagine now! This street was also the main western access route into Dundee before Perth Road was built. It runs past the northern flank of Dundee university and is enlivened by public art where an artist named Stan Bonnar created a pyramid over a now disused public convenience. Parts of what was the original Hawkhill, beside the university, are now called Old Hawkhill, with a street roughly parallel now known as Hawkhill.

Hayston Terrace

Named after Hayston hill in the Sidlaw hills, which means Hay's toun or farm. Hay was a famous name locally, with the Hay family apparently being instrumental in defeating the Norse in battle at Luncarty in the tenth century. The incident is probably apocryphal but was first recounted by a historian named Boece in 1527 so the tale has a history if nothing else. The originator of the Hay family may have been William de Haya in the twelfth century. Many Norman knights were awarded lands by Scottish kings in that period, often marrying into local families.

Hazel Drive/Gardens

Hazel Drive

Takes its name from Hazel hall, which stood here. Hazel hall was built in 1854 for Edward Baxter of the famous Baxter textile dynasty. The architect was Charles Wilson of Glasgow and the design was of an Italianate pavilion.

Hazelwood Close
Part of the Beechwood estate. Many of the streets in the area had the suffix 'wood' to tie in with Beechwood house, a Cox mansion on whose grounds the houses were built. The mansion is now demolished.

Hazlehead Place/Street, Ardler
As much of Ardler was built on what had been a golf course, many of the streets were named after famous golf courses. This street was named after Hazlehead golf course in Aberdeen.

Heathfield Place, Hawkhill
Takes its name from the Heathfield works of James Neish, pioneer of the jute carpet trade. He struggled to succeed at first but when he found a market in New York his sales grew. The name indicates that the original field here was of poor quality heathland.

Hedge Road, off Dudhope Street
The name suggests there was a notable hedge here, but in the 1880s this small street was noted for vice. However, salvation arrived in the person of three redoubtable Christian ladies. They selected one address that housed a brothel, shebeen and a shop for resetting stolen goods, and cleansed it of its sinful contents. Instead they imported Bibles and hymn books and created a mission station. They held their first meeting on a Tuesday evening in November 1884 where there was a lecture on temperance and social reform, with a closing speech by Revd Reid, the prison chaplain. Dundee being what it is, the place was crowded with supportive people.

Henderson's Wynd
From 'Rambles through Dundee', *Dundee Courier*, 1849: 'We are just entering a region which, last winter, gained the unenviable name of the 'Valley of Death' . . . from the dreadful ravages of typhus fever among its poverty stricken inhabitants. This place is comprised within Henderson's Wynd, Malcolm's Pend and Horsewater Wynd and is principally inhabited by poor Irish families engaged in the surrounding mills . . . Henderson's Wynd, of the three above mentioned lanes the worst.'

Hermitage Road, Broughty Ferry

Took the name from a house called the Hermitage, which was home to Peter Duncan (1798–1872). He named it for the Hermitage museum in St Petersburg, where he had worked in the flax trade.

Hermon Lodge, West Ferry

This is a B-listed, French-gothic-style mansion house, designed by Charles Edward (1816–90). Reflecting a more religious age, the name derives from Mount Hermon, which has at least fifteen mentions in the Bible.

Hermonhill Apartments

There was a Hermonhill cottage in Dundee and new cottages and villas were built here, between Perth Road and Hawkhill in 1890. The name, presumably, is from Mount Hermon in the Bible.

High Mill court

The name gives the clue. This mill is an A-listed building that stands prominently in the heart of the West End Lane's conservation area. Built between 1861 and 1864, this mill once employed hundreds of people but now is a highly desirable block of flats with a south-facing, glass-fronted elevator, car parking and excellent communal areas.

Owned by Thomson, Shepherd & Co., and known as Seafield works, this was a jute-carpet factory that operated between 1864 and 1986. It is an Italianate stone building and was neglected afrer its closure until restoration work began in 1992, with the upper floors first to be converted. When Dundee was the jute capital of the world, she was proud of her mills and factories; the conversion of buildings such as this creates a new type of civic pride.

High School

Boasts three parent establishments and a tradition of excellent education. Dundee High School was formed from three distinct institutions: the English school, the Grammar school (originally for training priests) and the Academy. The three schools combined under one roof as Dundee Public Seminaries, which evolved into Dundee High School.

In the 1830s Dundee Public Seminaries was in financial difficulties until a former baillie, William Harris, bailed it out with a grant of £10,000. The money was used to build the present school in Euclid Crescent, with George Angus (1792–1845), as the architect. The result was most satisfactory: it is a Greek Revival temple with a magnificent Doric portico that confers culture and prestige on the city centre while providing an excellent education.

As well as William Wallace, the precursors of the High School may claim the mediaeval scholar, Hector Boece, and the poet, Robert Fergusson, who could have rivalled Burns had he not died tragically young. On the sporting field there are Scottish rugby internationalists Andy Nicol and George Ritchie.

High Street
By the fifteenth century the tolbooth, market cross and the Tron were all situated here, making High Street the main market place. The name was not official until as late as 1876; before that it was known as Highgait, Marketgait or the Cross.

Perhaps because of its position, this street has long been central to Dundee's life, with incidents such as that of 16 November 1792 showing the temper of Dundonians. On that day the street was the scene of sedition when a small crowd gathered to celebrate the French revolutionary army's capture – or liberation as they termed it – of Brussels. The crowd also planted a symbolic tree of liberty. The next day a group of more loyal gentlemen pulled the tree back down. There was more trouble when the radical crowd tried to unload a cargo of meal from a ship in harbour, threw stones at the house of one of the gentlemen who had removed the liberty tree, rang the bells in the town hall until Provost Riddoch asked them to stop and built a bonfire. To drive their point home these terrible radicals then erected another tree in High Street.

There was a different type of excitement on 22 April 1944 when a German aircraft machine gunned the street but failed to hit anybody. Today the street still bustles but with families out shopping rather than with political agitation. Some may stop to examine the clock, which has a brass plaque inscribed with a verse from a jute-mill song:

Oh dear me, the mills gaen fest,
The puir wee shifters canna get a rest,
Shiftin' bobbins, coorse and fine,
They fairly mak' ye work for your ten and nine.

High Street is the beating heart of Dundee.

High Street, Clydesdale bank
Designed by William Spence and built in 1878, this fine building with its renaissance details is no longer occupied by the bank but many Dundonians still use that nomenclature.

Highland Chief Way, Claverhouse
This slightly fanciful name may seem out of place in pragmatic Dundee, but it is near Hebrides Drive and Chevalier's Pend as well as being within Claverhouse. The Hebrides are the island groups that lie to the west of the Highlands and the

name Chevalier is normally given to Prince Charles Edward Stuart, who led a confederation of Highland chiefs during the 1745 Jacobite rising while Claverhouse, as Bonnie Dundee, also had Highland chiefs in his army at the battle of Killiecrankie. A Highland chief was the head of the entire clan and therefore superior to a chieftain, who only led one branch.

Hill Street, Broughty Ferry
Dr Thomas Dick (1774–1857), the Christian philosopher and astronomer, lived in this street. The meaning of the name is obvious as this street is set on a hill overlooking the Tay.

Hill Street, by Dundee Law
Named after Dundee Law on which it sits, this street was on the lands of Richard Gardner of Dudhope. It was also the birthplace of George Kidd (1925–98). While serving in the Royal Navy during the Second World War, Kidd took up wrestling. With over a thousand bouts to his credit, and only thirty defeats, he was world lightweight champion for twenty-six years, retiring at the age of 51. This was a world record for the length of time a title has been held. He retired to Lawrence Street in Broughty Ferry. In 2015 Kidd was inducted into the Scottish wrestling hall of fame and there are plans for a plaque in his honour in Caird hall.

Hillbank Gardens, between Dens Road and Alexander Street
Takes its name from the mansion house of Hillbank that once stood at the brow of the hill. There is also a B-listed Hillbank mill or Blakey's mill, now converted into flats and known as Blakey's Mews.

Hilltown
A place of many names. It was once known as Bonnet hill, as it was inhabited by bonnet makers, one of the Nine Trades of Dundee. It was also known as Hilltown of Dudhope or Rotten Row and was a burgh of barony outwith the boundaries of Dundee. The name Rotten Row has nothing to do with the character of the people or the quality of the houses, but is presumed to mean infested with rats, with 'rotten' a corruption from the Scots word *rottan* or *rattan*.

In 1697 Dundee bought the Barony of Hilltown and incorporated it into the town. More recently Hilltown has had some famous inhabitants, including Jimmy Shand the accordionist. There was also Sarah Jane Gall, who was born at no. 64 Hilltown. Sarah Jane Gall, known as Ma, was a street missionary despite being blind from her teenage years. She played the organ as she helped the poor, the unfortunate and the homeless.

Hilltown clock, also known as Barrie's clock

An iconic site in the area, the Hilltown clock stands at the junction of Strathmartine Road and Mains Road. The clock was made in 1900 and is now a listed building; a public clock on a cast-iron ionic column, it carries the arms of the city of Dundee. An inscription reads: 'Presented to the Community of Dundee by Charles Barrie, one of the representatives of the Seventh Ward, December 1900'.

Hilltown Clock

Holly Crescent/Road, Broughty Ferry

These streets take their name from a mansion, the Hollies, owned by seed merchant and nursery owner Daniel Urquhart (1801–80). His son ran Blackness foundry.

Holly Blue Court

Named after the butterfly of that name.

Home Street, Broughty Ferry

Another street that commemorates the Earls of Home, a Border family who were also landowners in the Broughty Ferry area. They were ancestors of Sir Alex Douglas-Home (1903–95), who was prime minister in the Sixties.

Honeygreen Road

Named after Honeygreen mill, which stood on the banks of the Dighty water. Honeygreen mill was a plash, or washing mill, driven by water power.

Horse Wynd

This is a lane with an evocative name and a long history. Its origin is unknown but at one time it was the only route between Seagate and Murraygate and by 1449 had buildings on both sides of the wynd, which suggests it was already well-established. In 1465 it was known as the King's Vennel, which hints at a royal connection. At that time Horse Wynd was an elite area with many of the most important burgesses of the town owning properties here.

The lane led to the Market Cross (then in the Seagate and the centre of trade in the burgh), and it was opposite Sea Vennel, which gave access to the river Tay.

Horsewater Wynd

Presumably this is where carriers and carters were able to water their horses, so was a refuelling stop for the most important method of transport. It was also a place known for shebeens, or illicit drinking dens.

Howff, the

The Howff graveyard

One of the most evocative open spaces in Dundee, and surely unique in Britain, the Howff is a popular spot for strolling or having a quiet seat in the centre of the city. The name howff means a favourite haunt or meeting place, so the Howff lives up to its name, but this is Dundee, so nothing is quite what it seems. At first glance it will be obvious that the Howff has other functions apart from a place for gentle conversation. This is a burial ground.

Originally, this area was occupied by Greyfriars monastery, founded by Dervorguilla, Lady of Galloway, who also founded Sweetheart abbey in the Borders and Balliol college in Oxford. She was the mother of King John Balliol, the man who allegedly surrendered Scotland to King Edward Plantagenet of England, but nobody is perfect.

Greyfriars is said to have been beautiful but there are no surviving buildings or even a picture to prove that. The Scottish clergy gathered here in 1310 to recognise Robert Bruce as the legitimate King of Scots, so it occupies a vastly important place in Scottish history. The English tore it down in their 1547 ravage across southern Scotland, and, just twelve years later, Dundee council completed the destruction the English started. Officially sanctioned vandalism is nothing new.

In 1562 Queen Mary granted the land to Dundee for a public burial ground and the Nine Trades of Dundee used the Howff as a meeting place to discuss business. Earnest commercial consultations were continued around the grey stones that commemorated the dead. Each of the Nine Trades had a designated area of the graveyard, which retained its primary function of a repository for interring dead bodies until 1867. But there was more to the Howff than just business and death. It could be lively, especially at night. In the early nineteenth century grave robbers stole fresh corpses from graves and sold them to anatomists and the Howff was not immune from these practices. So where people now have calm walks and eat their lunchtime cheese sandwiches, great affairs of state and business transactions were discussed and evil men dug up corpses to sell for profit. Only in Dundee!

Hoylake Crescent, Ardler
Is one of many streets in the area named after a famous golf course. Hoylake is also known as the Royal Liverpool golf club.

Hunter Street
Takes its name from the Hunter family, owners of the Blackness estate. In 1882 David Hunter of Blackness house died at another of his properties in Portobello, Edinburgh. He had been a member of the Liff and Benvie parochial board and the Dundee harbour board.

Hutton Lane/Place, Broughty Ferry
Recalls John Hutton, a Caputh-born man, who came to the Ferry and opened a market garden. He won a number of gardening prizes.

Hyndford Street
John Carmichael was secretary of state for Scotland and Earl of Hyndford. He was one of the so-called 'parcel o' rogues' who voted for Union with England in 1707.

Ida Place, Broughty Ferry
Recalls the daughter of James Bell Archer, housing convener of Broughty, builder, stonemason and Conservative councillor.

Inchcape Place/Road, Barnhill
The names in this part of Barnhill were all selected with the prefix 'inch' which is the Scots word for an island. Inchcape is the alternative name for the Bell Rock, north-east of Dundee in the North Sea.

Inchcolm Drive, Barnhill
Inch is the Scots word for an island. Inchcolm is an island in the Firth of Forth, known as the Iona of the East as it houses an important religious site and is the burial place for many prominent people. The island means 'island of Columba' although that saint is not known to have visited the Forth.

Inchkeith Avenue, Barnhill
The names in this part of Barnhill were all selected with the prefix 'inch', the Scots word for an island. Inchkeith is the largest island in the Firth of Forth, with an impressive history that includes a sixteenth-century battle between French and English, gun emplacements in the Second World War and a legend of babies left there to see which language they spoke when they grew up.

Inchyra Place
Takes its name from Inchyra in the Carse of Gowrie. The name is Gaelic, meaning 'western island', which on first reading makes no sense, but it is possible that the hamlet was surrounded by boggy ground so was indeed an island of firm land. There have been Roman and Pictish archaeological finds here and the area was once famed for its apple orchards.

India buildings, 46 Bell Street
A reminder of Dundee's close connection with India due to the jute industry. The exterior detail is interesting but as the buildings are at the edge of a busy street, the viewer takes his or her life in their hands if they stand back to admire.

Industrial school, Courthouse Square
Intended as a home for children from challenging backgrounds, but no longer in existence.

Inglefield Street
As an ingle was a fire on an open hearth, the name means 'fire field'.

Institute of Sport and Exercise, University of Dundee
The university has state-of-the-art facilities, both indoor and outdoor.

Inveraray Terrace
Inveraray is a small village in Argyll, and means 'confluence of the Aray', which is the river that meets Loch Fyne just north of Inveraray castle.

Inverarity Gardens
Named after a parish on the Sidlaw hills. The name signifies the confluence of the Arity burn with the Corbie burn.

Invergowrie

Invergowrie means 'confluence of the Gowrie' so is where the Gowrie burn runs into the Tay. According to legend, when the Scots moved en masse from Ireland to Scotland to form the kingdom of Dalriada, the sons of Eirc (King of Irish Dalriada) grabbed various chunks of the land, which were named in their honour. Gowrie was named after a prince named Gabran. The village itself is old, and another legend states that the church here was the first Christian church in the northern part of Scotland, which, if true, means it predates Iona in Christianity.

There is a legend that early Scottish kings sailed from here and King Alexander I intended building a royal palace on this spot. If he had done so, perhaps Dundee would have become the capital of Scotland, with unimaginable consequences.

There was a major employer in the Bullionfield paper mill, now gone, with the proprietors also owning Greystane house, now a hotel. The buildings in today's Invergowrie are nineteenth century and twentieth century and are augmented by an agricultural-research station, pleasant walks and a railway station, primary school, churches and an inviting local inn. Mylnefield research station is an affiliate of the James Hutton Institute and specialises in plant breeding, creating disease-resistant varieties of fruit and vegetables.

There have been some prominent people associated with Invergowrie. A former premier of Queensland, Australia, William Forgan Smith (1887–1953), was raised in a cottage at Balbunnoch, at the back of Main Street. He came back to the village in 1934 to a hero's reception. More recently the author Rosamunde Pilcher lived in a large house just outside the village.

Invergowrie house

Close to Ninewells hospital, this very impressive mansion dates from at least 1600 but was extended and improved by William Burn in 1837. This house was owned by Patrick Gray and his wife, Anne Napier, whose initials are carved on the staircase tower. In Scotland it used to be the norm for women to retain their maiden names after marriage.

Inverlaw Place

The name Inverlaw would mean the confluence of a hill, which makes no sense. However, in this case the street is named after a large house named Inverlaw, situated on Dudhope Terrace. As so often in Dundee it was a jute baron, in this case David Halley of the Wallace Craigie jute works, who owned the said house.

Invermark Terrace, Broughty Ferry

Is named after Invermark lodge in Glenesk where Fox Ramsay, Lord Panmure, held his hunting and shooting parties. The guests included Queen Victoria and Prince Albert, which underlines the status of Lord Panmure.

Ivanhoe Place

Named after the novel *Ivanhoe* by Sir Walter Scott, in which Ivanhoe is a knight during the Middle Ages.

Ivory Place

One of Dundee's near-forgotten men, the mathematician James Ivory (1765–1842), was the son of a Dundee clockmaker. Educated in Dundee and St Andrews, he studied arts and theology. He intended to join the Church of Scotland but from June 1786 taught maths at Dundee Academy. After an abortive spell in the textile trade he returned to teaching as professor of mathematics at the Royal Military College. He taught there until he retired through ill health in 1819 but still obtained a full pension. He was made Knight of the Order of Hanover and in 1829 gave his scientific library of three hundred books to Dundee. The collection is held in the central library.

Jamaica Street

This now-vanished street reminds one of the local man, Thomas Wyse, who qualified as a doctor and emigrated to Jamaica in the early eighteenth century. He made a fortune there, returned to Scotland and bought the estate of Hillbank. It was not uncommon for Scots to make a fortune in the colonies and return home to enjoy it. Jamaica Square, off Ann Street, carries on the name.

James Place, Broughty Ferry

On the banks of the Firth of Tay, this street is neoclassical and faces toward Fife. It recalls James Mitchell (1807–58), railway contractor and local landowner. William Adams, whaling master, lived at no. 8 from 1874–8.

James Black Place

Is beside Ninewells hospital and commemorates Sir James Whyte Black (1924–2010), an Uddingston-born pharmacologist who created the physiologist department of the University of Glasgow. While working for ICI Pharmaceuticals he developed a beta-blocker named propranolol that is used to treat heart disease. He also developed cimetidine for treating stomach ulcers. In 1988 he received the Nobel Prize for medicine.

Black's Dundee connection was strong. He attended the then Queen's College Dundee, graduating in 1946. In 1980 Dundee University awarded him the honorary degree of Doctor of Laws and in 1992 he became chancellor of the university.

James Lindsay Place

Born near Arbroath, James Lindsay (1799–1862) was a prominent nineteenth-century mathematician and inventor. He started his working life as a linen weaver but gained a place at St Andrews University and became the science and mathematics lecturer at the Watt institute in Dundee. He was innovative, creating electric light in 1835, decades before Thomas Edison invented the light bulb. The motivation for his discovery was to make safe lighting for Dundee's mills, which were often ravaged by fire. He was a pioneer of wireless telegraphy and an astronomer, while also using his philology talents to attempt to prove how accurate Bible history was. Although he turned down a position at the British Museum in order to remain in Dundee and care for his mother, his talents were recognised as Lord Derby, the prime minister, recommended that Queen Victoria grant him a pension of £100 a year in recognition of his achievements. There is an obelisk to his memory in Dundee's western cemetery.

Janefield Place

Takes its name from a farm that the expanding city of Dundee swallowed.

Jetty Lane, Broughty Ferry

Not surprisingly, this was the lane that led to the jetty that belonged to the Perth Steam Packet company.

John Grahame Avenue

John Grahame (or Graham) of Claverhouse (c.1648–89), Viscount Dundee, was a man of many parts. He is either admired as Bonnie Dundee, the hero who led the Jacobites to victory at the battle of Killiecrankie in 1689, or vilified as Bluidy Claverhouse, the villain who persecuted the Covenanters in the Killing Times of the 1670s and early 1680s.

Grahame was born in 1648 or 1649 and succeeded to the title Grahame of Claverhouse at the age of fourteen. Educated at St Andrews, by twenty-one he was already a Forfarshire JP. In 1672 he volunteered into the army of King James and was a captain of horse with his own troop in 1678. However, he lost his command the following year when the Covenanters defeated him at the Battle of Drumclog. Even so, King James granted him lands in Galloway and appointed him Sheriff of Wigtown. Grahame was colonel of his own regiment in 1682 and a member of the Privy Council shortly after.

He advanced to the rank of major-general and in 1688 became Viscount Dundee and Lord Grahame of Claverhouse. When the Convention decided that Scotland should have William of Orange as king, and not James, Grahame remained loyal to James, and raised the standard of rebellion. The government put a reward of 18,000 merks on his head, dead or alive, but redcoat soldiers saved them the money when they shot him during his victory at the battle of Killiecrankie in 1689.

John Huband Drive

Commemorates John Huband (1942–2000) who began his fifty-year career as an accordionist when he was only eight years old. For a while he worked alongside the world famous Jimmy Shand at J. T Forbes, accordion repairer and tuners, in the Nethergate.

Jute

Was one of the three 'J's that are considered to have made Dundee, with the others being jam and journalism. Jute was grown in India and brought to Dundee to be processed into rough textiles that were used for articles such as sacking and wagon covers. In the nineteenth century Dundee capitalised from the various gold rushes, colonial expansions and wars with their demand for jute products.

There were three main areas for jute mills: Blackness, Lochee and along the Dens burn. Each became congested with mills and their attendant factories, with the workers usually finding accommodation close by. The streets were crammed with jute wagons and filled with the clatter of mill machinery while smoke from factory chimneys polluted the air. In time the owners and managers who could afford it left the city centre for leafy Broughty Ferry, the broad expanse of the west end or across the Tay to Newport.

Jute only became important to Dundee in the nineteenth century, with just over a thousand tons imported in the 1830s, but three hundred thousand tons in 1900. This huge amount had to be brought by sea, so the jute industry encouraged shipbuilding and an expansion of the docks as well as factory building and employment. A number of the jute merchants even owned their own ships.

Jute also helped the whaling industry. As other towns abandoned whaling, it was discovered that whale oil softened the brittle jute fibres and allowed them to be processed into textiles, giving whaling a new lease of life in Dundee, with associated benefits to shipbuilding and Arctic exploration. When Arctic whaling experienced a terminal decline in the early twentieth century, mineral oil replaced whale oil in the jute works.

Jute was a labour-intensive industry and people poured into the city for work in the mills and factories. In consequence, the population rose from 45,000 in 1841 to 160,000 in 1901, with consequent pressure on housing. Many hailed from rural Scotland, while others came from Ireland, creating tensions between 'Scotch' and 'Irish', but on a lesser scale than in the west of Scotland. Over-crowding continued until the twentieth century when vast peripheral housing schemes were built. There was also terrible child mortality, general ill-health and crime. However, it was not all bad, as the best jute works had high morale and sporting and social clubs.

Most of the fifty thousand jute workers were women, who could be very assertive despite, or possibly because of, working for some of the lowest wages in the country. Others were children, while a minority were men. The mills required machinery so Dundee developed a strong engineering sector. All these ancillary industries were endangered in times of slump and when the jute industry faded in the twentieth century Dundee experienced some very bad times.

Dundee was justifiably proud of her mills, not only because they provided employment for tens of thousands of people, but also because the best of them were architecturally distinguished. A jute mill was not a single building, but a number of different structures, each with its own function. There was a low mill in which the workers softened the brittle raw material with whale or vegetable oil, then prepared and carded before being transported to the high mill for the spinners to make it into yarn. From there it was another short journey to the factory for the weavers to create cloth from the yarn, and, finally, over to the calendar to be finished.

Added to that was a warehouse for storage, an engine house for the machinery, a cooling pond, schoolhouse for the many very young workers, a dye works and waste works and offices. The high mill was the most ornate, with campaniles, fancy decoration and an expression of company pride.

Despite the loss of the jute industry to India, some of the mill buildings survive and are now put to other uses in the city that was once Juteopolis. They are a monument to the entrepreneurs who had the business acumen to take Dundee to the apex of world trade, but mainly to the generations of workers who toiled and sweated and suffered within their sturdy stone walls.

Jute Mill Woman statue

By Malcolm Robertson, this bronze statue was erected in 2014 in Bank Street, Lochee as a memorial to the tens of thousands of women who worked in Dundee's jute mills. Lochee is an excellent site for the statue as it was the location of the massive Camperdown works, owned by the Cox family.

Keats Place

Located north of the Law it remembers John Keats (1795–1821), the English poet and leading figure of the Romantic movement. His work was not well received during his lifetime but his stature grew steadily in the centuries that followed.

Keiller shopping centre

Keiller Shopping Centre (Forum Centre)

This covered array of fascinating shops sits square in the centre of the city where Keiller's marmalade factory used to stand, between the High Street and Albert Square. The name Keiller means hard water.

Kelso Street

Kelso Street

A secluded little street in Dundee's west end. It was named after Kelso in the Scottish Borders, which is sometimes referred to as the most beautiful town in the Borders.

Kemback Street
Named after the Fife parish of Kemback whence John Walker, the owner of the nearby Dura works, originated. The name could mean 'field of battle'.

Kenilworth Avenue
Derives from a novel by Sir Walter Scott. In the first half of the nineteenth century Scott was arguably the most famous novelist in the world, with houses, streets, railway stations, pubs and even towns named after his books.

Kennoway Place, Barnhill
The streets in this part of Barnhill were named after places in Fife. Kennoway is east of Glenrothes and north of Leven.

Kerrington Crescent, Broughty Ferry
Among his other titles the local landowner, Lord Panmure, was 11th Lord Ramsay of Kerrington, inheriting the title from his cousin. Kerrington is in Midlothian and is now spelled Carrington; it is a delightful little hamlet a mile or so from Gorebridge.

Kerrsview Terrace
Commemorates the hard work of James Kerr in helping Dundee obtain Caird park for the city.

Kerrystone Court
The derivation is the one-time hamlet of Kerrystone bank in the parish of Murroes in Angus.

Kettins Terrace
Named after the village of Kettins beside the Sidlaw hills. The name is from the Gaelic *ceite ness* and according to David Dorward means mound of the assembly.

Kilmaron Lane, Broughty Ferry
Sir David Baxter of Kilmaron (1793–1872) owned Kilmaron castle in Fife. In June 1859 he also bought Pittencrieff, near Cupar, for £4,000. It was this Baxter who gave Baxter park to Dundee as well as generous donations to the University of Edinburgh.

Kilspindie Road

The village in the Sidlaws called Kilspindie is known to have existed in 1114 and was on the main road between Dundee and Perth. According to Dorward the name means 'at the end of the thorny place'.

Kilwinning Place

Refers to the Ayrshire town of Kilwinning.

Kincaldrum Place

Kincaldrum is a small village with a ruined house in the Sidlaw hills in Angus. In 1853 the Dundee connection began when the Baxters bought the property. According to Dorward the name comes from the Gaelic *ceann called druim* – 'at the head of the hard ridge'.

King Street

King Street

This pleasing, partly neoclassical, eighteenth- and nineteenth-century street was originally King's Road. The king in question was George III and the street was created as an alternative to the Hilltown route toward Forfar. The city architect David Neave created the most prestigious frontage.

King Street also has Weavers Yard, once one of Baxter's mills, but now converted to flats. On the wall of this building is a blue plaque, one of twenty-five distributed around the city. Each plaque highlights the contribution to society of a prominent woman of Dundee. This plaque is to Mary Brooksbank (1897–1978), a communist activist, poet and trade unionist who worked from the age of twelve and challenged malpractice by mill owners. She turned from Roman Catholicism to atheism and fought for women's rights.

King Street is further blessed with a second blue plaque at the Old Wishart church. This was once known as Heaven and Hell, with a pub named John o' Groats on the ground floor and the church above. This plaque is to Dundee's very own missionary, Mary Slessor.

King Street, Broughty Ferry
King George III was the monarch at the time that General Charles Hunter of Burnside planned the 'new town' of Broughty Ferry in 1801.

Kinghorne Road
Has a mixture of housing and was initially built in the 1880s using the labour of the unemployed, so in a way was an early job-creation scheme.

Kingoodie

Kingoodie

Until 1895 Kingoodie was home to quarries from which building stone was extracted to use in Dundee. Kingoodie is a lovely little place that faces onto the Tay west of Dundee, with memories of its industrial past in the old harbour wall. On a dull winter's day, the atmosphere can be quite impressive. The piece of land locally known as the Pointy that protrudes into the Tay was originally the jetty for the quarry. This is also a fine place to observe bird life as waders visit the mud flats.

King's Cross

According to legend this area, north of the Law, is where Alpin, king of the Scots, was beheaded by Brude, king of the Picts. The two peoples were at war, with Alpin defending a dun on the Law. Alpin appeared to be triumphant when a host of camp followers swarmed over from Clatto and Alpin thought it was a fresh Pictish army. His men fled, but the Picts captured Alpin and executed him – according to legend.

King's Cross hospital

King's Cross Hospital

Opened in 1889 as an epidemic hospital and named after King's Cross Road. There were only two wards when the hospital was first built, but it expanded with extra buildings including King's Cross hospital (west) added in 1893 specifically for smallpox and cholera sufferers. Both these diseases would spread rapidly in Dundee's crowded streets. After the creation of the NHS, King's Cross was the centre for infectious diseases for Dundee, Perth and Angus, but now it deals mainly with outpatients and administration.

Kingsway

The road around the north of Dundee, and, when it opened in 1919, Britain's first ring road. Originally the name was intended to honour King Edward VII but by the time the road was built, George V was on the throne. Kingsway was created in the mind of James Thomson, Dundee's city engineer. He planned for a wide, tree-lined road around the outside of the city, but expansion has put many areas of Dundee outside the Kingsway. It remains a very important route.

During the building process an inscribed stone, the Bullion stone, was discovered. It dates from the Dark Ages and shows a slightly worse-for-wear horseman with a shield and large drinking horn.

Kinloch, George

A statue to George Kinloch (1775–1833), landowner, justice of the peace, political reformer, one-time outlaw, civic reformer and Dundee's first MP, stands in Albert Square. As a man he hoped to better the conditions of his fellow human beings and as a politician he strove for greater inclusivity. He is worthy of his statue although it is doubtful if one person in a hundred knows who he was. When in 1817–18 his pro-reform speeches caused him to be accused of sedition he fled the country and was not pardoned until the visit of George IV to Scotland in 1822. After the Great Reform Act of 1832 Kinloch was Dundee's first MP, but he died the following year, aged 58. He is one of the forgotten pioneers of democracy in Scotland and deserves to be better known. According to Professor Christopher Whatley, money was available to erect a statue for Kinloch soon after his death but the Conservatives objected to a statue of a radical in any public space in Dundee, so it was nearly forty years before it was erected.

Kinloch Place/Street

Honours George Kinloch (see previous entry). *Kinloch* is from Gaelic and means 'head of the loch'.

Just before the Second World War there was a hairdresser's shop at 1 Kinloch Street called Jolly's Saloon. This shop was owned by Jessie Jordan, a Glasgow-born woman who had lived in Hamburg and married a German. She used the shop as a post office for the Abwehr – German military intelligence – and sent them mundane information about British docks. However, her assistant, Mary Curran, became aware of the number of letters she received with German stamps and wondered at the long periods when Jordan was in Germany. Curran reported her boss to the police and she was arrested and jailed. She was repatriated to Germany in 1945 where she became a missionary for the Christian Scientists. She died in 1954, Dundee's only known German spy.

Kinnaird Street

Situated on the sunny southern slope of Dundee Law, this street recalls George, 9th Lord and 1st Baron Kinnaird (1807–78), who was a landowner, Liberal politician and city benefactor. He succeeded to the lordship in 1826 and five years later became Baron Rossie of Rossie Priory, which lies between Dundee and Perth. In 1839 he became Master of the Buckhounds under Lord Melbourne, and the following year a member of the Privy Council. He became a Knight of the Thistle in 1857, and, finally, in 1860, Baron Kinnaird of Rossie.

His lands were in the Carse of Gowrie but he also donated Dundee the land that the corn exchange, later Kinnaird hall, was built on.

Kinnoull Road/Street

The parish and hill of Kinnoull is on the outskirts of Perth. Kinnoull hill is the last outlier of the Sidlaws and is a dramatic introduction to Perth, if coming from the east, or to the hills, if coming from the west. The building on top is a folly with no practical use except as a romantic ruin, while few people even know of the Dark Age monster that was once supposed to live in the Dragon's Hole. The name Kinnoull is from Gaelic and means 'at the head of the rocks'.

Kinpurnie castle

Not as old as it appears, this castle eleven miles north of Dundee was built as recently as 1911 although the style is seventeenth-century Scots, with a hugely attractive entrance between two circular turrets. The name means 'tree-covered headland'. Kinpurnie castle and over six hundred acres of land was up for sale in 2015.

Kinpurnie Place

Named after the castle that overlooks the planned village of Newtyle. The building on the top of the hill is the remains of an eighteenth-century observatory.

Kirkbuddo Place

Another Dundee street named after a small settlement in the Sidlaw hills. The original name may come from *caer buite*, with *caer* meaning fort and *buite* referring to the elusive St Buite, from the Dark Ages, who founded a church here.

Kirkton

Now a large housing scheme in the north of Dundee, the original Kirkton meant the settlement was around the local kirk, or church. The estate was built around two farms named West Kirkton and Magdalene's Kirkton.

There is a community centre, a supermarket and other shops and plans for an outstanding new Baldragon high school that is due to open this year (2016).

Kirsty Semple Way

Kirsty Semple (1924–95) was born in Edinburgh and graduated in medicine. She moved to Dundee where she became a general practitioner, but a visit to Canada gave her the idea to form Tayside breast care and mastectomy group in 1978. She was also an elder at the Steeple church, was instrumental in creating Tayside Council on Addictions and worked with the homeless.

Knapdale Place

In common with other streets in this area, there is no local connection to the name. Knapdale is a district of Argyll, just north of Kintyre.

Ladybank Place, Barnhill

The streets in this part of Barnhill were named after places in Fife. Ladybank sits a few miles to the south-west of Cupar. Its original name was 'Our Lady's Bog' but when the railway arrived the name Ladybank was considered more pleasant.

Ladywell Avenue

Ladywell Avenue

Between Victoria Road and King Street, this street recalls Our Lady's Well, otherwise known as 'the well of the Blessed Maria of Dundee'. The Wellgate steps and the Wellgate centre were also named after this well. This was one of Dundee's principal water supplies, along with wells at Logie Spout in Milnbank Road and Smellie's Wynd at Lochee Road. Water was collected each morning and brought in carts to the town, where it was sold to the inhabitants. The Dundee Water Act of 1845 created a private water company that brought water from Stobsmuir and Monickie but hardly helped the majority of people in the city. Things improved in the 1870s when the council took over and imported water from Clatto reservoir and the Loch of Linlathen.

Ladywell roundabout

On the inner ring road, this roundabout was named after 'the well of the blessed Maria of Dundee', which also gave its name to the Wellgate.

Laird Street

Commemorates Dundee's forgotten admiral, Admiral David Laird, who in 1785 bought Strathmartine estate for the then large sum of £15,000. The admiral was a local man, the son of a Dundee merchant who joined the Royal Navy and rose to the rank of admiral during the American War of Independence.

When he came ashore Laird spent much money and time in improving Strathmartine estate. He lived in Strathmartine castle, died in 1811 and was buried in the local churchyard.

Lamb's Lane

Recalls James Lamb, who lived in this lane in the late eighteenth century. His son was Thomas Lamb, who ran Lamb's Temperance hotel and his grandson was Alexander Crawford Lamb, a noted local historian and author of *Dundee: Its Quaint and Historic Buildings*.

Larch Street

In 1884 this street was the site of Dundee's first day nursery for working women. It was also home to a large number of mill workers, some of whom lived in the ten-storey Robertson's Land.

Largo Place, Barnhill

The streets in this part of Barnhill were named after places in Fife. Largo is in the East Neuk and was home to Sir Andrew Wood, the Scottish seaman who made his name with victories over English ships in the late fifteenth century. The name may mean 'village on a hillside'.

Laurel Bank

Built around 1851, this street contains fine Victorian villas that were intended for the middle classes. A high wall protected the houses from the neighbouring working-class Rosebank. The name is a reminder of the rural background of this part of Dundee.

Law The, Law hill or Dundee Law

The most prominent feature in Dundee, a green lung that dominates the skyline, the Law is an extinct volcano, four hundred million years old, that rises to 572 grassy feet. There is easy access by road for cars, bicycles or pedestrians and the views from the top over Dundee, Angus and the Firth of Tay are worth every step.

Dundee's principal war memorial is located on the summit, with a beacon that is lit on special occasions, such as 25 September, the anniversary of the Battle of Loos, in which the Black Watch played a memorable part. It is also lit on United Nations Day, 24 October, on 11 November and on Remembrance Sunday.

Law Hill War Memorial

The monument was built in 1924 and officially unveiled in May 1925. It is a plain and dignified memorial to the thousands of Dundee men and women who gave their lives in the First and Second World Wars and subsequent conflicts.

The name itself is unusual, as the word 'law' means hill, or more specifically a rounded hill, so it is misnamed 'Hill hill' but the people of Dundee do not seem to mind. It is their special hill and that is all there is to it.

As one would expect, there is a lot of history attached to the Law. There was an Iron Age fortress on the summit, and the Romans were also here as they sought to subdue the un-subduable Caledonians. Given the recent experiences of the British army in Afghanistan, one can almost feel sympathy for a Roman soldier standing guard on the summit, looking north toward the outliers of the Highland hills and wondering what sort of enemy he would be facing when the wild men descended.

There is also a legend of a Dark Ages beheading and traces of a sixteenth-century fortress from a later English incursion. That one ended in fire and blood as the invaders were very messily pushed out of the country. Bonnie Dundee unfurled the Stuart banner here before he began the campaign that saw his victory and death at the battle of Killiecrankie. His reputation among certain sectors of the population was so bad that it was said it needed a silver bullet to kill him.

There is also a tunnel that passes through the Law, part of the Dundee to Newtyle railway, but this is currently closed although there are suggestions that it could be opened as a tourist attraction.

In 1879, at a time when cities were keen on acquiring parks and open spaces to improve the amenity and health of the inhabitants, William Macbean Rankine sold the Law to Dundee council. At one time there was a custom on May morning for youths to ascend the Law to wash their faces with dew. In some years, such as 1877, this ceremony was augmented with various games and a choir led by Frank Sharp, which sang summer songs. Today it is Dundee's iconic hill, a mecca for citizens and visitors alike.

Law Crescent
Curls around the Law, after which it is named.

Law Road
Straight and direct for vehicles and brings them to the summit of the Law and one of the finest urban viewpoints in eastern Scotland.

Lawers Drive
The streets in this part of Barnhill were named after Scottish mountains. Ben Lawers stands at 1,214 metres and is Scotland's tenth-highest mountain. Owned by the National Trust for Scotland, it is in Perthshire and renowned for its Arctic-Alpine flora.

Lawrence Street, Dundee
The communist activist Bob Stewart lived at no. 21 when he first came to Dundee. Born in Eassie in 1877, he was the tenth child of twelve. At the age of ten, after only three years of schooling, Stewart started work as a shifter in Mitchell's jute mill. Either the wages were very low or he just liked to work, for Stewart also sold papers around the pubs of Dundee, an experience that encouraged him to join the temperance movement. He moved jobs and became a union man and a socialist. Against wars in principle he joined the No Conscription Fellowship.

Jailed for opposing the First World War, Stewart still served in the army from 1917 to 1919. He managed to be court martialled four times during that period, which must be some sort of record. On his return to civilian life he joined the Socialist Prohibition Party and was also a founder member of the Communist Party of Great Britain, gaining over six thousand votes when he stood in the 1921 Dundee council election. He was active in the communist cause, becoming Scottish organiser, and was so effective that the authorities jailed him for sedition in 1922. After a trip to Moscow, Stewart again stood for the Communist Party in three successive elections. He worked for Comintern (Communist International) around Europe and had contacts in China and possibly with the IRA. He was obviously a man of strong convictions.

Lawrence Street, Broughty Ferry
Commemorates Captain Lawrence Brown who died in 1809. He was the captain of the customs cruiser, *Princess Royal*, and married Elizabeth Henry, the heiress to the Woodend estate in Perthshire. Customs cruisers were responsible for controlling smuggling, which was endemic in the eighteenth and early-nineteenth centuries, with the coast of Angus a hotspot for illegal landings.

Lawside Road/Terrace
Not surprisingly, these pleasant streets are named after the Law, on which western side they sit.

Lawson Place, off Constitution Street
William Lawson was the proprietor of the area and had the street built. He modestly proposed that it was named Lawson Street and so Lawson Place it became.

Lawton Road/Terrace
Remembers Lawton and North Lawton farms, which stood here. The meaning of the name is simple: the 'farm or settlement by the hill'.

Leith Gardens, Menzieshill
Named after the Water of Leith, which rises in the Pentland hills and flows through Edinburgh.

Leng Street
Commemorates Hull-born Sir John Leng (1828–1906), Liberal MP for Dundee from 1889 until 1905, and knighted in 1893. From 1851 he was the editor of the *Dundee Advertiser,* which Dundee people with their genius for shortening words, called the *Tiser.* That paper had been founded in 1801 and had some interesting editors, including Perthshire-born Robert Rintoul, radical, founder of *The Spectator* and supporter of the 1832 Reform Act. He was known for saying 'the Bill, the whole Bill and nothing but the Bill'.

By the time Leng took over *The Advertiser* it had fallen on hard times. He modernised it, established an office in Fleet Street and launched the *People's Journal* and the *People's Friend.* As an MP, Leng announced firm support for Home Rule for Ireland. He left another lasting memorial in the Leng chapel, which is a French Gothic-style building off the Dundee to St Andrews Road. Finally, the Leng Charitable Trust gave more than £100,000 to the University of Dundee.

Lethnot Gardens/Street, Broughty Ferry
Another reference to Ramsay of Dalhousie; he was Baron Panmure of Brechin and Navar. Navar is a parish in Angus, which combined with Lethnot to form the parish of Lethnot and Navar.

Library, Queen Street, Broughty Ferry

Public Library, Broughty Ferry

This single-storey building has a pilastered central bay and is an attractive addition to the street.

Liddel Road, Menzieshill

Many streets in the area are named after Scottish rivers, in this case the Liddel, which runs through Liddesdale in the south-west. Liddesdale was once one of the most notorious areas of Scotland, home to some of the wildest reivers and outlaws.

Broughty Ferry Lifeboat Station

Lifeboat station, Broughty Ferry

Established in 1830, the Broughty Ferry lifeboat has had a busy life. The Tay is not an easy firth to negotiate with a plethora of shifting sandbanks and a strong current, a combination that has seen many shipwrecks at the mouth. The worst day for the lifeboat service was on 8 December 1959, when the lifeboat *Mona* was lost in the teeth of a 'strong south-easterly gale' and a 'westerly flood tide', together with all eight of her crew.

Mona had been launched to

rescue the *North Carr* lightship, which had broken free of her moorings in atrocious weather. At 04.48 all wireless communication from the lifeboat ceased. At dawn the coastguard began a search that included helicopters and shore parties. The lifeboat was found at 8.45 ashore, north of Buddon Ness, with five bodies on board, while three more of the crew perished in the sea.

Liff

A picturesque small village to the north of Dundee that was once known as Kirkton of Liff. It sits in an elevated position overlooking the Carse of Gowrie and the Tay. The meaning of the name is unclear; it is possible it came from the Gaelic *lighe*, meaning a flood, although the position of the village well above the flood plain would make that unlikely. Dorward thinks the name is from the Gaelic *cliatach*, the side of a hill, which seems to make more sense.

There is some interesting architecture, with the impeccable 1839 kirk, the recently restored manse, the Grade-B listed Hearse house looking fit for a Gothic romance and the Watt-Webster monument all attracting the attention of passers-by. Look for the clay-walled Red Roofs at Loch of Liff Road.

There is also a site called Hurly Hawkin, which legend claims had been the palace of King Alexander I. He could hardly have chosen a more favoured spot to live. This site is to the west of the kirkyard on a promontory between the confluence of two burns. An archaeological dig in the 1950s found evidence of a building here, but it predated Alexander's period by some centuries and contained a second-century broch and a prehistoric promontory fort.

Liff Crescent/Place/Road/Terrace

Take their name from Liff village.

Liff hospital

The Dundee Royal lunatic asylum opened in 1820 with three patients but it was not until the early 1880s that Liff hospital opened. It operated for over a century until new premises opened in the grounds of Ninewells hospital. The site is now used for private houses.

Lilybank Road/Terrace

Take their name from the small estate of Lilybank that stood here. The estate could have been named after a collection of lilies that grew here before the house was built.

Lime Street

Part of the highly successful 1919 Logie scheme. The name was chosen to reflect the garden-city theme, with lime trees deciduous and native to Scotland.

Lindores Place, Barnhill
Lindores is a small village in north-east Fife. The name means 'church by the water', which is fitting as the village is set beside a loch and has a twelfth-century abbey and the remains of an even older church.

Lindsay Lane/Street, Broughty Ferry
Commemorates William Lindsay, the last provost of the Ferry before it was taken over by Dundee in 1913.

Linen
Before Dundee became the world capital of jute, there was linen. It is often forgotten that in the early nineteenth century Dundee was one of the most important linen towns of the United Kingdom. Dundee vessels brought the raw flax in from the Baltic, it was converted into linen in the town and exported by sea to London and thence to the West Indies, or elsewhere. When the government bounty on linen increased in 1745, Dundee flourished, even as Glasgow rose to dominate the transatlantic tobacco trade. Scotland was learning how to exploit the less-than-four-decades-old Union. During times of war the Royal Navy escorted convoys of Dundee ships through the Kattegat and up to Riga, while Dundee-manufactured sailcloth pushed HMS *Victory* onward at the Battle of Trafalgar. There was also a thriving export trade directly to South Carolina.

Dundee specialised in 'osnaburgs,' which name was coined from the Hanoverian town of Osnaburg that manufactured a type of low-quality linen. The quantities produced in Dundee were impressive: in 1789 alone the town created seven hundred thousand yards of canvas.

Any linen manufacture needed a bleachfield, an area where cloth was spread out to be bleached by the combination of sun and water. Such places were common in eighteenth-century Scotland, with Dundee having a public bleachfield at Baldovie. In the closing years of the eighteenth century steam-powered calendering mills for the final touches of pressing and polishing were installed as hemp and flax imports and linen exports both increased. The jute industry may have made Dundee famous but linen was her staple product for a longer period of time.

Linlathen
One of the more successful council schemes of the interwar period. The houses were clad in cedar, which was highly unusual for a country whose building tradition was largely of stone. The name comes from a rural estate then outside Dundee, and is presumably from the Gaelic *lann-leathan*, 'broad enclosure or large field'.

Linlathen east footbridge

Linlathen east footbridge

Crosses the Dighty burn at the eastern entrance to the policies of Linlathen house at Broughty Ferry. This Grade-A listed structure is the oldest iron bridge in Scotland and one of the oldest anywhere, having been built at the turn of the eighteenth and nineteenth centuries. Its restoration resulted in a prize winner in the 2012 Historic Bridge and Infrastructure Awards. The judges were impressed by the technical quality, imagination and efficiency of the engineering.

Linlathen house

Originally known as Fintry, on Friday, 2 August 1940 the Luftwaffe dropped twenty-three bombs on this house and the general area. A few windows were smashed and some plasterwork destroyed. The Luftwaffe managed to kill a solitary cat. Later in the same war Polish troops were based here but there is now no trace of the house as it was demolished in 1990 and a nursing home built on the site.

Linlithgow Place, Kingoodie

A beautiful pair of stone and slate cottages built in the 1920s and since merged into a single house.

Lister Court/Place

Honours Joseph Lister (1827–1912), the London-born surgeon who was a pioneer of antiseptic surgery. It had been quite common for patients to survive surgery only to die from 'ward fever', an infection that was transmitted through dirt. Suitably, the street is within a stone's throw of Ninewells hospital.

Little Theatre, 58 Victoria Road

The Little Theatre, Victoria Road

The name gives an indication of the size of this theatre, which is based in a converted jute store. The theatre has been the home of the Dundee Dramatic Society since it opened in 1936. It has a hundred-seat auditorium as well as a coffee shop and bar; one of Dundee's little gems.

Lochee

Although there is no loch remaining, the name means 'eye of the loch' or loch eye. The loch in question was Loch Balgay, just west of the original village and seems to have been drained around the fifteenth century. There was a small settlement here named Backside of Invergowrie, but thankfully that name has long fallen into disuse! Backside merely meant the north side that faced away from the sun.

In the late-eighteenth and nineteenth century industrialisation came to Lochee. As early as 1791 most of the 276 handloom workers in Lochee were employed by David Cock (the family name was later altered to the more familiar Cox) and as the nineteenth century progressed the family tightened their grip on Lochee. By the latter half of the century their Camperdown works were thirty acres in extent. However, Lochee became part of Dundee in 1859. By that date many of the population were Irish-born, or of Irish ancestry, and even in the twentieth century there was a clear division between Scots and Irish in Lochee.

Perhaps because of the low wages paid to textile workers, Lochee was noted for its trade unionism with one strike in Camperdown works in 1923 lasting over six months. When the textile industry declined Lochee slumped but it is reviving again with the centre of Lochee now a conservation area.

Lochee has produced a number of prominent people including George Barnes (1859–1940), Labour leader between 1910 and 1911 and minister of pensions 1916–17, William Cooper who was speaker of the legislative assembly of Prince Edward Island from 1839–42, Michael Marra the musician and indie rock band The View. Another, more controversial resident was James Connolly, the Edinburgh-born founder of the Irish Socialist Republican party, who allegedly lived in Lochee in 1898. He was a turbulent man, a deserter from the British Army, a socialist and a leader of the 1916 Irish Rising that saw him executed by firing squad that same year.

Lochee library

Lochee Library

Donated by the Cox family to Lochee, this distinctive building is built with red stone adorned with Jacobean details and sits in the much reconstructed High Street.

Lochee park

This important green space is around twenty-three acres in extent and lies to the north of Balgay hill. The Cox family, owners of much of Lochee, presented the park to Dundee in 1890. It is a very popular place for football and a number of other sports and recreations, while younger children can enjoy the play park. As it backs onto Balgay hill, it helps provide a much-appreciated green oasis in this area of Dundee.

Lochee railway station
The station closed in 1955, but the building deserves a second look. It was designed by James Gowan and the north wall is built with units divided into two-foot squares. It is now a Burns club.

Lochee west church
Designed by James MacLaren, it can accommodate up to a thousand worshippers and was opened in September 1871. It is a prominent landmark in Lochee and harks back to the days when Christianity was central to the lives of huge numbers of people.

Logie Avenue
From the Gaelic *logan*, or *lagan*, meaning a hollow. The Logie housing scheme was erected in the aftermath of the First World War when the council tried to make the phrase 'homes fit for heroes' mean something. The Addison Act of 1919 provided subsidies for good-quality housing for ordinary people, and Dundee took full advantage.

The scheme was named after the sadly demolished Logie house, an interesting property that had a number of reincarnations. Its owners included the Read family, nabobs who made their money in the Honourable East India Company. Fletcher Read, one of their number, was said to have blown trumpets over the graves at Logie cemetery and to have had an Indian bride, who, as the Black Lady of Logie, haunts the road between Dundee and Lochee. Unfortunately for this folk tale he only had one wife and she was blessed with the very Scottish name of Jean Scott.

Logie was said to have been the first major municipal-housing development in Scotland after the Great War. It has a beautiful situation beside Victoria park and Balgay hill, with a viewing platform from which one can survey most of the scheme. The garden-city movement was undoubtedly behind both the planning and the naming of the streets. The central artery is wide, grassy and lined with trees, which must have been heaven for people from crowded slum tenements, or those men who lived here after surviving the hell of the Somme. The curved streets of four-in-a-block houses that run off the main street are supplied with gardens, while there was a common heating system. James Thomson, the city engineer, was the designer. However, the rents were too high for the lowest paid, so most houses were let to skilled or white-collar workers.

In 1991 Logie was designated an 'outstanding conservation area'.

Logie poorhouse
Stood on the corner of Blackness Road and Glenagnes Road. Known as Logie for the area in which it stood, this was the poorhouse for Liff and Benvie parish.

It opened in 1864 and in 1928 was replaced by Logie secondary school. Harris academy took it over but, in 2001, a fire destroyed the building. There is a new school building on the site.

Logie works

Logie Works, Coffin mill

Now known as Pleasance Court but maybe better known as the Coffin mill because of the distinctive shape of its courtyard. This flax mill at the corner of Horsewater Wynd and Brook Street was built in 1828 and is one of the oldest in Dundee still extant. The most distinctive part, save for the nickname, is the seven-storey tower, which combined with Venetian windows on the southern wall, give character to the building. Now converted into flats, the mill is also rumoured to be haunted by a female operator who was entangled in the machinery and killed.

Long Lane, Broughty Ferry
Named for its length, this street runs parallel to Brook Street in the Ferry.

Longcroft, 2 Panmure Terrace, Broughty Ferry
Built in 1922 this B-listed house is classical in appearance with a hipped roof.

Longforgan
A pleasant little village in the Carse of Gowrie, well within commuting distance of Dundee. The village has splendid views over the Carse to the Tay and beyond, while a bypass saves the village from the worst of the traffic on the main Dundee–

Perth road. Robert I granted the lands and barony of Longforgund to Sir Andrew Gray of Broxmouth in 1315, so there is a great deal of history here as well.

The streets have some lovely single-storey cottages, enhanced by the 1794 parish kirk with its tower of a century earlier and the 1823, David Neave-designed, manse.

Longhaugh Road/Terrace
There was a Longhaugh house in this area after which the streets were named.

Lossie Place, Menzieshill
The Lossie river flows through Moray and enters the sea at Lossiemouth.

Lothian Crescent, Whitfield
No local connection but refers to East, Mid and West Lothian, south of Edinburgh. Many streets in the area have names that originate in Lothian and the Borders.

Louise Terrace, Broughty Ferry
Recalls Princess Louise (1848–1939), who married the Marquis of Lorne in 1871, the same year that these houses were built. She was a daughter of Queen Victoria and became Duchess of Argyll.

Luke Place, Broughty Ferry
Takes its name from local Conservative councillor William Luke.

Lulworth Court
A pleasant area with neat flats surrounded by well-maintained grounds. In common with courts in this area, it is named after a butterfly or moth. The Lulworth Skipper first came to scientific notice in 1932 and is native to the south coast of England.

Luna Place
Part of the Dundee technology park, the name is from the Latin for moon and reflects the forward-looking thrust of Dundee. The place names in this area are all related to space exploration.

Lunan Terrace
The derivation is Lunan bay in Angus, once a favoured landing site of smugglers. Today dog walkers, casual strollers and families are more likely to stalk the sweeping sands.

Lundie Avenue
Lundie in the Sidlaws has a village, castle and a group of six lovely little lochs. Admiral Duncan was the most prominent owner, but the Duncan family left the old castle and moved to Gourdie house which was in what is now Camperdown park. Both Gourdie house and Lundie castle have been demolished; Camperdown house replaced Gourdie. Lundie seems to mean *lon dubh* – 'black bog or marsh'.

Lynch sports centre, South Road
Recalls the brothers John, Andy and Ned Lynch who founded the Lochee boys' sports club. The Lynch sports centre has two halls, named for Andrew Lynch and John Lynch, as well as a fitness suite. It caters for a variety of sports.

Lyndhurst Avenue/Place/Terrace
Named after Lyndhurst house, which was demolished some time before 1939. Edward Cox of the Cox dynasty was the proprietor and the house may have been named after the prominent politician, Lord Lyndhurst (1772–1863), who was born in Boston, Massachusetts a few years before the United States achieved independence and was Lord Chancellor of Great Britain three times.

Lynnewood Place
The paving committee decided on the name Lynnewood Place in August 1890.

Lyon Street
Baxters built houses here for their workers, which was unusual in Dundee.

Macalpine Road
Evokes the legend of the Scots King, Alpin, who was defeated in battle nearby and beheaded at Kings Cross. However, it is very unlikely that the Dundee Alpin was the father of Kenneth MacAlpin, reputedly the first king of a united Scotland with Scots and Picts combined.

Machrie Place
The name of this street has no local connection but refers to a village elsewhere in Scotland. There is a Machrie in the island of Arran, which could be the source.

Madeira Street
The lovely row of cottages built in the 1870s echoes the architecture of Morgan academy. In 1883 East End FC leased an area of land to use as a pitch from Mr Batchelor of Craigie. The ground was to be known as Madeira park and the first game played was against Strathmore.

Magdalen Green

Magdalen Green and bandstand

Undoubtedly one of the most atmospheric and interesting green areas in a city that abounds in atmosphere, the twenty-acre Magdalen Green is an open space on the western side of Dundee with views to the Tay and over to Fife. It is also Dundee's oldest public park and has a bandstand dating from 1890.

The name is said to originate from a chapel to St Mary Magdalen, which was situated at the foot of Step Row. In the medieval period, Dundee possessed many religious buildings but during the Reformation, all the lands of the Roman Catholic Church were annexed by various landowners. The lairds of Blackness took ownership of Magdalen Green. Eventually the town council paid £1,500 for the lands, which are now indisputably owned by the city of Dundee. The land was bought in the early 1840s, partly as a job-creation scheme as the unemployed were paid to create the park. The name Magdalen comes from Mary of Magdala, and refers to a reformed prostitute.

According to A. H. Miller, in his *Glimpses of Old and New Dundee*, this area may once have been known as Magdalen Gair, meaning the garden ground of the chapel, but that altered to Magdalen Guard and then Magdalen Yard, which is the name of the adjacent street. Naturally this area of open ground has an interesting history. In 1819 George Kinloch of Kinloch, the 'Radical Laird', spoke here to a crowd who wished to reform parliament. Kinloch was charged with sedition and had to abscond to France. He later became Dundee's first MP. There were other political meetings here, in 1832, and also in November 1838 when the Chartists gathered.

The garrison of Dudhope castle practised their musketry on the Green until the arrival of the railway made such events dangerous. In the years before the Second World War there was an outdoor swimming pool here, known as the Cowpers, but that was filled in and the area used to train Polish soldiers.

This is still a popular green space, used for impromptu games of football and also by students wishing to escape the rigours of academic study.

Magdalen Yard Road

In the early part of the nineteenth century a lodging-house keeper named Margaret Bower had a cottage built here. She was slightly eccentric, as she used her own coffin as a kitchen cupboard. The painter Mackintosh Patrick also lived in this street and created a splendid picture of the view from his window to the Tay bridge.

Maggie's centre

Maggie's Centre

Commemorates Maggie Keswick Jencks (1941–95), daughter of Sir John Keswick of Jardine Matheson. She suffered cancer and founded a programme to support others in her situation. She was a friend of the architect Frank Gehry, who designed this building, his first in the UK, and it opened in 2003. Situated in the grounds of Ninewells hospital, Maggie's centre is an oasis of hope and sharing, while its round tower echoes that of a lighthouse – a symbol of hope and life in perilous times.

Mains castle

Mains Castle

Otherwise known as Fintry castle, Mains castle stands proud on the sunny south side of the Gelly burn. The name 'mains' is an altered form of the Latin *dominium* but in Scotland it came to mean the principal farm of an estate, and that eased into meaning the home farm.

The area used to be known as Strathdighty after the Dighty burn, but in the fifteenth century Sir Robert Graham of Strathcarron and Fintry married one of the Earl of Angus's daughters and was granted Strathdichty as his dowry. He renamed his new lands Fintry after his Stirlingshire properties. Around 1582 Mains castle was completed in its present form although the foundations are much earlier. Graham of Fintry moved to South Africa in the nineteenth century and founded Grahamstown, a place that was prominent in many border wars in that country.

Maitland Street
Remembers Thomas Maitland, a jute baron of Baxter Brothers & Co., one of the most prominent textile manufacturers of Dundee.

Malcolm Street
Also named after one of Dundee's jute barons.

Mallaig Avenue
Many streets in the area have west Highland names. Mallaig is a fishing port and ferry terminal on the west coast of Scotland.

Malmaison hotel

Opened in February 2014 at the junction of Whitehall Crescent and Union Street. Originally this was Mather's temperance hotel, at a time Dundee was a curious mix with hundreds of pubs yet a strong temperance movement. Mather's hotel could hardly have been more central, a stone's throw from the railway station and with bedrooms that give fine views over the Tay.

The building has been restored to include many of the original features, including a beautiful wrought-iron staircase and a domed ceiling.

Malthouse Close, 58 Nethergate to Yeaman Shore

The name gives a clue to the use of the close. A malthouse is a building where cereal is soaked in water until it sprouts, and then it is dried and used for beer or whisky. Malthouse Close led to the site of the Earl of Crawford's lodgings. David Lindsay, Earl of Crawford married Elizabeth Stewart, daughter of King Robert III, giving the family royal blood. Crawford's Dundee town house was apparently both magnificent and huge but most, if not all, of it was destroyed to build Thistle hall in Union Street.

Manhattan Court

Takes its name from Manhattan works nearby, which in turn celebrated the links between Dundee and New York in the textile trade.

Manhattan works, Dundonald Street

Was a textile factory and is now a community, sports and dance facility after a £170,000 grant by Social Investment Scotland. The original twenty-acre works were owned by Sandeman, Keiller & Company and opened on 16 January 1874. James Carmichael & Co. of Dundee supplied much of the machinery. Thomson Brothers of Douglas foundry planned the building with the spinning machinery coming from Leeds, the looms were made by Parker & Sons of Dundee and the jute softeners by the Blackness foundry. This was an excellent example of the importance of the jute trade to Dundee.

Maplewood Drive

Part of the Beechwood estate. Many of the streets here have the suffix 'wood' to fit in with the mansion of Beechwood, on which grounds the houses were built.

Marchfield

Another name that evokes Dundee's rural past. It has nothing to do with the month of the year, for the word march was a mediaeval term for a boundary. Marchfield means 'boundary field'.

Margaret Crescent, Broughty Ferry
Remembers Margaret Makgill of Kemback, wife of Alexander Guthrie (1869–1929) who owned the nearby Craigie estate.

Margaret Harris building, Euclid Crescent
Dedicated to Margaret Harris, who founded the girl's school as part of the high school. Her husband founded Harris academy.

Mariner Drive
Part of the Dundee technology park with the name echoing space exploration. Mariner was a US space program intended to further explore Mars.

Marketgait
The street in which the market was held in old Dundee. It is now named High Street although the original name remains in an enclosed Marketgate centre for business. There was free entertainment in the old Marketgait as well, for this is where Dundee carried out its public beheadings at the 'Heding cross' in the less-than-good-old-days. This street is still central to Dundee, but although there may be a historic atmosphere there is little tangible evidence as Dundee has pulled down most of her ancient buildings, with Gardyne's Land a notable exception.

'Market gait' actually means the road to the market, and this is still an important place for shopping. Now the 'new' Marketgait indicates the A991 that runs through Dundee. It contains the long-closed Tay works of G. R. & A. Gilroy, which boasts a truly splendid pediment that shows the firm's pride in what was, at 650-feet long, one of the longest mill frontages in the country. There were eight mills in the original complex, plus a calender, dye works, factory and engine works as well as the office. The pediment has the initials of the firm and once was also adorned with a statue of Minerva, the Roman Goddess of wisdom, arts and trade. Sadly, the statue is no longer there but the building remains, now used as student accommodation.

On the corner of Marketgate and Nethergate is a plaque to Winston Churchill, who was a Liberal MP for the city. His daughter unveiled the plaque, which reads:

> Sir Winston Churchill, Prime Minister 1940–1945 and 1951–1955, Member of Parliament for The City of Dundee. From 9th May 1908 to 15th November 1922. This Plaque Was Erected to Commemorate The Centenary of His Election; 9th May 2008.

Winston lost the 1922 election to a temperance candidate with the very Dundee name of Edwin Scrymgeour. Churchill came fourth in that election, losing the seat due to a number of issues, including his views on votes for women – which would make him unpopular in Dundee with its large female workforce – his opposition to Irish home rule – Dundee has a large proportion of its people with Irish ancestry – and his supposed support in sending in troops to end miners' strikes. It has been claimed that Churchill never forgave Dundee and he is said to have stated he would 'see the grass growing in the streets of Dundee' before he returned. He refused the freedom of the city in 1943.

Market Street

At one time this street was known as Steam Loom Brae because Dundee's first steam loom was used here, a name that is much more evocative as it encapsulates Dundee's industrial history.

Marryat hall, City Square

Was named in honour of Mrs Emma Marryat (1849–1927), sister of James Caird the jute baron. She provided £75,000 to help fund the Caird hall and lounge.

Mars Lane, Broughty Ferry

A footpath that led to Marrs Land tenement. Alexander Marrs was a director of the Aberdeen Property Investment Building Society, which built the property in the 1870s.

Mary Ann Lane

Mary Ann Lane

Occupies the site of the old Mary Ann boiling yard, where whale blubber was brought to be boiled into oil. During that process, the pungent smell penetrated the whole area and was said to be so obnoxious that doors and windows were kept firmly closed. The Mary Ann boiling yard was one of a number of such places in this part of Dundee and so should be better known for its industrial significance.

Mary Slessor memorial

Mary Slessor Memorial

Unveiled outside Steeple church in 2015. Mary Slessor was born in Aberdeen but worked in a jute mill in Dundee and later became a missionary to west Africa. She was one of the most successful Scottish missionaries, known for her courage in standing up to aggression as she defended women and the weak.

There is also a stained-glass window in the museum dedicated to her, designed by a Londoner, William Aikman, but paid for by the people of Dundee.

Mary Slessor Square
Remembers the Aberdeen-born missionary who worked in a Dundee mill (see previous entry).

Maryfield Lane/Road, Broughty Ferry
Named after Maryfield cottage. Mary was the wife of William Webster (1782–1861), who lived here.

Maryfield Terrace
Carries the name of a house and farm that were swallowed up in Dundee's expansion.

Matthew building, University of Dundee
This brutalist building on Perth Road is part of the Duncan of Jordanstone College of Art. The exterior is of uncompromising concrete, which conceals the interior light and special divisions. The architect was Professor James Paul of Baxter Clark & Paul, who also worked on Edinburgh and Aberdeen airports and the stands at Tannadice stadium.

Mauchline Tower Court, 14 Murraygate
Now filled in, the name of this close harks back to a tower house that was the town residence of the Lords Mauchline and which formed part of the city walls. The Mauchline family were of the Loudon branch of the Argylls, after whom Argylegait was named (later to be known as Overgate). The building became the Mauchline Tower temperance hotel in the late nineteenth century, owned by the Lamb dynasty of temperance hoteliers.

Maule Street, Broughty Ferry
Another street that carries the name of local landowner Fox Maule Ramsay (1801–74) the 11th earl of Dalhousie. He was known as Lord Panmure until 1860 and then succeeded to the earldom of Dalhousie in Midlothian. He was at the War Office in the latter period of the Crimean War and was a supporter of the Free Church of Scotland.

Maxwelltown
The upper part of Hilltown was named after Maxwell of Tealing, who owned the land. There were a number of Maxwells who became provosts of Dundee.

Maybole Place
Has no local connection. It refers to the Ayrshire town of Maybole.

Mayfield Grove, Broughty Ferry Road
Continues the name of the mansion house of Mayfield that stood here.

McCheyne memorial church, 328 Perth Road
Built by Pilkington & Bell in 1870 to commemorate Revd McCheyne, the first minister of St Peter's, who was remembered for his inspiring sermons. He died tragically young at just 29. The church congregation merged with Dundee West church in 1999 and is now in private ownership and no longer used for Christian worship.

McDonald Street
Commemorates Bailie Duncan McDonald, who joined the town council in

1869 and served until 1897. He was on the school board from its inception in 1872 until 1908.

McGonagall's walk, Riverside

McGonagall's Walk

William Topaz McGonagall is arguably Dundee's best-known poet, no doubt because of his execrable verses. The eponymous walk is a stretch of around 150 metres along the Riverside, and it has one of McGonagall's poems ('The Railway Bridge of the Silvery Tay') embedded in the pavement.

Meadow Entry, 16–20 Murraygate

As the name implies, this close was a passage from the main street of Dundee to the Meadows to the north. It opened in 1775 to allow passage for carts as well as pedestrians. However, the construction of Commercial Street caused some realignment as the close headed west to connect to that major thoroughfare.

Meadow Mill, West Henderson Wynd

Also known as North Dudhope mill, this is an old jute mill with the upper storeys converted into art studios with dozens of artists and craftspeople. The building also has a Second World War firewatcher's shelter on its roof.

Meadowside

Formerly the public bleaching green for Dundee. Originally, the area extended from Albert Square all the way to Lochee Road, with the Scouring burn providing the water. Dundee's mill pond was here and the area was popular for fairs and market gardens, while Dundee drew its water from this less than healthy spot. In June 1803 Ward Road was opened but the area was still utilised for bleaching until as late as 1825. After that date bleaching was carried on in the Constitution Road area.

In the 1830s the Meadows was a large grassy hollow with a burn flowing through, around which women washed and bleached their clothes and children played. In the 1880s Meadowside was home to one of Dundee's forgotten companies, the Oriental Company, which blended tea and advertised in the *Army and Navy Gazette*. It has been a place of many identities.

There could be some geographical confusion here as the old Meadowside is now named Albert Square, and the 'modern' Meadowside is where the *Courier* building stands, then swings past the McManus to join the inner ring road.

Melville Place, Broughty Ferry
Commemorates John Melville, a farmer from Kirriemuir, who owned a tenement in the area. He later emigrated to the USA, where he died in 1885.

Menzieshill
This council estate is at the western extremity of the city. The name comes from a farm on a hill, at one time owned or worked by a man named Menzies. The surname Menzies – pronounced Mingis – has been known in Perthshire for centuries. It was a Norman name, originally *mesnieres*, to do with a manor. The original owner of the name Menzies of Menzieshill has been forgotten, but there may be a clue in the nearby estate of Invergowrie.

That estate was owned by a family named Clayhills. In 1766 Margaret Clayhills of Invergowrie married James Menzies of Woodend, who adopted the Clayhills name, but Menzies was retained as Menzies-Clayhills for some decades after. There was also a field or open space known as Menzies park, which was west of Balgay hill. These uses of the name Menzies indicate that it was a local name to this part of Dundee.

Menzieshill is airy and well-planned, built in the 1960s with a mixture of terraced, low-rise and five high-rise blocks of flats; it included a secondary and two primary schools, with a local church, police office and a few shops. There were also green spaces and views to the Tay or the Carse of Gowrie. As in every area, things have altered in fifty years. In June 2015 a council decision to close Menzieshill high school was greeted with a mixture of tears and anger by pupils and local residents, and a pledge to fight on. The high-rises have been levelled and the houses are no longer all council owned, but overall the area is still a pleasant place in which to live. Although the council scheme is fairly modern, there has been a settlement here for thousands of years. There have been ancient stone coffins found and a legend of a royal castle nearby.

One distinguished resident is Christina Rae, who was the telephone operator responsible for sending the message that declared the war in Europe was over.

Menzieshill Road
See the entry, Menzieshill.

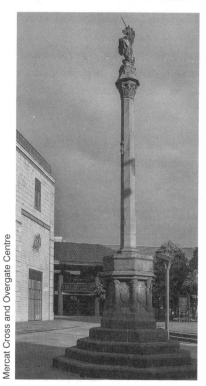

Mercat Cross and Overgate Centre

Mercat Cross

At one time the Mercat (or Market) Cross was the centrepiece of the merchant world in Scottish towns and cities. The Dundee Mercat Cross sat in the west end of the High Street for generations but with trade and traffic increasing, and the pattern of life altering, it became an obstruction to commerce. It was removed to its present position outside the city churches in 1874.

The B-listed cross, as it is now, is not all original. The stone shaft by John Mylne is ancient and dates from 1586 but the unicorn that surmounts it is of resin-bronze and was created by Scott Sutherland RSA in the 1960s.

Methven Square, Broughty Ferry

Named after local shoemaker and oil merchant John Methven (1789–1871).

Michelin, Baldovie Road

Makes tyres; the company came to Dundee in the early 1970s and employs some seven hundred people. The factory is powered by two large wind turbines that dominate this part of the Dundee skyline and can be seen from Fife. In November 2015 Michelin announced a £50 million investment plan at the plant that could create up to a hundred new jobs.

Microcomputing centre, University of Dundee

This building no longer holds computers but has music-rehearsal rooms and a Freeshop as well as Op-soc, the university's lively musical-theatre society.

Mid Craigie

Originally there were three farms in this area, with the name Craigie possibly coming from craggy, 'rough'. The farms were Old Craigie, Milton of Craigie and Strips of Craigie. The housing scheme of Mid Craigie occupies what was the central of the three farms and was begun in 1938.

Miley urban wildlife reserve

More commonly known simply as the Miley, this city-centre reserve follows a disused railway track. The Scottish Wildlife Trust developed it and it is now a peaceful and interesting daylight walk where one can observe wild flowers, red squirrels and birds of prey.

Mill Street, Broughty Ferry

Takes its name from a windmill that stood here. The mill gave power to a carpenter's workshop.

Mills Observatory

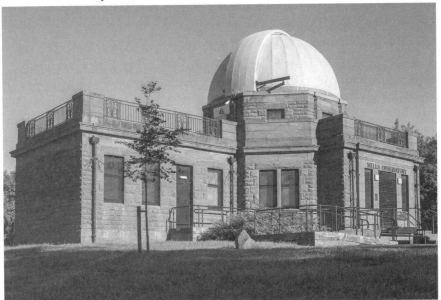

Mills Observatory

The only observatory in Great Britain that was created for the use and education of the general population. It is named after John Mills, who was a nineteenth-century textile industrialist. He was a follower of Revd Thomas Dick, who wrote on Christian philosophy and astronomy, and advocated that every city should have an observatory, public parks and public libraries. Mills owned a small observatory on Dundee Law, where Adelaide Place now stands, and when he died he left money for an observatory.

Mills observatory was built on Balgay hill in 1935. It has a classical design and a seven-metre dome, a Dobsonian reflector as well as a Victorian telescope and a twelve-inch Schmidt-Cassegrain telescope. It fulfils Mills's request perfectly, with a public observatory within a public park.

Milnbank Road

Takes its name from a small estate and mansion house that was in this area. There was a request for extra street lamps at Milnbank in the winter of 1845, which suggests the roads in this area were particularly dark.

Milton Street
References the seventeenth-century English poet, John Milton, who wrote *Paradise Lost*.

Minnie the Minx
This famous character from the *Beano,* created and published by DC Thomson in Dundee, stands on the fringes of City Square, catapult in hand, ready to minx any passers-by.

Mission Lane, Broughty Ferry
Stretches from the west side of St James church to Fisher Steet. The name originates from the fact that St James was originally a beach mission church.

Moncur Crescent
The name comes from Alexander Hay Moncur (1830–1905), provost from 1880–3. Dundee-born, he was a jute manufacturer in the Victoria works in Ure Street. He was chairman of the school board for fifteen years and known for his philanthropy. In 1885 the street was one of a number of others, such as Mayo Terrace and Hastings Place, opened partly to provide work for the unemployed. The paving committee selected the name.

Morgan academy

Morgan Academy

Known familiarly as 'the Morgan,' this school is part of the legacy of John Morgan, a native of Dundee who made his money in India. He returned to Scotland a wealthy nabob and in his will left money for the city. After a legal dispute regarding his bequests, the council built what was then known as the Morgan hospital, with a spectacular design based on a combination of Flemish guild hall and French chateau. In 1889 Dundee school board bought the building.

In March 2001 there was a disastrous fire that gutted the building and took seventeen hours to extinguish, but Dundee refused to lose one of the jewels in its educational crown. Calling in the assistance of Historic Scotland and builders Mansell, the Morgan was triumphantly restored.

Morgan Place

Takes its name from the nearby school, this 1930s development consists of a courtyard with flanking towers. It was built to give working families a better quality of life.

Morgan Street

Was also named after the Morgan. In 1910 this was the home of Dundee's first cinema, the Stobswell cinema theatre. Dundee soon fell in love with this form of escapism and within two years there were thirteen cinemas in the city, a number that rose to thirty by the mid-1930s, plus another in Broughty Ferry.

Morgan tower, 135–139 Nethergate

Morgan Tower, Nethergate

City architect Samuel Bell designed this block of quality flats in 1794. They are distinguished by a five-storey bow with Venetian windows, which protrude to narrow the pavement, but provide a focal point for the street. According to tradition, Captain Morgan, who had the tower built, specifically asked for the interesting 'saracen's hat' roof and Muslim-moon weathervane.

Mormons, or Church of the Latter Day Saints, Bingham Terrace

The Dundee Stake (branch) of the Mormon Church was created in 1975. There have been Mormons in the area since the nineteenth century and the church seems to be thriving with a growing number of members and a tuneful choir.

Murraygate

Murraygate

Originally spelled Murraygait, this street takes its name from Randolph, Earl of Moray, one of the nobles who supported King Robert I in the First War of Independence.

The Murraygate was the main business centre of Dundee, with the Town House Square in the middle. It dates from at least the mediaeval period and in the eighteenth century the local gentry had their town houses here, a safe sanctuary during the wild winter weather. The street must have been very attractive then as the houses had timber-fronted piazzas and gardens with trees, wells and bushes.

There is some fine architecture in the Murraygate, including the 1868 building at nos. 35–39, for which David Cousins was the architect, and commissioned by the British Linen Bank. It is a classical palazzo with a grand hall inside, complete with Corinthian columns stretching to a rotunda. It must have been worth checking a diminishing bank balance merely to view the interior.

Murraygate also has the remains of the 1913 La Scala cinema, built at a time in which Dundee had a plethora of such places of entertainment. This cinema used to have a tower and golden globe but both are now sadly gone.

Today the street is pedestrianised and lined with a variety of shops, with character pieces such as retained tramlines and ornamental lamp standards to supplement the varied architecture. It leads to the Wellgate centre and is still very much at the heart of Dundee.

Murroes house, Murroes, Angus

Built in the sixteenth century, with additions in 1600 and a roof replacement in 1942. The name Murroes is a corruption of Muirhouse, 'the house on the moor'. There was also a Murroes farm, which was tenanted by a Mr Arklay in 1895, and was the scene of an annual ploughing match.

Mylnefield

The name indicates that the Mylne family owned the estate here. In the seventeenth century the Mylnes were the royal master masons, which may account for the extensive quarrying at neighbouring Kingoodie. Seven members of the Mylne family were master masons to kings of Scots and their work includes the palace of Holyroodhouse and a bridge over the Tay at Perth.

Mylnefield research centre, Invergowrie

One of the world's leading centres for agricultural research. There is a complex of buildings and glass houses, with a number of very well-tended fields in which to grow the experimental crops.

Mylnefield Road

Takes its name from the old estate and village of Mylnefield Feus. The road runs through the heart of Invergowrie to the public park.

Myrekirk Road, Lochee

The name means the kirk beside a myre or area of bog land. Perhaps the bog was a result of Loch Eye drying up.

Mystery house

This is the house that Jack, or rather James, built. James Thomson was the redoubtable city architect who did so much for Dundee in the period after the First World War. In 1919 he suggested that the council should experiment with new building materials and methods for a prototype house that would be the model for future local-authority housing. The council agreed and this was the result. It stands proud on the corner of Glamis and Blackness roads, with the first occupant being Thomson himself.

National Cash Register, Fulton Road

National Cash Register is an American company that came to Dundee in 1946. Within twenty years the workforce had risen to some 3,400 skilled people and in 1979 the company paid for a chair of electronics and microcomputer systems at Dundee University. Today NCR is not the major city employer it once was but there is still a sizeable workforce and the company is an important component in the commercial life of Dundee.

Navarre Street, Broughty Ferry
The name comes from the local landlord, Baron Panmure of Brechin and Navar. He later became the Earl of Dalhousie.

Neish Street
Situated near Tannadice park, Neish Street takes its name from the local landowner, William Neish of Tannadice and Easter Clepington.

Nelson Street

Nelson Street

Commemorates Horatio, Lord Nelson, the victor of Trafalgar. However, that had not been the original plan. The authorities were going to name the street after Sir Henry Parnell, who had been Dundee's MP from 1837 until 1841. Unfortunately, Parnell inconveniently committed suicide and the council altered the name to honour the great British hero.

Nethergate
The lower 'gait' or way out of Dundee to the one-time hamlets of Westfield and Springfield and on to Perth Road. The original name was Flukergait, or Fluckergait, after a type of fish caught in the Tay, so possibly fishermen from the Tayside villages carried flukers into Dundee.

The south side of the Nethergate used to be a steep slope leading to the sea, and is partially lined by what were once the houses of eighteenth century merchants. That at nos. 170–172 was built later, in 1840, and is named Caird Rest. It was once the home of William Brown, a flax manufacturer, but James Caird bought it and presented it to the city as an old folk's home. It was later taken over by the university and is currently in private hands. Further along the Nethergate was Green's Playhouse, reputedly the second largest cinema in Europe.

At 136 Nethergate a blue plaque informs the reader that, in 1795, this was the birthplace of Frances Wright, one of twenty-five Dundee women commemorated in this manner. Wright was the daughter of a radical and she emigrated to the United States, where she became renowned for her support of women's rights, free love and the emancipation of slaves many years before the American Civil War.

At no. 93 is a plaque to Margaret Fenwick (1919–92) who became a trade-union activist while still in her teens. A mother of four children she became the first female general secretary of any British trade union, in her case the Dundee & District Union of Jute, Flax & Kindred Textile Operatives. As a former mill worker she knew exactly what life was like on the shop floor and forced through improvements in working conditions and pay. As if that was not enough she was also a justice of the peace and served on industrial tribunals. Her contribution to society was marked with an MBE. The plaque is at the site of the union headquarters.

Nethergate house

Clydesdale Bank, Nethergate House, 158 Nethergate

Samuel Bell, the town architect, was most likely the designer of this 1790 house, which at the time of writing is a branch of Clydesdale bank. This very pleasing building was occupied by Provost Riddoch, arguably Dundee's most famous eighteenth-century politician, and in office from 1788–1819.

Riddoch was one of the most interesting people in a city full of characters. Love him or loathe him, he is impossible to ignore. He was undoubtedly a skilful politician as he guided Dundee through the quagmire of the revolutionary years when all Europe was ablaze but Dundee was relatively quiet. Riddoch was also something of a dictator, who surrounded himself with yes-men and manipulated council business to his own advantage. At the same time, he improved the burgh by adding new streets without raising taxes. Rightly or wrongly, he is today associated with political corruption.

Netherton Terrace
Named after Netherton in Aberlemno parish, Angus. The name 'nether' means lower and 'ton' indicates a settlement or farm, so lower farm would make sense. The fact that the neighbouring street is named Overton indicates that the two were named in conjunction, with one over, or above, the other.

Nevay Terrace
The name comes from the parish of Nevay in the Sidlaw hills. The name is interesting as the *nemeton* was the supposed home of a Celtic god, often in a grove, and *nevay* is from that root. To add to that, Nevay parish had an ancient tree called the Templar Tree, which suggests some sort of connection to the Knights Templar, while nearby was St Bride's Well. St Bride was the Christian version of the pagan Bride, who was a very powerful pagan goddess (hence the He-Brides islands). The area obviously had great spiritual significance.

New Howff, Bell Street
Created in 1834 for the victims of the plague, of whatever variety, and because the Howff was overcrowded. It was originally a picturesque place, with curving walkways and quiet trees. The graves are still here, but buried deep beneath what is now a multistorey car park.

New Inn Entry, 67 High Street
Quite simply, this was the entry for an inn off the High Street in the early nineteenth century. It also held a theatre that was later converted into a church. Until Reform Street was built, this was the main thoroughfare between High Street and the Meadows. Today it leads to the Arctic bar, one of the most evocative pubs in Dundee with tales of whaling men being paid here. Presumably the Arctic bar was the new inn, as the lane had existed long before under a different name.

New Inn Entry and Arctic Bar

New Road, Broughty Ferry

This road from Castle Green to Brook Street could well be called Old Road. The thoroughfare was an ancient right of way between the castle and the lands of Broughty but the Dundee & Arbroath Railway Company closed it off. It was not until 1861 – when the war department was modernising Broughty castle in view of a possible French military threat – that the street was officially reopened to the public. Only three years later the road was nearly lost again. Lord Dalhousie had sold off much of the sand on Broughty beach at one shilling the cart load, so when an especially high tide occurred in January 1864 the recently reconstructed New Road was flooded and much of it was swept away.

Newport-on-Tay

Newport-on-Tay, Old Ferry Slipway

Directly opposite Dundee, this Fife village was the southern terminal of the ferries from Dundee. An attempt to call it New Dundee failed, but it was a preferred location for some of the city elite during a time that industry filled streets with smoke and choked the roads with horse-drawn traffic. Newport has a large number of substantial Victorian villas that stand proud on the hillside looking north, yet deer still wander close to the southern fringes and the occasional seal can be seen on the beaches. The opening of the rail bridge encouraged settlement in the town, as did the road bridge, but people now tend to shop in Dundee to the detriment of local businesses.

The mileposts, old ferry terminus and Victorian drinking fountain are all worth a second look.

Newtyle

Newtyle Walkway

With a name that could mean 'sacred place at the hill', Newtyle is a planned village twelve miles north of Dundee. This small village was the terminus of the Dundee and Newtyle railway. Early trains were mainly horse-powered, although winches were used to haul the carriages up the steep slope of the Law and the Sidlaw Hills. From 1833 steam locomotives were employed, but the railway was never a commercial success. It impacted on Dundee with a station beside the Howff and a line that bisected road traffic as it carried traffic to the harbour.

The settlement at Newtyle is at least eight hundred years old and has a church on an ancient site, a gridiron pattern for the village centre and some new and council housing spread around. Add a brand-new primary school, a few fine shops and some of the loveliest countryside in Scotland and you have one of the finest villages possible.

Things to look for: the present church was built in 1872 and has the most welcoming atmosphere. The old railway line is now a walkway from which the surrounding country and a plethora of wildlife can be seen: deer, buzzards, red squirrel, woodpeckers, wrens and even frogs.

Nicoll Street, Broughty Ferry
Takes its name from the one-time landowner, James Nicoll Constable of Balmyle. There are Constable family gravestones in the Howff.

Ninewells hospital

Ninewells Hospital

Part of NHS Tayside and situated at the western extremity of the city, Ninewells hospital is one of the finest in the country. Opened in 1974, it is a teaching hospital so there are students as well as doctors, nurses and patients. It has strong links with the University of Dundee and the local community and a reputation for research and innovation. Ninewells was a pioneer of laparoscopic surgery in the UK as well as of robotic surgery and cancer care.

There are two possible derivations of the name. The first comes from a piece of local folklore that there were nine wells in the area, while the second, and more plausible, is that it derives from Ninian's well, 'Ninwell'.

Norrie Street, Broughty Ferry
Takes its name from the Norrie family of Camphill house. William Norrie broke with the family tradition of working, and perishing, at sea. He stayed on land and became a linen merchant.

North Carr lightship

North Carr Lightship

Moored in Victoria dock, *North Carr* is Scotland's last remaining lightship, effectively a floating lighthouse. Built by A. & J. Inglis of Glasgow in 1932 – the same company that built the paddle-steamers *Maid of the Loch* and *Waverley* – she is 101-feet long. She spent her working life moored off Fife Ness, from 1933 to 1975, to warn passing vessels away from the North Carr rocks.

Before her service began, she tested her foghorn in the Firth of Forth, keeping the good people of Edinburgh and Leith awake night after night, but came to public attention when she broke free of her mornings in 1959 and the Broughty Ferry lifeboat lost all hands in a rescue attempt. Retired in 1975, she became a tourist attraction in Anstruther before coming to Dundee, where she now sits a short step from *Unicorn*.

North Street
The name of this street has nothing to do with geography. It was named after Frederick, Lord North, 2nd Earl of Guildford (1732–92), prime minister during most of the American War of Independence. His Tea Act of 1773 helped to spark that conflict.

North Ellen Street
A house in this street had carved heads on the wall. Naturally, this being Dundee, the building is called the 'Facey Land'.

North Lindsay Street

In the seventeenth century the original street here was known as School Wynd, when it was the location of the grammar school. In the 1830s Provost William Lindsay (1767–1849) persuaded the council to flatten the wynd and build a wider street. The council agreed and used the ancient Corbie (crow) hill as a quarry, with the stones used to build the new street, named Lindsay Street in honour of the Provost.

North Lindsay Street is now home to Dundee house, the administrative centre for the city.

Northwood Court, Broughty Ferry

The name comes from the mansion of Northwood, owned by William Thomson of DC Thomson newspaper fame.

Nursery Road, Broughty Ferry

The name is a reminder of the nurseries that once spread out in this area.

Oakley Place, Broughty Ferry

Revd Arthur Oakley was the pastor of Broughty Baptist church from 1883–6.

Observation platform

A few yards to the east of the Tay road bridge, this observation platform facilitates excellent views of the river Tay, the Firth of Tay and Fife. There is also a blue plaque on the platform, one of twenty-five around the city. Each plaque is dedicated to a woman who has played a prominent part in the story of Dundee. This plaque is to Bella Keyzer (1922–92), one of the many women who worked as welders with the Caledon shipyard during the Second World War. Keyzer was the daughter of a baker and pressed for equality for women in the shipyard during the war. She was committed to the trades unions and to the Labour Party.

The platform is a mecca for lovers. The rails are decorated with padlocks, each one symbolising a romantic union.

Ogilvie Court/Road, Broughty Ferry

Named after John Ogilvie of Harecraig House in nearby Dundee Road, the factor for the Earl and Countess of Home.

Ogilvie Street

Although the spelling is different, takes its name from a jute baron associated with Malcolm, Ogilvy & Co. The name was chosen in June 1869 at a meeting of the paving committee. It could be significant that the firm was based in neighbouring Jura Street.

Old Burial Ground, Broughty Ferry

This fascinating graveyard is surrounded by a stone wall and is off Fisher Street. To help kindle interest, kindly hands have placed information boards inside the graveyard. The Ship inn holds the graveyard key.

Old Glamis Road

At one time it led from Clepington Road to Glamis.

Old Steeple

Old Steeple

If there was ever history in stone, then the Old Steeple in Dundee would be a fine example. Dating from 1470, this solid structure is the steeple of St Mary's in the centre of the town, right outside the sparkling glass of the Overgate centre. The foundations possibly stretch back as far as the twelfth century, but the church has been reincarnated more than once. Edward Plantagenet, King of England, was blamed for the destruction of the original while he was striving to subjugate Scotland.

Around 1440 a massive new church was built on the same site and from 1460 the tall steeple was added. The steeple, properly a tower, was adorned with a crown spire, which is now lacking. According to Professor Charles McKean the crown spire or 'imperial crown' proclaimed that the King of Scots was emperor of his own country and owed allegiance to no one; a clear message to any who sought to impose alien rule.

The steeple must have seemed like a wonder but such a building inevitably attracted adverse attention. It was damaged in the English invasion of 1547: the crown was lost. Forty years later the steeple was used as a prison for those people who fell foul of the kirk in matters moral, but worse was to come.

The seventeenth century was arguably Dundee's most violent. First there was the 1645 assault by the Marquis of Montrose and his royalist Highlanders, and then the even more bloody attack by Cromwell's General Monck in 1651. On the latter occasion Dundee's defender, General Lumsden, had his last stand inside the Old Steeple. Monck piled wet straw outside the tower and set it alight to smoke Lumsden out. When Lumsden surrendered on terms, Monck promptly massacred the defenders, murdered Lumsden and displayed his head on the southwest corner of the tower, a reminder to the citizens of Cromwell's clemency.

For a while the steeple was used as a jail but it was not ideal for the purpose. For example, in January 1836, the police had to quell a fight between the sixteen prisoners confined on the second floor. Five of the prisoners were dragged to Dundee's main prison in the Town House and put in irons.

Today peace has returned to Dundee. The steeple is open to visitors and provides outstanding views of the city. It remains the oldest standing building in Dundee, and children skateboard where once soldiers disputed king or commonwealth.

Olympia, East Whale Lane

The original Olympia vanished with the Riverside improvements, but a new one has risen on the memories of the old, if slightly smaller and a few hundred metres to the east. There are four flumes here with a fifty-metre swimming pool as well as a toddler's pool for the little ones. Add to that an impressive studio with fitness classes and a public café and Dundee has a fine addition to her many attractions.

Orchar art gallery, Beach Crescent, Broughty Ferry

31 Beach Crescent, Broughty Ferry

Once contained the art collection of Provost James Guthrie Orchar (1825–98), who had been provost of Broughty Ferry from 1886–98. However, the contents passed to Dundee museum and art gallery in 1979. The building no longer functions as a gallery.

Orchar park, Broughty Ferry

Orchar Park Gateway, Broughty Ferry

Another derivation from James Guthrie Orchar (see previous entry). A joiner's son, Orchar moved into engineering and eventually owned the Wallace foundry, making machinery for the linen and jute trade in both Dundee and Calcutta.

Orchar also built the wall and railings around this park and worked hard to bring it into public ownership.

Orleans Place, Menzieshill

Named after Orléans, Dundee's twin city in France. It is a short street with a number of shops, the local library and community centre. Orléans is the capital not only of the Loiret *département* but also of the whole Centre Val de Loire region. The city has been badly damaged a number of times, not least in the Second World War, suffering even more than Dundee, but has managed to retain some, if not all, of its historic buildings – again like Dundee.

Overgate centre

A shopping centre rebuilt in 2001 and named after the Overgate, once a major route in, and out, of Dundee. The name 'over' gait is in contrast to the lower or 'nether' gait. The original Overgate, or Overgait, was once known as Argylegait

Overgate Centre

as it passed the town house of Campbell of Balruddery who was related to the Campbells of Argyll. Country gentry once used this street for their town houses but, by the mid-sixteenth century, weavers and spinners were beginning to move in and, in consequence, the mansions were subdivided.

The Overgait gave access to Dundee from the west, with the southeast of the street termed the luckenbooths after the locked booths or shops that lined the thoroughfare. By the middle of the nineteenth century the street was beginning to earn a less than savoury reputation. In the *Diary of John Sturrock* one passage of February 1865 states: 'Went up the Overgate and came down again and don't think I was ever so disgusted with it as I was tonight, for what with the smell of spirits and tobacco I thought I would have choked before I got out of it.'

The present Overgate is surely one of the most distinctive shopping centres in the country with a great curved wall of glass giving splendid views of the City Churches and the Old Steeple. It has a plethora of shops and eating places in sheltered and vibrant surroundings.

Overton Gardens

Sits beside Netherton Terrace. As *nether* mean lower and *over* means upper, it is logical that both were named together, as upper and lower streets. Ton is a settlement or farm.

Panmure Street/Terrace

In the early nineteenth century Dundee was becoming very congested and the council decided to create more streets to ease the flow of traffic. One street was to connect the Cowgate to the Meadows. Panmure Street was opened in 1839 and named to honour William Maule Ramsay, 1st Baron Panmure, who had given large sums to help fund the infirmary and to other good causes.

Panmure is thought to be Pictish, from the original inhabitants of the area. According to David Dorward it is from *pant mawr* – 'large hollow'.

Panmure Terrace has a number of fine houses, with no. 3 boasting several art nouveau details. In July 1848 the provost of Dundee praised Lord Panmure for his gifts to, and interest in, Dundee, prompting cheers from the members of the council.

Panmure Street/Terrace, Broughty Ferry
These are also named after Fox Maule Ramsay, the 11th Earl of Dalhousie. He was originally known as Lord Panmure until 1860 and then succeeded to the earldom of Dalhousie in Midlothian.

Paradise Road
The site of Dundee's first orphanage and the manse of Revd George Gilfillan of the United Presbyterian church from about 1838 to 1878. His church was located on what was then School Wynd. The building at no. 6, Marrbank, is listed. The name 'paradise' is said to refer to the time when this area was part of the pleasure gardens of Dallfield estate.

Park Place
Was built beside Hospital park on the then western fringe of Dundee. It was originally conceived around 1818 as an area of high-quality villas for the elite of Dundee at a time when industrialisation was creeping into the town. David Neave was the architect and his houses faced westward to what was then a patchwork of fields. Today this street is dominated by university buildings, the dental hospital and Park Place primary school.

Park Road
Runs beside Fairmuir park, after which it is named.

Parker Street
Honours Charles Parker, provost of Dundee from 1861–7. He moved to Dundee from Yorkshire in 1849 and founded an engineering works and an iron foundry. In 1857 he was elected to the town council and must have been an energetic member because within two years he was appointed treasurer and, after another two years, provost. He died in office, aged 71. One of his pet projects was free public libraries.

Pasteur Lane
Honours Louis Pasteur (1822–95), the great French chemist and microbiologist.

Patent Slip Way
One of the new streets being created with the waterfront development. Patent Slip Way will be beneath the ramps of the bridge and refers to the method by which ships were moved from the docks to the Tay. The 1837 harbour workshop used to be at this spot.

Paton's Lane

Paton's Lane

In this street, William Topaz McGonagall, possibly the world's worst poet, first decided he was a literary genius. He is not always recognised outside Dundee but in his lifetime he wrote many pieces of doggerel and was the butt of many jokes.

Patrick Blair Place, Ninewells
Named after Dundee-born surgeon Patrick Blair (c.1680–1728), whose Jacobite tendencies saw him cast into jail during the 1715 rising. Once released, he moved to England and settled in Lincolnshire. He is perhaps best known for his treatise in dissecting an elephant on the outskirts of Dundee, although he also wrote treatises on other scientific subjects, including *Botanick Essay* of 1720.

Peel Street
One of many Dundee streets named after prominent nineteenth-century prime ministers. It was Robert Peel (1788–1850) who passed the Police Act that

brought uniformed police officers to the streets of London and of course the slang words 'bobbies' and 'peelers' are references to him. However, many Scottish towns had uniformed police long before Peel's legislation. Peel was also responsible for the Mines Act of 1842 that made it illegal for women and children to work underground, and the Factory Act of 1844 that limited working hours for women and children. He was also involved in the repeal of the Corn Laws, which kept the price of bread artificially high.

Peep-o'-day Lane

Peep-o'-Day Lane

Takes its name from a mansion house that stood on the site. According to folklore, the house was situated to catch the dawn rising over the Tay. The Ogilvy family lived here until David Ogilvy of Clova became the Earl of Airlie and moved to grander surroundings. The house was knocked down when the gas works was established but the name survives.

As a young woman, Mary Wollstonecraft Godwin (1797–1851) visited the Ogilvy family in 1813 in Peep-o'-day when she lived with the Baxters in Broughty Ferry, where she began work on her great horror novel *Frankenstein*.

Penguins

Only in Dundee would there be penguins strutting in a line along the side wall of a church. These sculptured birds walk beside the City Churches, a reminder of Dundee's important role in polar exploration. More penguins are on view outside Discovery Point at Riverside, highlighting the fascinating exhibits inside that establishment. (See photograph on facing page).

Pentland Avenue/Crescent

Named after the Pentland hill range that runs south and west of Edinburgh.

Penguins outside Town Churches

Perrie Street

Bailie Perrie was born in Burreltown in Perthshire but came to Dundee in 1846 when he was eleven. After completing his apprenticeship Perrie started his own bakery. He became councillor for Lochee in 1876 and by the time he died in 1917, aged 82, was known as 'father of the council'.

Perth Road

One of the most pleasant thoroughfares in Dundee, Perth Road is named after

Perth Road

its eventual destination. There is a whiff of the bohemian among the shops, bars and restaurants in the eastern part of the street, with many students living here in what is sometimes termed Dundee's 'cultural quarter'. The western end has some very desirable property.

Binrock, at no. 465, is a lovely villa, built in the late eighteenth century, when no one thought the city could expand this far. Note also the distinguished Ardveck at no. 516, a 1907 Arts and Crafts house, designed by Dundee architects Mills and Shepherd. The name comes from the evocatively positioned Ardvreck castle in Assynt.

Peter Street

Peter Street

This short street from the Seagate to the Murraygate appears to have been named after John Peter, who, in 1793, was the wright who created the frontages at both the north and south sides. It is likely that the present street comprises a number of older closes that were knocked together.

The street is decorated by a mosaic on the ground that shows a fire, and also by a plaque on the wall dedicated to Grisel Jaffray, who was burnt at the stake for witchcraft in 1669. In Scotland witches were not burned alive but were 'worrit', or strangled, before being cast into the flames.

Peters building, Unesco Centre, University of Dundee

The UNESCO centre for water law, policy and science is for postgraduate students, and aims at poverty reduction with the slogan: 'water for all'.

Pitairlie Road

Derived from the place near Newbigging in Monikie parish, Angus. In 1853 a gentleman named Alexander Kinnear owned Pitairlie. The prefix *pit* hints at a Pictish origin while Airlie is very much a local name: 'the place of Airlie'.

Pitalpin Court/Street

The name Alpin is famous in Scottish history. He was the father of Kenneth, the man who, according to tradition, united Scots and Picts into a single nation. The name *pit* means 'place of' so this street name means 'the place of Alpin', the King of Scots. There was a Pitalpin mill in Lochee, owned by James Donald.

Pitfour Street

The source is Pitfour castle in Perthshire, one of the homes of Lord Panmure. When Lady Panmure died in the castle in November 1853 her body was taken to the family burial ground at Panbride, and the ships in Dundee harbour wore their colours at half-mast while church bells tolled. In the 1850s when Panmure house was being improved, Lord Panmure made his home at Pitfour, and took a house in Edinburgh for the winter.

Pitkerro Court/Drive/Road

Pitkerro Road was once the road to Pitkerro.

Pitkerro house

A house with many royal links: according to folklore, Robert I gave the land here to the Durham family. Mary, Queen of Scots stayed here in 1562 on her way north to put down Huntly's rebellion. The author Charles Kingsley lived here, and it was one of the first houses in the country to have electricity. The house was restored in the early twentieth century by Sir Robert Lorimer and is now divided into flats.

Pitroddie Gardens

Takes its name from the abandoned settlement of Pitroddie in the Sidlaw hills. There is still a farm of the name but once there was an entire community with a church, inn and blacksmith's shop. There are tales of William Wallace having been here, and a seventeenth-century murder in the Den of Pitroddie. More pertinent to Dundee, in the latter part of the nineteenth century the works committee of the Dundee police commission leased Pitrodie quarry (note the single 'd' in the name of the quarry) from Sir Thomas Montagu Steele of Evelick, so there is a strong possibility that Pitrodie stone is used in Dundee buildings.

Playhouse cinema

When Green's Playhouse in the Nethergate opened in 1936 it was the second-largest cinema in Europe. George Fairweather, who also helped with Blackpool tower, designed the foyer, which still exists.

Pleasance Court

A pleasance was a pleasure garden, in this case part of the gardens of Dudhope castle.

Polepark Road

The name is a mystery. A. H. Miller, in *Glimpses of Old and New Dundee*, conjectures that it came from a park that had a pole on which flags were occasionally hung. On the corner of Polepark Road, Lochee Road and Lower Pleasance there is a reminder of Dundee's whaling heritage in a sculpture by Alistair Smart that is made of three teeth from a whale.

Police Scotland, 59 West Bell Street

Police Scotland HQ Dundee

Dundee's official uniformed police came into existence in 1824, and have developed into one of the most efficient forces in the country. Today the Tayside division of Police Scotland protects nearly 390,000 people in Dundee, Angus and Tayside – 2,896 square miles of very varied and often rough terrain that includes city streets, mountains, coast and farmland. At the time of writing (2016) the division has 1,078 officers with another 151 special constables and over 500 additional staff with about 200,000 incidents a year.

At the Marketgate entrance to the police headquarters there is a blue plaque, one of twenty-five throughout Dundee. Each plaque commemorates a woman who was prominent in her own field. This plaque highlights the career of Jean Thomson, a Lochee minister's daughter, who became Dundee's first policewoman.

Poorhouse

Otherwise known as a workhouse or combination. Dundee had two of these establishments: combination poorhouse east, off Mains Road in Maryfield; and combination poorhouse west, on the corner of Blackness Road and Glenagnes Road. On 28 December 1881 there were 587 inmates in 'east' and 154 in 'west'. That year the poorhouse committee recommended that, due to the prevalence of opthalmia, each child should be allowed an extra two ounces of boiled beef per week.

Many individuals, firms and organisations gave what they could to these establishments, in the form of money, food or clothes. Poorhouses had a bad reputation and in some cases that may well be deserved, but they also did a lot of good work. For instance, in March 1882, the police picked up a young girl named Isabella Shand who was 'in a very wretched condition, being nearly naked and crawling with vermin'. She was sent to the poorhouse whose workers cleaned her, removed the infestations, clothed her and reintroduced her to her mother, who lived apart from her father. The mother had no furniture in her house and lived by sewing sacks; the father lived with another woman, by whom he had a child, and in July that year he was convicted of assaulting a third woman who was the mother of another of his children.

Poplar Grey Court
The poplar grey caterpillar lives off the leaves of poplar trees before it becomes a moth.

Postbox Road, Birkhill
This is obviously the road in which the postbox was situated. However, the fact that it is so named highlights the importance of the Royal Mail.

Powrie Place, Hilltown
Takes its name from the lands and castle of the same name in the Sidlaw hills. The name extends to at least the twelfth century.

Princes Street
Was named after Prince George, later King George IV.

Princes Street

Prospect Place

Created around 1851, this street was intended to house the middle-class families who were migrating from the increasingly congested town. The name probably refers to the views over the Tay, while a high wall protected the houses from working class Rosebank.

Provost McGowan Place

Commemorates Norman McGowan (1926–2005). There is an Angus McEwan portrait of him in Dundee art galleries and museum. He was lord provost of Dundee in 1995–6 but was known to all and sundry as Norrie. Married to Florence, he was a butcher, a mattress maker, a councillor and a dedicated Labour man.

Pullar's Close, 62 Murraygate

Takes its name from James Pullar (1735–1811). He was a baker who founded a charity to educate ten poor boys by the name of Pullar.

Quaker meeting place, 7 Whitehall Crescent

Whitehall Crescent

The Quakers have been in this building since 1891 and the words 'Meeting House' are carved into the lintel above the Solicitors' Property Centre on the ground floor. The original intention was for the Quakers to have an institute, library, classrooms, recreation and reading room, but financial pressures resulted in the space being let out in the difficult years between the First and Second World Wars. Now the Quakers occupy the first and third floors and allow other like-minded peaceful groups to use the meeting room.

Queen's hotel

Was intended to be beside the railway, but when the station was built in a different position to that originally planned the hotel was out of place in Nethergate. However, it redeemed itself by becoming one of the finest in Dundee, boasting splendid architecture and high-quality service. In the late nineteenth century, circuit judges stayed here before giving their decisions in court, Churchill used it as his base in his successful 1908 attempt to become Dundee's MP and more recently it has been a favoured hotel for those visiting Dundee University. Visitors and guests have private car parking at the back and should look for the splendid wooden staircase.

Queen's Hotel, Nethergate

Queen Mother building/research centre, University of Dundee

In 1967 when Dundee University gained independence from the University of St Andrews, Queen Elizabeth became the chancellor. Situated behind Campus Green, the spanking new Queen Mother building hosts the school of computing.

Queen Street

Takes its name from the consort of King George III, Charlotte of Mecklenburg-Strelitz, a grand duchy in northern Germany.

Queen Street, Broughty Ferry

Queen Street, Broughty Ferry

Also named after Queen Charlotte of Mecklenburg-Strelitz, wife of George III, who was on the throne in 1801 when General Hunter of Burnside planned the new town of Broughty Ferry. This is the main street through the Ferry, and boasts a number of notable buildings including Broughty Ferry library and Camphill house, a neo-Jacobean mansion of 1850. It also has the Bughties at no. 76, an 1882 building that, with its half-timbered frontage, would not be out of place in Worcestershire.

Queen Street church, Broughty Ferry
Now a restaurant, this church was opened in 1876 as the Queen Street United Presbyterian church. In 1953 the congregation merged with St Luke's.

Queen Victoria and Regent works, Blackness
This two-storey structure was built in 1834 as a water-powered flax mill but was altered for jute production and closed as late as 1990. Originally known as Lower Pleasance mill, it was renamed in 1887 in honour of Queen Victoria's jubilee, a year of great celebration throughout the country as communities marked fifty years of her rule. There are now (2016) plans to turn the Queen Victoria mill into flats, as has happened to many Dundee mills.

Raglan Street
Commemorates Fitzroy Somerset, 1st Baron Raglan (1788–1855), who commanded the British Army in the early part of the Crimean War (1854–6). The street was opened in 1854, when Raglan was still in charge, but he died during the campaign. The war in the Crimea was characterised by significant mismanagement by the military hierarchy – including of course the disastrous Charge of the Light Brigade – so perhaps another name could, and should, have been chosen.

The paving committee first selected Guthrie Street, after the proprietor, but that name was rejected as it was already in use. Subsequent suggestions included Athole Street, after Athole brose, a mixture of oatmeal and whisky, and Foggie Street after councillor Foggie, but eventually Raglan Street was chosen.

Ralston Road, West Ferry
Has the Grade-B listed house, Sunningdale, which, with its flat roof, balconies and a fretted parapet suggests North Africa rather than eastern Scotland. The street was named after Claude Ralston (1867–1928) factor to the Earl of Home on his Angus estates.

Ramsay Street, Broughty Ferry
Nothing to do with the famous Ramsay Street in the Australian soap opera, this area was owned by Lord Panmure, whose family name was Ramsay.

Rankine's Court, 79 High Street

Takes its name from a burgess named Andrew Rankine who lived here in the early seventeenth century. In 1607 he built a prominent house, named Andrew Rankine's tower, in a part of Dundee known as the Vault. George Dempster, a prominent merchant and banker, also had his town house in this close. He bought land in Angus (then Forfarshire) and was known as George Dempster of Dunnichen. In February 1720 the people of Dundee were angered when Dempster exported grain at a time of famine, so they sacked his house and shop, boarded two of his ships in harbour and distributed the grain to the hungry of the town.

Dempster's son, also George (1732–1818), was born in Rankine's Court and became the local MP in 1761. Among his many achievements he improved Scottish fisheries and so helped to shape an industry that eventually employed over fifty thousand people. In Dundee terms he was the head of the banking firm, George Dempster & Co. He lent the town money on easy terms, purchased land for housing, established the Dundee Banking Company, and, as president of the Whig club of Dundee, sent a message of congratulations to the revolutionary National Assembly in Paris.

Rankine Street

Honours William Macbean Rankine (1848–79), the landowner of Dudhope who sold the Law to the city in 1878. It cost Dundee £3,888 for the privilege of giving free access to the Law. Even though that was a great deal of money at the time, it was well spent as the Law would be a splendid asset to any city.

The Rankine family originated in Perthshire and they married into one of the many branches of the Argyllshire Campbells. William Macbean Rankine was born William Macbean Campbell but assumed the name Rankine when he succeeded to the lands of Dudhope. He married Rose MacLaine, of the MacLaines of Lochbuie.

Rannoch Moor Gardens, Brackens Road, Balgowan

Dundee City Council named this street in 1982, 'To associate with the name of the house (*Rhoineach Mohr*) on this site which was previously demolished.'

Ravenscraig Gardens, Broughty Ferry

Continues the name of the mansion of Ravenscraig, which was the home of Colonel Frank Sandeman, a jute lord of the Manhattan works. In 1876 Sandeman bought the Stanley cotton mill in Perthshire and improved the cotton driving belting. Although F. Stewart Sandeman went into voluntary liquidation in 1932 the Stanley Belting companies continued to trade.

There is a Ravenscraig castle near Kirkcaldy in Fife and this may be the inspiration for the house and street name. It means 'ravens rock'.

Red Admiral Court
Named after the butterfly of that name. All the courts in this part of Dundee were named after types of butterflies or moths.

Redwood Avenue
Part of the Beechwood housing estate. Many of the streets in this area had the suffix 'wood' to fit in with the mansion of Beechwood, on whose grounds the streets were built. The mansion of Beechwood was owned by the Cox family and is now demolished.

Reform Street

Reform Street

One of the most pleasant thoroughfares in central Dundee, Reform Street commemorates the (Great) Reform Act of 1832, which extended the vote to a large proportion of the middle classes. News of the Act caused great celebrations in Dundee, which eventually ended in a near riot. The disorder was such that the 78th Highlanders were drafted in from Perth, helped by a thousand locally recruited special constables.

In the nineteenth century people liked to promenade in Reform Street, and window shop at the quality establishments that lined the pavements. It was the famous architect William Burn who first suggested this street be built, but an Edinburgh architect named George Angus was the actual designer. He had been responsible for the High School, which closes the vista to the north, and the Bell Street court buildings, so his style was well known and respected in Dundee.

The name Reform Street was chosen above Kinnaird Street and Jobson Street

– which are fine names in their own right and celebrate Dundee political figures – but do not have the historical punch of Reform Street. Other, tongue-in-cheek, suggestions included Mortgage Street and Bond Street because of the expense to the town.

Reform Street held Lamb's hotel at no. 64, which in the 1880s was the first hotel in Dundee to have electric light. This was also the setting for the meeting of the Dundee-based Oregon Railway Company in December 1880, with the Earl of Airlie as chairman.

Finally, Reform Street was the birthplace of David Coupar Thomson (1861–1954), founder of the D. C. Thomson empire.

Educated at Dundee High School, Thomson began work in his father's shipping company. In 1886 he became general manager of the *Dundee Courier and Daily Argus*, in which his father was the major shareholder. In 1905 Thomson founded D. C. Thomson Ltd. He opposed the Liberal MP Winston Churchill through the columns of both his newspapers, which may have been instrumental in Churchill losing his seat to temperance campaigner Ned Scrymgeour in 1922. Thomson was anti-union, deputy lieutenant of Dundee, a governor of University College and a member of Dundee chamber of commerce.

Regent Place, Broughty Ferry
Dundee council named this street after the Prince Regent, who later became King George IV.

Reres hill
A public park in Broughty Ferry. Provost Orchar put in a number of improvements and there is an archway into the park, adorned with a bas-relief structure of the head of Queen Victoria. At the back is an inscription that reads: 'this gateway and fountain were erected in commemoration of Her Majesty's Jubilee by James Guthrie Orchar Esq, Chief Magistrate of Broughty Ferry and were presented by him to the community on nineteenth September 1887.'

Orchar intended to build an art gallery in the park to hold his own collection, which he gifted to Broughty Ferry, with the gateway as an impressive entrance.

Reresmount Place, Broughty Ferry
Perpetuates the name of a mansion that stood here. In November 1883 Alexander Buist of Reresmount donated £100 to Dundee Royal Infirmary.

Richmond Terrace
In the Victorian era there was a deep reverence for things royal. The street was named after the royal dukedom of the same name, indicating that the street was intended to be of high status.

Riverside Drive

Riverside Sculpture

The name speaks for itself; this is the road that runs beside the river Tay. This walkway and road provide some of the finest views in any city in Britain, over the always-altering Firth of Tay to the fertile fields of Fife. It also provides a striking, and amazingly green, entry into Dundee from the west.

What should be remembered is that much of this area has been reclaimed from the Tay. Dundee is dynamic, a city that never keeps still as it reinvents itself. As this is being written (2016) there are vast works on Riverside including the building of a splendid new museum, an offshoot of London's Victoria and Albert, and a new railway station. Add to that new flats being developed, as well as business opportunities: this area is set for a new lease of life.

Rockfield Crescent

Commemorates a large house of that name. The owner in the 1860s and 1870s was a Perthshire-born solicitor, Peter Reid. He started the Dundee Property and Investment Building Society in 1851, the first of its kind in Dundee. In the 1870s there was a cricket club named Rockfield that played at Magdalen Green, with 14-year-old William Lyle as captain.

Roodyards burial ground, Broughty Ferry Road

The name is simple; with a rood being the holy cross, rood yards is the yard of the cross. This burial ground was created for victims of the plague of 1561, although the tombstones date mainly from the mid-nineteenth century. The ground also holds the Grade-B-listed Guthrie mausoleum.

This area was once known as St John's chapel and was on a headland known as Kilcraig: Rock Point.

Roseangle

The area was named after a small estate. At the bottom of Roseangle, where it meets Magdalen Green, is a state-of-the-art play park.

Rosebank Road
Takes its name from the estate of Rosebank that stood here.

Rosedale Crescent/Rosemarkie Crescent/Place, Broughty Ferry
Dundee Council works committee gave all the streets in this private-housing area the prefix 'Rose'.

Rosefield Street

Rosefield Street

Continues the name of Rosefield cottage, a mansion that stood here. In 1859 Mr Blyth, proprietor of Bank mill, was the owner. He seems to have been a decent employer and paid for a holiday for his workers to Lindores in Fife.

In 1873 the property of Rosefield was described as: 'about five aces of ground . . . between Milnbank Road and Blackness Road . . . bounded on the west by the Liff and Benvie Poorhouse and on the east by the works of Messrs Boase and Mudie.'

On 5 November 1940 a German air raid destroyed an electricity substation and badly damaged a tenement building in Rosefield Street. A visit to the street will easily reveal which building was damaged by the different style of architecture. The 'new' tenement is also slightly brighter inside than its neighbours.

Rosemount Crescent, Ardler
In common with other Ardler streets, this was named after a famous golf course. Rosemount golf course is in Perthshire.

Rossie Avenue

Takes its name from Rossie priory and Rossie hill near Inchture. There is also Rossie Old Kirk and a Rossie village.

Rowanbank Gardens, Broughty Ferry

Was built on the grounds of the mansion of Rowanbank, owned by the Gilroy jute lords. The rowan was a sacred tree of the Celts and was often planted to keep homes safe from witches and other creatures of the night.

Rowantree Crescent

In old Scotland, a rowan tree was thought to protect from witches, fairies and general bad luck, so that many crofts and houses, particularly in the Highlands, had rowan trees planted close by. Calling a street Rowantree Crescent continues the tradition.

Royal Arch

Now demolished, the first Royal Arch was a wooden structure built to commemorate the visit of Queen Victoria in 1844. The Queen and Prince Albert passed under the arch as seamen clambered onto masts in the harbour for three loyal cheers. Victoria and Albert graced Dundee for a spell before travelling to Highland haunts in Aberdeenshire.

A competition was held to replace the temporary wooden arch, with plans for a number of structures presented to a panel headed by Lord Panmure. As a major local landlord, who had given a great deal to the town, including cut-price land for the Dundee–Arbroath railway, his opinion carried much weight. He selected the design of the Glaswegian Thomas Rochead, who also designed the Wallace monument near Stirling. The result was an elaborate stone structure sometimes known as the Pigeon's Palace. This archway was the largest of its type in Great Britain and stood beside the docks opposite the Exchange coffee house. It has been demolished but a tiny replica exists in City Square. The front cover of this book has a fine painting of the Royal Arch.

Royal Exchange

Situated in Albert Square, this Flemish-style building is underappreciated but has a style of architecture unique for Dundee. The so-called Baltic merchants had traditionally worked from the historic Cowgate but, in 1850, decided they needed somewhere grander and the idea was to have a Dundee version of Glasgow's Royal Exchange Square. David Bryce, one of Scotland's foremost architects, designed the building to be similar to a Dutch cloth hall, but the ground was boggy and so the original plans had to be altered. A crown steeple was also mooted but when that proved too heavy it was removed. Now the

Royal Exchange, Panmure Street

building is at an angle; Dundee's leaning tower of Pisa. Among the items sold in the Royal Exchange auction rooms was whale oil, with that of the whaling ship *Nova Zembla* fetching up to £28 per ton in 1878. The building is no longer used for its original purpose.

Royal Tay Yacht club, Fort William house, West Ferry
Founded in 1885 the club has sailing, rowing and powerboat racing. There is top-class sailing tuition and an extensive social calendar. Fort William house is in a prominent position for those people who enter Dundee by rail from the north.

Rugby Terrace, Broughty Ferry
Among the councillors who named this street in 1887 was Edward Cowan who was vice chairman of Invertay rugby club.

Russell Place
Commemorates the prominent Victorian statesman, John, Lord Russell (1792–1878). He was the Whig (Liberal) prime minister from July 1846 to February 1852 and from October 1865 to June 1866. Educated at the University of Edinburgh, Russell was instrumental in drafting the mould-breaking Great Reform Act of 1832 that extended the franchise, and after which Reform Street is named. He also passed the Factories Act of 1847 that limited working hours in factories and passed a public health bill in 1848 and eased restrictions on colonial trade, all of which would have benefitted Dundonians.

Rustic Place

Once part of the pleasure gardens of Dallfield estate, the name refers to the old rural charm of the area before industrialisation crept in.

Ryehill church, Perth Road

Now converted to residential flats, this church was built in 1878 and boasts a lovely gabled façade that faces Perth Road. The interior is not always easy to navigate for the visitor, however.

Ryehill Lane

This street is notable mainly for the painted gable that passers-by cannot fail to see. The paintings show the history of Dundee and were created by the Edinburgh Artists Collective. Quite rightly it won the Saltire Society's Art in Architecture award in 1983. The 1821 map of Dundee marks the small estate of Ryehill in this location.

Saggar Street

Commemorates a doctor who may have been Dundee's first permanent

Ryehill Lane

SAGGAR STREET

Saggar Street

resident from south Asia. Born in the Punjab in 1898, Jayanti Saggar left India to study medicine at St Andrews University and afterward settled in Dundee. As well as a medical degree he obtained diplomas in ophthalmic medicine, surgery and public health and topped that with a keen interest in education. Seeing the poverty in Dundee he became concerned about social welfare, joined the Labour party and became Scotland's first Asian-born councillor. He married a lady named Jane Quinn and when he died in 1974 the Lord Provost said that 'no son of Dundee had greater love for its people or worked harder in their interests'.

Sailors' home, 62 Dock Street

Built in 1881, at the same time as the neighbouring seaman's chapel, the Grade-B listed sailors' home is a distinctive landmark. It was created to help seamen escape from the temptation of public houses and prostitutes and also to provide protection from crimps and others who sought to part them from their hard-earned wages.

Sailors' Home, Dock Street

The first sailors' home in Dundee was at the bottom of Union Street and opened in 1851 but financial pressure caused it to close two years later. The Earl of Dalhousie opened the 'new' sailors' home in December 1881. Seamen and ships' captains were all welcome, with the higher ranking living in the upper storeys. The building stands five-storeys high with the names of prominent sea captains inscribed on a wallhead frieze. After the First World War fewer seamen used the home and it catered for general travellers. It has now been converted into twelve apartments.

St Aidan's church, Brook Street, Broughty Ferry

Built in 1824, this church boasts a distinctive square tower. Aidan was probably Irish, moved to Iona but spent most of his life converting the pagan Angles of Northumbria to Christianity. The church was originally known as Broughty Ferry parish church but the name was changed in 1929. It was built to cater for the spiritual needs of the holidaymakers who came to the Ferry during the summer. At the time of writing (2016), it was not open for worship.

St Alban's Terrace

One of a number of streets in the St Mary's area named after saints. St Alban was said to be one of the first four Romano-British Christian martyrs. He helped a Christian missionary to escape Roman persecution, converted to Christianity himself and later refused to give offerings to the Roman gods, saying he only believed in 'the true and living God who created all things'. He was beheaded for his faith.

St Andrew's church, Cowgate

Designed by the Dundee-born city architect, Samuel Bell, in 1739, this church was funded in part by the Nine Trades of Dundee. The church was built in 1772 and is undoubtedly one of the most visually pleasing churches in the city. There are semi-circular windows, mingled with Venetian, but the western tower with its steeple is the masterpiece. St Andrew was one of Christ's apostles and the patron saint of Scotland.

St Andrew's Roman Catholic cathedral, Nethergate

Built in 1835, and opened in August 1836, this church has six pinnacles protruding skyward in an otherwise quiet exterior but the interior is spacious and has an atmosphere of spirituality. It is the oldest surviving Roman Catholic church in Dundee and has seating for a thousand worshippers. In February 1923 it became a cathedral.

St Andrew's Street

Takes its name from the nearby St Andrew's church.

St Boswell's Terrace

St Boisil was the abbot of Old Maelros, or Mailros, in the Scottish Borders, now known as Melrose. History has altered his name to Boswell and the town of St Boswell's in the Borders is named after him.

St Clement Terrace

St Clement was said to be the third bishop of Rome around 91 AD and was martyred by being exiled to the Crimea marble quarries and subsequently thrown into the Black Sea. Clement was the original patron saint of Dundee and there is a legend that David of Huntingdon attributed his survival in a storm to him. Dundee had a St Clement's church before St Mary became the patron saint of the town. The original St Clement's church was where City Square is now. Dundee still has a St Clement's church, in Charleston, and a St Clement's primary school.

St David's high kirk, Kinghorne Road

Can be seen from many points in the south of Dundee as it stands on a magnificent site on the slopes of Dundee Law. St David was from Cardigan in Wales, which country claims him as her patron saint.

St David's High Kirk, Kinghorne Road

St David's Lane

Off North Tay Street, this narrow lane was named after the local St David's church.

St Dennis Terrace

During one of the many periods when Christians were persecuted, around 250 AD, Saint Denis (sic) or Dionysius, Bishop of Paris, was beheaded with a sword. The legend that states he then picked up the head and walked six miles while preaching a sermon is probably apocryphal.

St Edmund Place

The twentieth of November is St Edmund Day, and there are some who claim that this Saxon is the true patron saint of England, with St George a Norman imposition.

St Fillans Terrace

Fillan was an Irish saint of the Dark Ages and a missionary to the Picts. It is believed that he lived in Perthshire, near the present-day village of St Fillans by Loch Earn.

St Francis friary, Tullideph Road

St Francis Friary

231

This red-brick, Grade-B-listed building was completed in 1933 and dominates the street and the area. City Church Dundee is now the owner and it is still a centre of Christian activity. Francis of Assisi was an animal-loving saint from Italy.

St Giles'(s) Terrace
St Giles was a Greek Christian who lived as a hermit in what is now the south of France. He was a vegetarian and became the patron saint of the disabled.

St Helens, 474 Perth Road
An explosion of Scottish baronial architecture from 1850, complete with corbie-stepped gables. It was a grand house, now converted to flats.

St James'(s) church, Fort Street, Broughty Ferry
Designed by T. S. Robertson, built in 1889 and opened in 1890, this church was originally intended as a mission for the large fishing community in the Ferry. The saint after whom this church is named is in doubt as there were a number of saints named James.

St John's church, Roseangle
Built in 1884 with James Hutton as the architect and now called Roseangle Ryehill parish church. It is currently a place of worship.

St John's Cross Church, Blackness Avenue
Properly known as Logie and St John's Cross, this church replaced the Cross Church that a fire of 1841 destroyed. The congregation is apt to call it 'Logie's'.

St Joseph's convent, Gardner Street
This B-listed building is the home for Sisters of Mercy nuns. Archibald McPherson was the architect.

St Kilda Road
As there never was a saint called Kilda, the street is named after the island group off the west coast of Scotland. There is a community centre on this street in an area known as the Green.

St Leonard Place/Terrace
Leonard was a Frankish noble who converted to Christianity and became a hermit. His oratory became the site of the Benedictine monastery of Noblat. Leonard was interested in the plight of prisoners and became the patron saint of those imprisoned, midwives and expectant mothers.

St Luke's Episcopal church, Baldovan Road
Built in 1901, this B-listed Scottish Gothic church has unusual harled walls.

St Luke's and Queen Street, Church of Scotland, Broughty Ferry
A lovely red sandstone church built to a traditional cruciform design. This is a very forward-looking church with an excellent website.

St Margaret's Lane, Broughty Ferry
Takes its name from the nearby St Margaret's church. St Margaret (c.1045–93) was the Hungarian wife of King Malcolm IV of Scotland and introduced the Catholic faith into Scotland in opposition to the Culdee Celtic Christian church.

St Mark's church, 158 Perth Road
Pilkington and Bell built this church in 1868–9. It is the home of Gate Church International, an evangelical church full of joyous people with their own brand of Christianity.

St Martin's Stone, Balkello farm
The remains of a cross slab that shows carvings of a horseman and a serpent. The weather-worn carving of the serpent is undoubtedly the origin of the local dragon legend.

St Mary's Close, 30 Nethergate
Reputedly named after an ancient church that stood here. In 1882 five carved panels were discovered behind plasterwork and eventually found their way to Dundee museum.

St Mary, 164 Queen Street, Broughty Ferry
This B-listed, Gothic church was designed by Sir George Gilbert Scott in 1858–70 and later extended by Robert Lorimer. Scott is one of our finest architects, responsible for a wide array of iconic buildings including the Albert memorial, the Foreign and Commonwealth office, Glasgow University and St Mary's cathedral, Edinburgh.

St Mary's housing scheme
Built in the aftermath of the Second World War in an attempt to alleviate the bad housing in Dundee, St Mary's is in the north-west of the city. As with other council developments, the street names follow a theme, in this case they are all prefixed by 'St'. There is a community centre and Dundee West FC has its home here.

The area has been home to Mick McCluskey the author and the Whitbread poetry prizewinner, Don Paterson.

St Mary's Lochee Roman Catholic church, 41 High Street, Lochee
Designed by Londoner Joseph Aloysius Hansom (1803–82), who also created the Hansom, the nineteenth-century taxi. This Grade A-listed, Gothic-revival church is, according to the Pevsner architectural guide, 'one of Dundee's most arresting edifices, mixing the ethos of a mission church with that of a cathedral'.

St Mary Magdalene's, Blinshall Street
Bishop Forbes of Brechin founded a mission in a thatched cottage in this area, intended to bring God's word to the workers of Blackness mills. The linear descendant of the mission is this Grade-B listed structure of 1854, which, when it opened, was Dundee's first Episcopal church since 1690. In time the congregation outgrew the church and moved to the present building at Dudhope Crescent Road. At present the Blinshall Street site is home to the Avertical World climbing centre.

St Mary Magdalene's Episcopal church, Dudhope Crescent Road
Once the Catholic Apostolic Church but the Episcopal church took over as the premises were larger than their previous accommodation in Blinshall Street. However, shortly after they moved, Dundee council decanted thousands of people from congested areas in the centre of the city to peripheral housing schemes where walking to church was no longer easy and the congregations slumped. Rebuilding the congregation as well as maintaining the fabric of the 1867 church, which is by Edward & Robertson, has been a Herculean but successful task.

St Mary's manse, 69 Dalkeith Road
Built in 1890 in beautiful red stone, this house has fascinating decorative features with a pillared entrance and Dundee's coat of arms above the door. It is privately owned and no longer a manse.

St Mary's Road
St Mary is the patron saint of Dundee. Mary was the mother of Christ and as such enjoys a special position in Christianity.

St Mary's Roman Catholic church Forebank, Powrie Place
Also known as Our Lady of Victories, George Mathewson was the architect of this 1850 church. It has a highly impressive Romanesque interior and outstanding twin campaniles, added in 1901, that form a local landmark.

St Monance Place
St Monance was a Celtic saint murdered by Vikings around AD 875. The Fife village of St Monance is also named after him.

St Nicholas Place

St Nicholas was one of the people on whom Santa Claus was based, so this street is Santa Claus Street: a cheerful name for any place.

Nicholas, or Nikolaos of Myra (270–343), was the bishop of Myra in Anatolia and devoted his life to helping the poor. The Roman Emperor, Diocletian, persecuted Christians, but brave men and women such as Nicholas spread the Word and gradually Christianised the area. Anatolia remained Christian until Muslim Turks invaded in the tenth century, the catalyst for the counterattack of the Crusades.

St Ninian's church, Kingsway East

A bright and cheerful buttressed Episcopal church built in 1938 for the Mid Craigie scheme. It is still fully operational and hosts the Girl's Brigade.

St Ninian's church, Methven Street, Lochee

This B-listed, David Neave-designed church was built right at the gates of the Camperdown works. It is straightforward, but attractive, with a simple pediment and spire. It is no longer used for worship and has an alternative name of Lochee old parish church.

St Ninian Terrace

Ninian was one of Scotland's earliest saints. While the precise facts of his life are disputed, he is said, after being trained in Rome, to have founded a religious community in Whithorn, Galloway, in southwest Scotland, around 397 AD. His monastery there was known as Candida Casa, the 'white house', and the name lives on in 'Whithorn'. It was from here that he set about converting the southern Picts. Whatever the truth about Ninian's life, Whithorn became an important place of pilgrimage in Scotland, and its devotees included several Scottish kings, most notably Robert the Bruce.

St Patrick's Roman Catholic church, 3 Arthurstone Terrace

Built in red rubble with an octagonal belfry, this church is still used for Christian worship. British-born St Patrick was said to have been captured by Irish slavers, escaped back to Britain and returned to Christianise Ireland. He is the patron saint of Ireland.

St Paul's Court, 23 Murraygate to 36 Seagate

This close is traditionally named after a Culdee (Celtic) church, established very early in Dundee. There are no remains of this church, if indeed it ever existed, but anyone who enters the close will see later architectural relics.

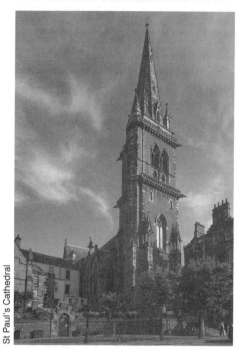

St Paul's Cathedral

St Paul's cathedral, 1 High Street

Built on what remains of the castle rock, the church was completed in 1855 and was given the status of a cathedral in 1905. Sir George Gilbert Scott was the architect, and the style is Gothic revival, conforming to what some architectural historians describe as 'Catholic' Anglican. The position of the cathedral – it is hemmed in by other buildings – unfortunately conceals much of the detail, but there is no disguising its elegance. An exception to this is the magnificent north steeple, which is clearly visible from a distance and rendered even more dominant by the approaching steps. The tall, airy interior is equally impressive and there is an outstanding reredos over the high altar as well as fine stained-glass windows.

St Paul's is the mother church of the diocese of Brechin in the Scottish Episcopal Church, and, as such, the seat of the bishop of Brechin. While it welcomes worshippers from all faiths and none, the style of worship is distinctly High Church, with vestments being worn and incense burned.

St Paul's Nethergate

Built by Charles Wilson of Glasgow in 1850 this church stands right beside the inner ring road. It is known as Meadowside St Paul's and replaced the earlier Mariners' Church. It is in full use for Christian worship.

St Peter and Paul Roman Catholic church, Byron Street

Was built in 1928 of red brick, which is unusual for a Scottish church. It could be categorised as Arts and Crafts and is next to a primary school of the same name.

St Peter's Free church, St Peter's Street

Built in 1836, this is a Free Kirk church with an impressive spire, designed and constructed in 1836 by David Hean & Sons. It was originally conceived as a chapel-of-ease and is next to a small graveyard.

St Peter's Street
Takes its name from the church that stands in the street.

St Ronan's Avenue
Celebrates the novel by Sir Walter Scott, *St Ronan's Well*. St Ronan's Well, in the Borders village of Innerleithen, is noted for its healthy mineral content. Ronan is said to have driven the devil out of the Leithen valley by thumping him with his staff whereupon Ronan blessed the natural spring of Dow well, now known by his name.

St Roque's Lane
A lane near where St Roque's chapel once stood. St Roque, or Roch, was the patron saint of plague victims, with infected people isolated outside the East Port in case they infected the healthy within the town. The area was known as Sick Men's Yards, with the dead buried at Roodyards cemetery. The name St Roque's was used for a garage, a library and a mill, all sadly gone.

At the corner of St Roque's Lane and King Street there is a blue plaque dedicated to Ethel Moorhead, a suffragette and painter. There are twenty-five of these plaques throughout the city, each one highlighting the career of a prominent woman from Dundee. Moorhead was known as the most talented female artist in Dundee and worked at the now vanished King Street arcade. She was also a suffragette who smashed windows and attempted arson attacks.

St Peter's Free church

St Roque's Lane

St Roque's library, Blackscroft

Reading Room, former St Roque's Library

Was a Carnegie library and is currently (2016) a nightclub, known as the Reading Room. Created by James Thomson in 1910 in an Italianate style, it was an attempt to give some sophistication to what was then known as a 'sordid district'. The single-storey building was an oasis in this part of Dundee, with a Mediterranean terrace, garden, sundial and fountain.

St Roque's Place, Broughty Ferry

Takes its name from the saint who cared for plague victims.

St Salvador's church, Hilltown

An Arts and Crafts-style, Episcopalian church of 1868, built to bring hope and colour to the millworkers of Hilltown. Bishop Forbes of Brechin was the man who instigated the church, which interior is a riot of colour and the Christian welcome is genuine. George Frederick Bodley (1827–1907) was the architect and the brother-in-law of Sir George Gilbert Scott.

St Salvador Street, Hilltown

Was named after the church in the street.

St Stephen's church, Broughty Ferry

Was built in 1871 to a traditional cruciform design. The architect, Thomas Robertson (1835–1923), was a founding member of the church while the Morris & Co. stained-glass windows are a joy to behold.

St Vincent Street, Broughty Ferry
Commemorates John Jervis, Earl of St Vincent (1735–1823), a British admiral who gained his title after defeating the Spanish at the battle of St Vincent in February 1797.

Sandeman Street
Frank Stewart Sandeman (died 1898) was another nineteenth-century industrialist who brought jobs to the city. He was a jute magnate who, in 1874, founded the highly successful Manhattan Works in Dundonald Street. Sandeman was a focused businessman who concentrated on New York state, hence the name of his works. Sandeman Street is his memorial.

Sandy Loan, Broughty Ferry
This name was chosen by residents of the Ferry in 2013 and confirmed in 2014. The new road was built beside Churchill Place and other suggestions included a further use of the name Churchill or a mention of Agnes Forbes Blackadder, a local surgeon. The local area was known as Sandy Hole, which was perhaps not appropriate as a street name.

Scotscraig Lane, Ardler
One of many streets in the area named after a famous golf course; Scotscraig is near St Andrews and is a qualifying course for the Open.

Scotscraig Place, Barnhill
The streets in this part of Barnhill were named after places in Fife. Scotscraig is a golf course near St Andrews.

Scott Court
In common with other streets in the vicinity named after a literary figure, in this case Sir Walter Scott.

Scott Street
Was part of the Balgay estate, which was owned by the Scott family. The street was laid out in the 1860s, when Harry Scott was the proprietor, and he also named it, presumably after his father, William Scott.

Scouringburn
Was a highly industrialised area in the west of Dundee. The name comes from the burn that ran here and is now culverted under Brook Street. This burn, a major source for the water-powered mills of the town, flowed through the Pleasance and past Dudhope until it was dammed in the Meadows and altered course to gush under Murraygait and Seagait.

Scrymgeour Building, University of Dundee

Scrymgeour building, Park Place, University of Dundee

When this building was opened in 1911 it was a teacher's training college. It is an impressive length of red sandstone and was given its present name in 1979 to honour Dundee man Henry Scrymgeour (1506–72), professor of law at Geneva. Not surprisingly it now houses the law department of the university, which teaches both Scottish and English law and has frequently been named as the best law school in Scotland and one of the best in Britain. College hall, inside, has some scintillating stained-glass windows. The building also houses the school of psychology.

Seabourne Gardens, Broughty Ferry

The street was built where the gardens of Seabourne house used to be. The house was owned by John Brown, a Montrose shipbuilder.

Seabraes

Seabraes

The name says it all. This very pleasant area is set on the top of a brae and overlooks the river Tay. Situated directly opposite the University of Dundee, this oasis has flower beds and a grassed area plus a number of seats that look both toward the university and over the Tay. It is very popular with students temporarily escaping their studies as well as with passers-by. There are also examples of Dundee's ubiquitous public art here, with a number of lemmings creeping around to the fascination of visitors.

Sea captain's house, 48 St Andrews Lane

Sea Captain's House, St Andrew's Lane

The first building restored by the Dundee Building Preservation Trust, now the Tayside Building Preservation Trust. It was built around 1770 and may have been owned by a seaman named Captain Rattray, who operated three vessels in the Baltic trade.

Seafield Close/Lane/Road, between Roseangle and Perth Road
The name says it all, 'the field beside the sea', when this area was a rural or semi-rural suburb of Dundee. It is named after the mansion and lands of Seafield that stood here.

Seafield works, Magdalene Yard
Built in 1861, this mill – a prominent building – was owned by the firm of Sanderson, Thomson, Shepherd.

Seagate

Seagate

An ancient street with roots that stretch back to the eleventh century, Seagate was originally St Mary's gait. The present name is a clue: the eastern end of the Seagate ran parallel to the Firth of Tay; hence the 'sea' part of the name, while gate, or gait, indicates this was a road. At one time the west end of the Seagate was closed by the castle and the east end by the Seagait port, roughly where Sugarhouse Wynd is.

It was a rich thoroughfare then, with the local gentry inhabiting town houses along its length until industrialisation choked the town centre with noise, smoke, traffic and noxious smells from the nearby whale-boiling yards. Near here Grisel Jaffray, Dundee's most famous witch, was burned.

Despite its name, the Seagate is no longer at the sea. So much land has been reclaimed that the coast is a fair step to the north. There have been some interesting people born here, with a plaque marking the birthplace of Sarah Weideman, mother of Robert Browning. George Mealmaker (1768–1808) was also born in this street. He was a weaver and a radical who supported the French Revolution and in 1793 produced a broadsheet that denounced the 'despotism and tyranny' of the British government. He was secretary of the Dundee Friends of Liberty and tried to persuade people not to join the militia. He also wrote the constitution for the United Scotsmen, which had such seditious aims as annual parliaments and universal suffrage. He was arrested in 1798 and, after a mockery of a trial, transported for fourteen years. Mealmaker died in 1808.

Seagate no. 2 warehouse

A bonded warehouse of 1868 but to appreciate it properly it is necessary to leave the Seagate and walk up Candle Lane, where the true façade of the building faces.

Seaman's Chapel, 15 Candle Lane

Built in 1881 at the same time as the neighbouring sailors' home, the chapel is at present (2016) roofless but the Tayside Building Preservation Trust hopes to take responsibility. The combination of home and chapel is the best surviving grouping of its kind in Scotland. Such buildings were erected across the country in the nineteenth century in an attempt to help the physical and spiritual welfare of seamen, often a neglected class of men.

David MacLaren was the architect, which hints at the Arts and Craft style.

Seaplanes

Dundee was a seaplane base in the First World War and again from 1941 until June 1944. The base was named HMS *Condor* and was sited at Stannergate. The first flight, in February 1914, nearly ended in disaster when the aircraft narrowly missed a barge on landing and there was another incident when a Tay gale sunk the rescue launch in the Fish Dock. Nevertheless, operations continued and during the First World War aircraft from Dundee were used on convoy escort and anti-submarine patrols. Squadron commander Christopher Draper seemed to be quite a character as he flew under the Tay bridge on a regular basis and challenged his pilots to do the same.

Despite the wartime exploits, the area's greatest fame came on 6 October 1938 when a flying boat, *Maia*, took off from the Tay, carrying a Mercury seaplane piggyback style. However, the two aircraft only remained together for a few miles before the Mercury – under an Australian, Captain Donald Bennett – roared southward toward Africa. Bennett's flight to the river Orange in South Africa was a seaplane record flight of 6,045 miles. In 2008 a stamp was issued to commemorate the flight and there was a ceremony in City Square. There is also a small plaque near the present Tay road bridge mentioning the event.

Selkirk Gardens

In common with many streets in this area, the name has no local connection but refers to the town of Selkirk in the Scottish Borders. A royal burgh since the thirteenth century, Selkirk has many connections with the great and good of Scottish history: William Wallace was appointed overlord of Scotland in the town's Forest kirk; Sir Walter Scott was sheriff of Selkirk for thirty-three years; and Mungo Park, the great explorer of Africa, was born four miles away, in Foulshiels.

Sensation, Dundee Science Centre, Greenmarket

Sensation, Greenmarket

This spectacular, wedge-shaped building houses scores of interactive exhibits designed to establish the visitor's understanding of the importance of the senses. It also houses touring exhibitions that appeal to adults and children alike.

Session Street

In the 1670s Gilbert Guthrie ordered that ten acres of his lands in the western side – westfield – of Dundee be mortified (bequeathed in perpetuity) to the church to enable a number of poor boys to be educated. That situation continued for the best part of a century but in the 1760s the town council attempted to take over the Guthrie lands. Revd Dr James Blinshall, minister of St Paul's, led the kirk session in a campaign against the council's proposal, a protest that was ultimately successful. Three streets were named in honour of the campaign: Blinshall Street, Guthrie Street and Session Street.

Seven arches viaduct

North of Dundee, this viaduct carried the railway between Dundee and Forfar from its opening in 1870 until the closure of the line in the 1960s. In common with most pieces of Victorian railway engineering it is solid, impressive and enduring.

Seymour lodge, 259 Perth Road

Built in 1880 this six-bedroom mansion is now A-listed. At one time it was a private school for girls and there is still an old-girls' association. It was later utilised as child-protection unit until a new facility, Seymour house, opened in 2010.

Shelley Gardens

Like other streets in this area, named after a poet, in this case Percy Bysshe Shelley, one of the leading exponents of the Romantic school.

Shepherd's Loan, off Roseangle

A reminder that this area was rural before Dundee expanded westwards.

Sherbrook Street

A tribute to Robert Lowe, Viscount Sherbrooke (*sic*) (1811–92), a prominent Victorian politician. He was a Liberal who became chancellor of the exchequer and home secretary during the premierships of William Ewart Gladstone.

Sheriff Court, West Bell Street

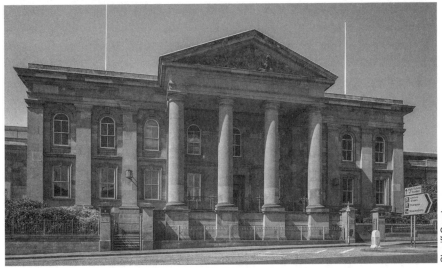

Sheriff Court

Designed by George Angus in 1833, and altered by William Scott in 1863, this is a neoclassical building with an interesting square courtroom. It was renovated in 1996 and the Princess Royal formally reopened it the following year.

Shiell Court/Street, Broughty Ferry

Remembers John Shiell who was a solicitor and the factor of the Earl of Dalhousie.

Shore Terrace, at City Square

Although this street is now a long way from the sea, this was the original shore line before land reclamation pushed Dundee further south into the Tay.

Shrubbery, the, 67 Magdalen Yard Road

David Neave designed this lovely B-listed villa, which has an ionic doorway. It was built in 1817.

Sidlaw Avenue

The Sidlaw hills shelter Dundee from the worst of the northern winds. They also offer some delightful low-level walking, folklore, history and views that stretch from Fife as far as Schiehallion and far out to sea.

Sinderins

Sinderins

From the old Scots word *sundering*, meaning the separation of the roads. The Sinderins is where Hawkhill merges with Perth Road and Blackness Avenue. It is an evocative name for a busy junction with the shops of Perth Road leading to the centre of town in one direction and out to Perth in the other, and Hawkhill, 'the Hawkie', leading back to Dundee. At one time this area had the alternative name of 'Blacknessgate', although this seems to have vanished from the collective memory and certainly from popular usage.

Sir James Black centre, University of Dundee

Opened in 2006 this £20 million centre promotes interdisciplinary research in life sciences. Brian Cox, the then rector of the University and a diabetes sufferer, supported the opening of this building that is connected to the Wellcome centre. Around 250 scientists work here, including Professor Sir Philip Cohen, as they research into cancer, tropical diseases and diabetes. This establishment is Scotland's first Cancer UK research centre.

Slessor Gardens

With the redevelopment of Dundee's waterfront there are new streets being formed. There was a request to the public for suggestions for names and five hundred were handed in, from which the best suggestions were chosen. The alterations will create a public space with show gardens behind Caird hall, which will be known as Slessor Gardens, after Dundee mill girl Mary Slessor, who became a missionary in West Africa.

Small Copper Court

Named after the fast-flying butterfly, which has bright copper forewings.

Small Meadow Court

Takes its name from the meadow brown butterfly, which is sensible enough to feed on ripe brambles.

Soapwork Lane

Joseph Sanderson established a soap-making workshop here at the beginning of the nineteenth century, which was continued by his widow, Elizabeth Smith, and their sons.

Somerville Place

Commemorates Margaret Somerville, the wife of Charles Carmichael, co-founder of James Carmichael & Co. in 1810. Margaret Somerville was born in Lasswade, Midlothian and bore nine children. Her husband's firm built the steam engine for the Newport ferry, *George IV*, as well as the first two engines for the Newtyle railway, *Earl of Airlie* and *Lord Wharncliffe*. Carmichael & Co. was one of the first locomotive manufacturers in Scotland and James Carmichael also invented the fan blast. The street was built in 1830 and has a row of delightful regency villas.

South Baffin Street

Has a plaque: 'On this site stood the cottage (mentioned in *Frankenstein*) visited by Mary Wollstonecraft Godwin 1812–1814.' The street name is a reminder of the long-gone Dundee Arctic whaling industry, when ships sailed to Baffin Bay to hunt for whales and seals.

South mills, Brown Street

Now residential flats, this mill was built in the 1860s and boasts a fine cornice and a courtyard. Founded by J. & W. Brown and expanded by his son-in-law, O. G. Miller.

South Road park

Located on the slope between Menzieshill and Charleston, and on the level ridge beyond, this long park includes football pitches and allotments with a bowling green, allotments and a games area. It is a pleasant place to walk and for children to play. The Lynch sports centre is close by, as are a couple of supermarkets.

South Tay Street

South Tay Street

An elegant street – a mixture of residential and office use – with many fine buildings. The street was originally designed (1792) to pass through the then Dundee hospital grounds, thus enabling easier access between the Nethergate and the Hawkhill. Few of the original buildings survive, but those on the east side were designed by David Neave (1773–1841), who moved into one of his own houses.

Soutterain, Tealing north of Dundee

A souterrain is an underground earth house; this one is some eighty feet in length and dates from the Iron Age. Perhaps structures like this led to stories about dwarves and fairies living under the ground.

Space, the

A custom-built facility for the Scottish School of Contemporary Dance, located at Kingsway campus, Dundee and Angus college. Opened by the Queen in 2003. It has seen top-quality companies performing as well as college students learning dance skills.

The Space, Kingsway campus, Dundee and Angus College

Speckled Wood Court

In common with other courts in this area, was named after a butterfly, or moth, in this case the Speckled Wood butterfly that lives in wooded areas.

Spence Gardens/Lane/Place, Broughty Ferry

Commemorates Andrew Spence (1774–1859), a builder and wood merchant. He was active in local affairs and hoped for a better harbour for Broughty Ferry.

Spey Drive, Menzieshill

Named after the river Spey, one of the finest fishing rivers in Scotland, which flows through the Highlands and Moray.

Springfield

A lovely street beside the University of Dundee. The name means 'field of the water source' and the 1821 map of Dundee has a small estate named Springfield from which this street was named. According to Charles McKean, nos. 2–32 Springfield make up Dundee's finest regency development and these houses, a stone's throw from Perth Road, are complete with Greek Doric porches to make them like miniature mansion houses.

The Canadian politician, William Lyon Mackenzie (1795–1861), was born in Springfield and is commemorated by a stained-glass window in nearby St Mark's church. After emigrating in 1820, Mackenzie became a radical campaigning journalist, fiercely critical of the colonial regime, and a powerful advocate of American-style democracy for Canada. When the party he supported, the

Reformers, won control of the newly created Toronto city council in 1834, he became its first mayor and was also a member of the provincial parliament. However, his popularity did not endure, and, by 1837, he was out of office. Mackenzie, a fiery character, promptly launched an armed revolt, which he was sure would attract popular support, but his indisclipined and poorly organised rebellion was easily quelled by the authorities. Although he ultimately failed in his objectives, he is remembered as a principled champion of democracy and is part of the well-established Dundee tradition of radicalism.

Springhill

In the early 1860s, the proprietor closed this road with a chain. The rights-of-way society investigated and discovered that the public had used the road for more than forty years and thus it was free for public access.

Today there is no dispute. There is a group of 1930s flat-roofed houses that enjoy an enviable location as they face the Firth of Tay. Strangely, there is also a Springhill mall in West Dundee in Illinois: an interesting transatlantic coincidence – or an exiled Dundonian pining for home?

Sri Guru Nanak Sikh Temple, Nelson Street

The main temple for Sikhs in north-east Scotland. The Sikhs are a vibrant community, originally from Punjab. Sikhism was founded in the sixteenth century and is a religion that believes in working hard and treating everybody equally, while helping the less fortunate.

Stannergate Road

The name extends back at least to the fifteenth century, while the street extends from the docks to West Ferry. A. H. Miller suggests it could be from stanner, or 'stoney gait'. The name would be more logical without the suffix, for as gait means road, Stannergate Road means Stanner-road Road. According to David Dorward, *stanner* is the Scots for shingle and suggested it was where people collected shingle for building.

In 1878 workmen dug up stone coffins that were around two thousand years old and also found kitchen middens that were dated to around 6,000 BC, which would make Stannergate the site of one of the earliest settlements in Scotland. Dundee is indeed a city of many discoveries.

Step Row, Roseangle

Has a fine Scottish Special Housing Association development of harled and pantiled houses. William McGonagall lived at no. 48, from which property he was evicted in October 1894.

Step Row

Stevenson Street, Lochee

Another street named after a prominent manufacturer, Perthshire-born George Stevenson, who founded the firm of George Stevenson & Sons at the Ancrum carpet works. The firm held an annual festival in the Lochee UP church hall for hundreds of its workers, while George Stevenson became a bailie in 1900.

Stewart Street, Broughty Ferry

Remembers the seed merchant John Stewart of Forthill, Camperdown and Seafield nurseries.

Stirling Street

Has nothing to do with Stirling. The name came from Skirling's Park, being the property of Bailie Alexander Skirling as far back as the fourteenth century. The street ran through Skirling's lands. The word 'bailie' is an interesting one. In his learned book on Scots law Erskine defines it thus: 'Where lands, not erected into a regality, fell into the king's hands, he appointed a bailie over them, whose jurisdiction was equal to that of a sheriff'. Another definition holds that a bailie was a Scottish municipal officer equivalent to an English alderman and, in fact, some local-authority councillors in Scottish cities are still described as bailies, although it is now a courtesy title. The word itself appears to have its roots in the old French word, bailli, or perhaps the Middle English word, baillie.

Stobsmuir park

Stobsmuir (Swannie) Ponds

Contains ponds that are also known as Swannie ponds because swans are often resident here. These ponds also acted as the water supply for Dundee before a much improved service was introduced. The park is a popular recreational area.

Stobsmuir Road

At one time this area was well outside the town boundary. The name *muir* is self-explanatory – moor – while 'stob' may come from the old name for a wooden cross, a stob cross or a post. This was the site of an annual fair that became notorious for drunken violence and pocket picking. In 1809 it was the scene of a full-scale battle between soldiers and local men, which saw one killed and others badly hurt. In 1824 there was another murder when a mob attacked a group of masons. Not long after, and partly because of the unrest, the fair left Stobs Muir for Fair Muir.

Stobswell Road

Stobswell was once a small village outside Dundee. Stob means 'a post' and the well here served the nearby farms of Maryfield and Janefield. Stobswell school alumnus Peter Lorimer was one of the greatest players Scotland ever produced. He made 676 appearances for Leeds United during that club's golden age, winning many honours, including two league titles, and scoring 238 goals in the process, an incredible tally for a winger. Lorimer represented Scotland twenty-one times and played in the 1974 World Cup finals in West Germany, putting in a man-of-the-match performance against then world champions

Brazil. It is said that Peter Lorimer had the hardest shot in football – earning him nicknames such as Lash and Hotshot – with one of his penalties recorded at over a hundred miles per hour. Clearly, he got a good grounding at Stobswell, where he scored 176 goals for the school team in a single season.

Stracathro Terrace, Broughty Ferry

The council chose this name possibly because Stracathro is geographically close to Edzell, which was the name of an existing nearby street. Stracathro is a historically important place, the site of a Roman camp, and in 1130 was the scene of a battle when a royal army defeated a force from Moray.

Strathaven Terrace

In common with most street names in the area, Strathaven has no local connection. It refers to the Lanarkshire town of the same name.

Strathdee Terrace, Broughty Ferry

Near a street named Strathearn so it was named with a *strath* prefix for the sake of continuity or to create a sense of local identity.

Strathern Road, Broughty Ferry

The paving committee named this street in 1885, either after the strath itself or in honour of Prince Arthur, Duke of Connaught and Strathearn, or the equally noble Edward Duke of Kent and Strathearn.

Strathmartine Road

Strath is Gaelic for a broad valley and Martine relates to the personal name, Martin. The standing stone called Martin's Stone beside Balkello farm has a carving of a man and a snake, so naturally a legend grew that Martin killed a dragon – there is a Baldragon close by. Did Martin's name spread until the whole strath was named after him? The old name was Strathdighty which makes more sense – the 'strath of the Dighty water'. The road leads from Hilltown to the Sidlaw hills and passes through what were once the lands of the Earls of Strathmartine, who had a town house in the centre of Dundee. At one time the whaling master, Harry McKay, lived in this street; he was the man who rescued Commander Scott of *Discovery*.

Strathmore Avenue

Is a mid-1920s housing development. The name Strathmore refers to the wide strath – or wide valley – that covers much of Angus and part of Perthshire.

Strathmore Place/Street, Broughty Ferry
Takes its name from the strath that crosses Angus and east Perthshire.

Strawberry Bank, Perth Road
A reminder of the market garden that was situated here when the area was on the outskirts of Dundee.

Strome Terrace, Broughty Ferry
A street within a 1960s housing scheme. All the streets are named after places in the Highlands.

Submarines
There had been a submarine base in Dundee during the Edwardian period but in 1912 the vessels were relocated to Rosyth. In the autumn of 1939 the 2nd submarine flotilla moved to Dundee, later joined by the 9th submarine flotilla. Unlike other units, the 9th was composed of submariners of different nationalities, including French, Norwegians, Poles and Dutch. For a time in 1944 there was also a Russian contingent based in Dundee. The depot was known as HMS *Ambrose*.

Under Captain James Roper, Dundee-based submarines were engaged in patrol activity along the coast of Nazi-occupied Europe and attacked the German naval vessels *Prinz Eugen* (HMS *Trident* damaged her stern) and *Gneiseneu*. HMS *Venturer* made history by sinking a German submarine while both were submerged, a feat that has never been repeated. Dundee-based submarines helped escort allied convoys, attacked enemy shipping and landed agents in occupied

Sugarhouse Wynd

Europe. Indeed, they caused so much damage to German shipping off Norway that the German garrison in the north of that country had to be withdrawn due to lack of supplies. One of the submarines, the Free French *Rubis*, was one of the Allies' crack vessels with thirty-one confirmed kills. On the other side, six submarines from Dundee were lost.

There is a memorial between Victoria and Camperdown docks to the men who did not return.

Sugarhouse Wynd, Seagate
In the eighteenth century Britain owned a number of West Indian

islands whose main crop was sugar cane. Much of the sugar came into Scotland to be processed. Although the Clyde was the main artery for imports, Dundee also got involved and in 1766 the town imported a sugar master from London to set the business up.

From around 1770 a Mr Wiedemann from the Netherlands was the manager of Dundee's sugar house in this area. His son became a Dundee shipowner. His daughter Sarah married a London man named Robert Browning and their son was the famous poet of that name. Competition from Greenock forced the sugar factory to close in the 1820s.

Previous to the sugarhouse, this wynd was Fintry's Wynd, and, before that, Our Lady's Wynd.

Sunadale Court
Sunadale is a tiny settlement on the east coast of Kintyre, opposite the island of Arran.

Swallowtail Court
Was named after the largest butterfly in the United Kingdom. All the courts in this area are named after butterflies or moths.

Sycamore Place
Is in the successful post-First World War Logie scheme. All the street names have a garden-city theme.

Symers Street, Downfield
Commemorates Helen Haliburton Symers, one of those people who dedicated her life to helping others. Her father was John Symers, agent of the British Linen Company bank. She contributed to many charities, including the infirmary and the industrial school. She was also president of the Dundee Ladies' Union, treasurer of the Female Society for Visiting and Relieving Aged Females in Distress and was in the Industrial Schools Society and aided the Home for the Reformation of Females, among others. As if that was not enough, she also donated the site of Arthurstone library to the city. Designed by William Alexander and completed in 1905 (by James Thomson, after the death of Alexander in 1904), the library is described as being in the Scots Jacobean Renaissance style in polished red sandstone ashlar and it is without doubt an impressive edifice. Interestingly, Andrew Carnegie – the Scottish-American steel magnate and perhaps the most famous philanthropist in history – paid for the construction of the library building. Little wonder that Helen Symers was made an honorary burgess of Dundee in 1899.

Synagogue, 9 St Mary's Place

Synagogue, St Mary's Place

Ian Imlach designed this synagogue, which opened in 1978. The first known Jews in Dundee arrived from Europe as representatives of Hamburg textile firms in the 1840s. Many became agents and merchants with their own companies, and in 1878 they opened the first Dundee synagogue. From the 1880s persecution in Eastern Europe forced many Jews to flee to Britain, with some settling in Dundee. These impoverished refugees were different from the earlier German Jews, who had assimilated without difficulty and were generally middle class. The later arrivals gave Dundee the third largest Jewish community in Scotland, but they spoke only Yiddish, making it harder or them to fit in. Many settled in the Hilltown and ran pawn shops, lodging houses or market stalls. Although there was no animosity between Jews and locals, rival Jewish factions occasionally fell out.

The present Jewish community is not as large as it once was. However, Dundee's synagogue has survived and continues to maintain a very welcome Jewish presence in the city.

Tannadice Park

Home to Dundee United FC. The name comes from William Neish of Tannadice, who bought the Clepington estate in the early 1850s.

Founded in 1909, Dundee United was originally Dundee Hibernian and was associated with Dundee's substantial Irish community. The team moved into Clepington park at the expense of Dundee Wanderers, who had played there, altered the name to Tannadice and forged one of the most important clubs in Scotland. In 1923 they toyed with the idea of Dundee City before adopting the suffix United.

The best period for United to date was under the reign of Jim McLean in the

1970s and 1980s when, together with Aberdeen, they became one half of the New Firm, challenging Celtic and Rangers for dominance of Scottish football. The pinnacle was season 1982/83, when, for the first time, McLean's team became champions of Scotland. United also built a considerable reputation in Europe. In 1984 the team progressed to the semi-final of the European Cup, losing 3–2 on aggregate to Italian giants Roma. Three years later, in 1987, McLean's men went one better, reaching the final of the UEFA Cup, in which they played Gothenburg home and away, but lost narrowly by an aggregate score of 2–1.

Incidentally, by reaching the European Cup semi-final in 1984 United set the seal on yet another Dundonian triumph. It was only the second time in the history of British football that two clubs from the same city had reached that stage of the elite tournament (Glasgow being the first). Dundee, under manager Bob Shankly, had achieved the feat in season 1962/63, advancing to the last four and meeting one of the biggest clubs in world football, AC Milan.

The club can also boast a notable showbusiness triumph: the captain of the 1930s team, Neil Paterson, later won an Academy Award for his screenplay of the novel *Room at the Top*. No other football club can match having a club captain who was also an Oscar winner.

Tannadice Street
Takes its name from the landowner, William Neish of Tannadice and Easter Clepington, the son of a Dundee merchant.

Tay

Tay Rail Bridge and river Tay from the Law

Rivers tend to keep their names even when the human population that surrounds them changes. At 119 miles the Tay is the longest river in Scotland. It rises on Ben Lui in central Perthshire, and the name is so old that people cannot identify the language except to claim it is pre-Celtic, meaning it probably predates even the Picts. Ptolemy calls it Tawa and in Gaelic it is Tatha. Only one thing is certain: the original name goes back thousands of years.

If it is true to say that Glasgow made the Clyde and the Clyde made Glasgow, then it is equally correct to say that without the Tay there would be no Dundee as we know it.

Trade in various forms from whaling to linen and jute, armies bent on conquest, ferry-loads of visitors and locals, ideas and inspiration all come across or along this ribbon of water with its wondrous, ever-changing light. There was a sea battle fought at the mouth of the Firth in 1332 as Scots tried to repel yet another English invasion and there was triumph in 1490 when Sir Andrew Wood of Largo brought three captured English ships into Dundee.

At any time of day and night, a walk by the Tay is a delight. During summer the sun reflects from the fast-flowing river; in winter the mood can be sombre as the waves break creamy-brown against the retaining walls or the fields of Fife can be frost-white and more attractive than any Christmas card. There may be small craft out on the water, or even a ship sailing to Perth. If the tide is right the sandbanks will be revealed and the lucky observer may spot a seal or two basking there. At night the lights of Newport glisten to the sky and reflect on the dark water, a surreal picture when seen only a few hundred yards from the centre of Scotland's fourth largest city.

At one time there were a dozen salmon nets stretching along the sandbanks, waiting to catch the fish as they swam upstream to spawn or back to the ocean. These salmon were not to be sneezed at: one caught in a stake net at Buddonness, Carnoustie in July 1878 weighed a whopping forty-nine pounds. At that time the wildlife was impressive: contemporary accounts written in the early 1800s tell of 'flocks' of seals that occupied every sandbank from the Sands of Tay to Flisk while pods of grampus and porpoise hunted the salmon. The grampuses appeared in the Firth from July to September, moving upstream with the flow of the tide and withdrawing with the ebb, while porpoise season was April to August. All these fish were hunting the salmon 'like a pack of hounds' as Mr Stuart, the shepherd of Balmerino stated. There were also whaling ships and jute clippers, colliers and coasters, fishing boats and flax carriers . . . and smugglers.

War came to the Tay on more than one occasion. There were French privateers through the various encounters in the eighteenth century and German minefields in the First World War. In December 1939 the Second World War started with a bang as a German U-boat torpedoed two ships in the firth; one vessel was sunk and the other was towed into Dundee. That same month the

RAF shot down a number of German aircraft over the Tay. There were also German mines placed across the entrance of the Firth, which badly damaged the ship *City of Marseilles*.

But these were only incidents in a war that lasted six years. The Tay defences usually proved adequate to discourage German attacks but there were tragedies such as the loss of the Broughty fishing boat *Ben Attow* to a mine off the Isle of May in March 1940.

All in all, the Tay is a wondrous river, used for commerce and pleasure and with a history that stretches as far as time. It may be hard to imagine a time when it was thronged with shipping and the flax ships queued to get into harbour, yet it is still used and still very much a part of Dundee's heritage.

Tay rail bridge disaster memorial

Tay Rail Bridge Disaster Memorial

Near the spot where, on 28 December 1879, the original Tay bridge collapsed, taking a train and all on board into the river below. There were no survivors from seventy-five passengers. There is an identical monument in Wormit on the Fife side of the bridge. Perhaps surprisingly, it took no less than 134 years, until 2013, for the disaster to be commemorated. It is to the great credit of the Tay rail bridge disaster memorial trust, which campaigned effectively for a monument, that those who perished have now been permanently memorialised. The six granite panels – three on either side of the Tay – have been carefully positioned so that they face the spot where the central span of the bridge stood.

Tay mills, originally Tayworks, Marketgait

Tay Mills, Marketgait

This building is now student accommodation but when built it was among the largest textile mills in the country and possessed the longest frontage. The façade, with its arched entrance and carved pediment showing the initials of the Gilroy brothers, emphasises the splendour of the dynasty and the pride of the jute barons at the height of their power.

Although the popular image of the Industrial Revolution is of dark satanic mills, this building and others of its type were the repositories of great civic pride, equal in status to museums and public buildings. It was no wonder that workers boasted of the mills in which they laboured when the quality of this solid building is seen.

Today the Gilroys are little known outside of Dundee but in their prime they were princes of jute with land in India, a shipping line and the palatial mansion of Castleroy in Broughty Ferry. Like so much else, the jute industry slid into terminal decline after the First World War, dry rot destroyed Castleroy and the Gilroys, in common with other Dundee jute barons, bowed out before competition from Calcutta. Only the memory remains; and Tay mills.

Tay rail bridge

The most poignant tragedy in Dundee's history was the collapse of the first Tay bridge, when a passenger train was crossing on the night of 28 December 1879.

When Thomas Bouch's Tay bridge opened in the summer of 1878 it was viewed as one of the most important engineering triumphs of the era. However, a combination of poor design and poor quality materials coincided with a force 10 or 11 storm that terrible December night the following year. Seventy-five people perished when the train fell into the Tay, and, despite a massive search,

Tay Rail Bridge

no survivors were found. The piers that held the old bridge are still visible as a sobering reminder of the disaster, so anyone crossing the second, and much safer, bridge can look down at the Tay and wish their journey across the river was over.

The second and present bridge was designed by William Henry Barlow and built by William Arrol & Co. At 2.75 miles long it opened in 1887 and was improved and strengthened in 2003.

Tay road bridge

Tay Road Bridge from west

Designed by William Fairhurst and opened by the Queen Mother in August 1966, the Tay road bridge is nearly a mile-and-a-half in length, and one of the longest in Europe. On the Dundee side it was built on the site of the Earl Grey dock, the West Graving dock and the King William dock, all famous when Dundee was a major port. The bridge connects Dundee to Fife and the south, replacing the old Fifie ferries that had served the crossing for centuries.

There is also a central walkway that can be used by pedestrians and bicycles, giving a fine easy passage in either direction, if the user does not mind the constant throb of traffic.

Tay Square, off South Tay Street

Tay Square and Dundee Rep

Home to the Dundee Rep and named after the river Tay, the square was designed by Samuel Bell, the burgh architect who created many admirable buildings in late-eighteenth-century Dundee. Intended to be a gracious classical square, it never realised its full potential but is still a handsome area.

At no. 4 there is a blue plaque, one of twenty-five in Dundee that highlight the city's most prominent women. This plaque proclaims that, at this address, Alice Moorhead and Emily Thomson set themselves up as doctors, 2 of only 101 female doctors in the United Kingdom at the time. The pair had been doctors at 93 Nethergate before moving here. Thomson was also Dundee's first female driver and helped found a hospital exclusively for women, while Moorhead was better known for looking after the many impoverished women of the city. She married, moved to Leith and died in childbirth while Thomson worked as a doctor in Windsor Street before retiring to the country.

Taylor's Lane, Perth Road

In the 1850s this street was known for its cheeping shops, or illegal drinking dens.

Tayport

At the very corner of Fife was originally known as Portincraig, which is itself a corruption of *port na creage* or 'port of the rock', or possibly from *partan craig* or 'crab rock'. It has also been known as Ferryport on Craig as it was the home of a ferry to the Dundee side of the Tay. Finally, it could be known as South Ferry: a lot of names for a small village.

At one time there was a castle here, opposite the guardian of the Tay at Broughty, but Tayport also had shipbuilding, a textile industry and a golf course.

Tealing

A small village a few miles north of Dundee. It is notable for the Tealing doocot in the home farm, the souterrain (underground chamber) known as the Tealing earth house and the 1806 parish church and hearse house. St Boniface is credited with the first church here in AD 710, while John Glas of Tealing formed the nonconformist Glasite church.

During the Second World War there was a prisoner-of-war camp here. There was also an aerodrome, where, in May 1942, Vyacheslav Molotov (of Molotov cocktail fame) the Soviet foreign minister, landed on a secret mission to meet Churchill. The upshot was the British–Soviet treaty of May 1942.

Templeton woods

Templeton Woods

An area of beautiful, wooded, public land on the northwest outskirts of the city. There are walks and trails, small ponds, wildlife and peace, while the ranger centre is worthy of a visit.

Tentsmuir Place, Barnhill

The streets in this part of Barnhill were named after places in Fife. Tentsmuir is a large wooded area just north of St Andrews.

The Aspens

This area of Whitfield consists of a number of streets prefaced by 'the' and containing the name of a tree. As well as Aspens, the streets are named: The Beeches, The Cedars, The Hawthorns, The Larches, The Oaks, The Maples, The Pines and The Spruces.

The Crescent, Whitfield

The Crescent, Whitfield

Received a commendation at the Scottish Awards for Quality in Planning in 2014, as well as the Campbell Christie Public Sevice Reform Award and the Dundee Civic Trust Award. The Crescent is just what it says; a crescent-shaped building that includes community health and social-care services with shops, the very welcoming Whitfield community library and a café. It is a double-fronted building of two storeys with a friendly central foyer and is linked to Ballumbie primary school by a plaza that includes seating, landscaping and public artwork.

The Pillars

The affectionate name that Dundonians gave to their old town house and jail, which was completed in 1734. Designed by the eminent architect, William Adam (1689–1748), the Pillars was multi-functional, with cells in the attics and rooms for the town council, the guildry and the magistracy on the first floor. The ground floor had retail space and also the town guard. Unusually, the town house faced both ways, towards the town and towards the docks, showing the Janus approach of Dundee where shipping was essential for the wealth of the burgh.

In February 1834 there were one hundred prisoners held in Dundee, most in the town house and others in the old steeple. That contrasted with a period in 1808 when there was not a single person in jail, but crime rose from the time of the end of the French War in 1815, presumably with unemployment. The town house was demolished in 1932 to make way for Caird hall. A commemorative paving stone in City Square marks its site, and there is a pub named The Pillars in Crichton Street, with a model of the town house above the door. In such diverse ways does Dundee remember her past.

Thirlestane Place

In common with other streets in the area, there is no local connection. Thirlestane is a castle in the Scottish Borders.

Thistle hall, 11–19 Union Street

Thistle Hall, Union Street

Little remains of what must have been an impressive building, but there are still fine Venetian windows and Ionic pilasters to admire. This hall was owned by the Thistle Operative Lodge of Masons, hence the name, and was used as assembly rooms. David Neave, town architect, was the designer and it opened in 1828.

The Thistle hall was the venue for a variety of meetings, including political groups such as the gathering in January 1844 that advocated universal suffrage. Four years later the Chartists met here at a time of great political upheaval across Europe.

On the site of the hall there is a blue plaque, one of twenty-five throughout the city. Each plaque highlights the achievements of a prominent Dundee woman, or in this case a group of women. In the nineteenth century one of the largest fields of employment for women was in domestic service, where hours were long and wages low. The servants met in the Thistle hall to try and form a trade union to fight for better conditions. That simple meeting sounds like a very poor excuse for a blue plaque, but if the servants had been caught it would have resulted in instant dismissal.

Some gatherings were ethnographical, such as that in February 1845, when a party of what were termed Iowa Indians was presented to an interested audience. Others were botanical, as the Dundee Floral and Horticulture Society also used the hall.

Thomas Maclagan Way

A stone's throw from Ninewells hospital, it commemorates the pioneering physician and medical researcher, Thomas John Maclagan (1838–1903). The scion of a well-known Perthshire family, his father had managed slave plantations in Jamaica before returning to Scotland. Thomas Maclagan was superintendent of Dundee Royal Infirmary from 1864 to 1866, when Dundee was hit by a succession of fevers including typhus. He was also involved in the development of thermometers and the use of salicin, which, after being synthesised, is the major active substance in aspirin.

Thomas Wise Place

At the entrance to Ninewells hospital, this street was named after Thomas Alexander Wise (1801–89), a Scottish surgeon of the Bengal medical service, who wrote many medical books, including *Commentary on the Hindu System of Medicine* and *The History of Medicine*. He also wrote *History of Paganism in Caledonia*.

Thomson Park

The home of Lochee United, a football club in the Junior leagues. Known as the Bluebells, the club was established in 1892 but did not move into its present home at Thomson Park until 1959. They had success during the 1960s, 70s and 80s and at the time of writing (2016) are performing well in the East Region Superleague.

Thornbank Court/Park/Terrace

Takes its name from the mansion of Thornbank that stood here and which was sold to the council in 1894 for £5,000. The name Thornbank indicates that the surrounding landscape sloped and was infested with thorny vegetation.

Thorter Row

This name was known as far back as the fifteenth century. One theory suggests that it is a corruption of the nautical term 'athwart', as the street ran at more or less right angles to the main streets. The *Concise Scots Dictionary* gives the term Thorter as 'cross the path of' or 'do something in a direction at right angles to what one has done before'. Thorter Row sits in the regenerated Waterfront area of Dundee, overlooking the Tay.

Timex Brae

This steep street led to the Timex factory in Harrison Road. The company came to Dundee in 1946 after the Second World War, beginning with eleven people in a makeshift factory that had been a farm. As Timex expanded it became as much a part of Dundee as the jute mills had once been, with entire families employed and social events geared around the works. At its peak in the 1970s Timex employed up to seven thousand people, a large proportion of them female.

However, by the 1980s the company faced competition from the Far East and had to reduce the workforce. In 1993 Timex announced that it would pay off 110 workers, a move that was resisted by the union. Timex responded by sacking 243 workers who gone on strike and hired others at lower wages. The union reacted with a 92 per cent vote for strike action. The workers offered to return but were told there would still be a 10 per cent reduction in staff; they refused the terms and the management locked them out and bussed strikebreakers through picket lines.

The strikers, naturally bitter about losing their jobs, surrounded the buses chanting 'scab, scab' as the strike breakers tried to hide their identities. Known activists came in to support the strike and on 17 May 1993 there were thirty-three arrests in what was termed the worst picket-line violence since the miners' strike. The dispute continued until August that year when the factory closed and the company left Dundee.

Tircarra Gardens/Place, Broughty Ferry

Built on the site of the mansion of Tircarra. This was the home of export merchant John George Zoller who came from Frankfurt to Dundee to work in the linen trade. Mrs Zoller gave to charity, including to the Dundee convalescent home. In June 1897, Tircarra house, with its ten bedrooms and two public rooms, was put up for sale at £2,200.

Tofthill, Lochee

The name is shared with a farm north of Errol. It is possible that people from that area moved into Lochee for work.

Tom Johnston Road

Tom Johnston (1881–1965) was a prominent Scottish Labour politician. Kirkintilloch-born, he was involved in the socialist journal, *Forward*, was a prominent member of the group known as the Red Clydesiders while his 1909 book *Our Scots Noble Families* is distinctly anti-establishment. In 1922 he became MP for Stirling, the first of many stints as an MP. In 1939 he became Scotland's regional commissioner for civil defence, and two years later he was secretary of state for Scotland. Johnston was involved in the St Kilda evacuation and after his retirement from politics was chairman of the North of Scotland Hydro-Electric Board.

Tower Building, University of Dundee

Tower building, University of Dundee

Opened in 1956, this is the administration centre of the university and nerve centre of the entire complex. The building has lecture theatres, a café, classrooms, exhibitions, archives and the headquarters of the schools of humanities and school of the environment.

Trades hall

Samuel Bell designed the Trades hall, which stood at the joining of Murraygate and Seagate. It was an iconic building with a pedimented façade and was topped by a cupola. Inside was the hall, 15 metres by 10, and a separate chamber for each of Dundee's nine trades, while income from shops on the ground floor helped pay for running costs.

St Andrew's, or the Trades Kirk

Trades Lane

Was named 'the most important thoroughfare of the town' in a meeting of the paving committee in December 1844. It was originally known as St Andrews Street as it led from the Shore to St Andrew's kirk, which was also known as Trades kirk. A meeting of the harbour trustees renamed the street Trades Lane in January 1844.

Traill Street, Broughty Ferry

Commemorates Captain Anthony Trail, shipping master with the Board of Trade. Captain Trail was the son of the Revd Dr Trail of Panbride, and was at sea for most of his life. He was a midshipman on the East Indiaman *Kent* when she was burned in the Bay of Biscay in 1825, during which event he commanded one of the lifeboats that carried passengers from the blazing vessel. The episode was painted by William Daniell and commemorated by none other than William McGonagall:

> *Good people of high and low degree,*
> *I pray ye all to list to me,*
> *And I'll relate a harrowing tale of the sea*
> *Concerning the burning of the ship 'Kent' in the Bay of Biscay,*
> *Which is the most appalling tale of the present century.*

Captain Trail died at his home of Seafield, Broughty Ferry in December 1878.

For many years the street had two signs, on opposite sides of the road, one of which spelled it as Trail and the other as Traill. Dundee city archives has explained that Broughty Ferry council mis-spelled it with two 'l's, after which date the twin 'l's remained.

Tranent Gardens/Grove

The name has no local connection but refers to a town in East Lothian.

Traquair Gardens

In common with many streets in this area, the name of this street has no local connection but refers to a village in the Borders. Traquair is an ancient name and the village is home to Traquair castle, one of the oldest inhabited castles in Scotland.

Trinity House, 14 Yeaman Shore

Home to the Fraternity of Seamen, one of Dundee's Nine Trades. The name 'trinity' is a corruption of the word ending of fra-*ternity*. The fraternity is a benefit society for seamen to guard their rights and pay a small amount to widows in case of death. Trinity house was also known as the sailor's hall and opened in 1792 with a variety of uses that included hall, church and the vitally important school of navigation. It then stood alone, with a flag displayed outside and a fine, pillared gateway.

Troon Road/Place, Ardler

In common with most streets in Ardler, was named after a golf course. Troon is on the Ayrshire coast

Tullideph Road

Remembers Dr Walter Tullideph, who owned the estate of Logie, Baldovan and Balgay. He was from an Aberdeenshire family, undertook medical training in Edinburgh and in 1726 sailed to Antigua to act as physician and factor. He borrowed money, married a widow named Mary Burroughs and inherited her 127-acre estate with its sixty-three slaves. He bought a number of estates from bankrupt owners and thus, as a major landowner, the most important attorney in Antigua, a shipowner and sugar merchant, became the richest man on the island. He also sent collections of Antiguan plants to London, where they now form part of the collection in the Natural History museum.

In 1739 he paid £10,000 for the Baldovan estate, with Baldovan hall being renamed Tullideph hall for a time. He also bought the estates of Balgay and Logie and later gave the Baldovan and Balgay estates to his daughters as wedding presents. Charlotte married John Ogilvy and received Baldovan estate; Mary married Colonel Alexander Leslie and was granted Balgay. Tullideph returned to Scotland in 1758 and lived off the profits of his West Indian estates, so Tullideph Road is probably the only Dundee street named after a slave owner.

Tummel Place

In common with many streets in the area, this one is named after a Scottish river, in this case the Tummel, which flows from Loch Rannoch to the river Tay.

Turnberry Avenue

Turnberry Avenue, Ardler

This street runs straight through Ardler and is named after Turnberry golf course in Ayrshire.

Tweed Crescent

Tweed Crescent, Menzieshill

Takes its name from the Tweed, a famous salmon river that flows through the Borders and in places marks the frontier between Scotland and England.

Ullapool Crescent

Ullapool is a small town on the shores of Loch Broom in Wester Ross and the ferry port for Stornoway in Lewis. The name is from the Norse, Ulla-Bolstadr, or 'Ulla's steading'.

Unicorn

HMS *Unicorn*

This frigate is the oldest British-built ship still afloat and experts consider she is the best preserved early-nineteenth-century wooden ship in the world. *Unicorn* was launched in 1824 at Chatham but never saw service on the world's oceans. After being used as a powder hulk, she came to Earl Grey dock in Dundee in 1873 to be used as a drill vessel.

During both world wars *Unicorn* was the headquarters of the naval officer-in-charge, Dundee. Three men held that position during the Second World War, including Rear Admiral Eric Robinson who had won a Victoria Cross in the Dardanelles during the First World War.

There was some consternation on *Unicorn* when the Navy gave an aircraft carrier the same name and a number of Royal Navy airmen arrived in Dundee expecting to see a modern vessel but instead were ushered to a ship that would have fitted well with Nelson's fleet at Trafalgar. After that incident the Dundee *Unicorn's* name was altered to the very unsuitable *Cressy* for the duration of the war but when the aircraft carrier was scrapped, her bell came to Dundee.

Unicorn also served as a temporary prison for German airmen who had been shot down off the coast of Fife. The first such action was in 1940 when a Hurricane claimed a German aircraft that had attacked a convoy. James Dickson of Broughty Ferry commanded the trawler *Shelomi* that rescued the German survivors. There were more prisoners in 1941, and, finally, in May 1945, U-2326 surfaced off the Tay and hoisted a black surrender flag. The U-boat was taken to the eastern wharf and the officers brought to *Unicorn* for questioning. The war had been over for a week.

There is a blue plaque on *Unicorn*, one of twenty-five around Dundee, each dedicated to the memory of a prominent Dundee woman. The plaque here is for Mary Buik, who joined the Royal Navy when her husband, a Cellardyke fisherman, was pressed into service at the beginning of the nineteenth century. She was present at the battles of Copenhagen and Trafalgar and helped embalm Nelson after the latter battle. Women in the Royal Navy helped tend the wounded in battle and often carried powder to the cannon.

When Earl Grey dock was filled in with the building of the Tay road bridge, *Unicorn* was threatened with the scrapyard but instead was taken to Victoria dock, where she still floats. She is fascinating to visit, reveals what life was like for early-nineteenth-century seaman and has a small shop. She is also used for functions. The Unicorn Preservation Society looks after this vessel.

Union Street

Built in 1828, the name has nothing to do with either Scotland's union with England or the union between Great Britain and Ireland. The street was named after the Union hall that was sited at the head of the street, although the street also united Craig Pier and the Nethergate. It was intended to be a quality street with high-class shops and flats above, similar to Newington in Edinburgh. In 1876 Union hall was demolished to widen Nethergate.

Union Street, Broughty Ferry
Named after the formation of the United Kingdom of Great Britain and Ireland after Ireland joined the union on 1 January 1801.

Upper Constitution Street
When the paving committee debated the name of this street in August 1854, there was considerable disagreement. The road leads from Constitution Street to the Law and it was originally proposed to name it Law Street, but others did not like the sound of the word 'Law'. One member of the committee suggested naming it after Provost Rough, as the street was in a 'rough state', but the provost dismissed that idea and eventually the present mundane, yet accurate, name was agreed.

Ure Street, Broughty Ferry
Remembers George Ure (1812–98) owner of Camphill lodge, who was a wine-and-spirit merchant and pigeon fancier.

Ure Street, Dundee
References a nursery garden owned by James Ure at the turn of the eighteenth and nineteenth centuries. His sons carried on the business, but it had ended by 1820.

Urquhart Street
Derives from the owner of large nursery gardens that once existed in this area. William Urquhart was a seedsman who owned the Dundee Nursery ground. He became a burgess in 1817, and the land passed to his second son, Daniel.

Verdant works, West Henderson's Wynd

Verdant Works Museum

This fine museum is dedicated to the jute trade and is situated in the former industrial area of Blackness. It is well worth a visit with its old machinery and a step-by-step account of how jute was transformed from a brittle plant imported from the Indian sub-continent to a textile used in sacks and bagging, wagon covers and tents. Keep at least a couple of hours aside for this establishment!

The building itself has an entrance courtyard and a chimney stack incorporated into the walls. The oldest part dates from 1833 but as the business expanded more buildings were added until it reached its present size in 1870, when the industry was at its height. Originally a flax mill, it altered to jute around 1850 and employed an impressive five hundred workers. Most were women or children, who had nimble fingers and drew less pay than men. In the mid-1880s jute experienced a downturn and the factory diversified into the likes of jute waste products. At that time Alexander Thompson and sons were the owners.

In the twentieth century it was used by a number of companies until in 1991 Dundee Heritage Trust bought the site and created the museum. Some of the machinery was brought from what is now Abertay University, whose predecessor Dundee College of Technology ran courses in textiles for a century. As this is being written (2016) there is an ongoing project by Dundee Heritage Trust to extend the museum by developing the adjacent High Mill.

Victoria docks
Commemorates Queen Victoria. It once thronged with jute ships, whaling ships, coasters and Baltic traders. Now it is home to *Unicorn*, the Quay shopping complex and the *North Carr* lightship. On the west side stands the welcoming Apex hotel.

Victoria park

Victoria Park

Named after Queen Victoria, this park is on the southern side of Balgay hill and has a very pleasant atmosphere with flower beds, rose gardens and mature trees. The path that circles Balgay hill is home to squirrels and the occasional fox.

Victoria Road

Another street that honours the Queen-Empress. Its predecessor was known as Bucklemaker Wynd and was a major highway but too narrow for the volume of traffic it had to carry. Improvements were needed and Bucklemaker Wynd was widened. By that time the bucklemakers had long gone; in their prime they had made buckles for shoes, sword belts and saddles.

Victoria Road, West Ferry

Victoria Road, West Ferry

There is a weather-worn plaque in Victoria Road stating that Princess Charlotte Augusta – only daughter of George IV and in line for the throne – gave birth to a stillborn child here and then died the following day.

The Dundee version of events is that, in 1817, Charlotte and her husband, Prince Leopold of Saxe-Coburg, had been visiting Germany but she wanted to return home for the birth of her child. A storm forced their ship to seek shelter in the Firth of Tay – a not uncommon occurrence – and the disturbance forced Charlotte into labour. She was rushed ashore and gave birth in a West Ferry cottage, where both mother and child died. The remains of the princess and her child were rushed off to Windsor and the story was hushed up and altered to the 'official' line, which holds that the princess died in just such tragic circumstances but in Windsor.

The true facts may never be known.

Victoria statue, Albert Square
Erected in 1899 as a tribute for Queen Victoria's diamond jubilee. Harry Bates (1850–99) was the sculptor.

Victoria and Albert museum
Due to open in 2018, this branch of the eminent London museum will be a tremendous asset to the city. The museum is a centrepiece of the Waterfront development, next to *Discovery*. It is to be the only museum of design in the country outside of London with Kengo Kuma as the architect, his British building. The museum will showcase both Scottish and international design.

Vine, the

The Vine

This truly amazing building at 43 Magdalen Yard Road dates from the 1830s. It was created as a combined house and art gallery for the eccentric MP, George Duncan (1791–1878), who wore full court dress to greet Queen Victoria when she came to Dundee. The building has superb classical detail and is elevated to provide splendid views over the Firth of Tay. The interior has a domed hall with ionic columns. It is presently a meeting room and function suite.

Viscount's Pend, Claverhouse
Another street named after John Grahame, Viscount Dundee.

Vorlich Drive
The streets in this part of Barnhill were named after Scottish mountains. At 985

metres Ben Vorlich ranks as a Munro and as it is near the central belt is deservedly popular with weekend mountaineers.

Walker Street, Broughty Ferry

The shortest street in the Ferry is named after Robert Walker, a councillor and coal merchant. In 1887 he was one of a number of people who volunteered to find subscriptions to enable the 'deserving poor' of the Ferry celebrate Queen Victoria's jubilee.

Wallace Street

Although William Wallace was said to have been educated in Dundee, this street has no connection with the great Scottish patriot. Rather it was named after the estate of Wallace Craigie.

Wallace Craigie Works, Blackscroft

This B-listed building has been an eyesore for some time as it slowly crumbled into ruin but in 2014 it was decided to restore and transform it into flats. The owners, Craigie Estates, planned the restoration for years but the financial crisis delayed the project. The façade of the works, also known as Halley's mill, is readily identifiable with its gold lettering on red brick, and will be central to an area of high-quality housing.

The mill was built in 1835–6, employing hundreds of workers, and was the last surviving independent jute mill in Dundee. William Halley was originally a flax manufacturer but became one of the owners of Wallace Craigie works, which expanded significantly during the American Civil War. The firm of William Halley remained owners until 2004 when the factory and its outbuildings shut down.

Ward Road

A ward was an enclosed pasture, although the meaning later altered to an administrative area, as in a voting ward. The wards became public recreation ground that stretched from Guthrie Street to Barrack Street and were surrounded by a stone wall. This was open land until Ward mill was built in the early nineteenth century. The mill operated for decades but the original lengthy street has been truncated by the inner ring road.

Ward Road once held an industrial school to which boys and girls were sent if they had strayed from the path of righteousness, were homeless or because their parents could not afford to keep them.

Waterfront Place

With the development at the waterfront, new streets are being created. The

Dundee public were asked their opinions for new names and around five hundred were suggested, from which the best were chosen. The new public space beside the river will be known as Waterfront Place. Most of the land in the Waterfront development area is owned by the council and the buildings will be design-led in accordance with Dundee's enhanced status as the UK's first Unesco City of Design.

Watson Street housing
In 1981 this housing group won a Saltire Society award and in 2012 the sheltered housing in this street won a food-hygiene award.

Watt institution
James Brown, one of Dundee's major flax spinners, was the driving force behind this institution. It was founded on 11 November 1824 as the Mechanic's institute, with Provost Anderson as a major backer. Initially in Barrack Street, it was an educational institute for skilled workers and gave a series of lectures for an annual subscription of ten shillings. In 1838 the institution moved to Constitution Road. The elegant neoclassical building contained a thousand-volume library, lecture theatre, museum and laboratory. It closed for financial reasons, but this, Dundee's tentative dip into higher education, was not forgotten and laid the groundwork for the later universities.

Waverley Terrace
Sir Walter Scott's *Waverley* novels put the country firmly on the tourist trail and helped create the tartan, romantic scenery and shortbread image of the nation that even some Scots have. The books were so popular that streets, such as this one, were named in their honour.

Weavers Yard, between Princes Street and Victoria Road
Sits on the site where the Dens works were, a reminder of the importance of weavers to Dundee. Dens works were founded in 1822 and became the largest linen sailcloth and canvas manufacturers in the world.

Wedderburn Street/Place, off Strathmartine Road
Wedderburn is a name that has been associated with Dundee for centuries. It is fitting that these streets should carry the name of a family that supplied generations of town clerks.

Wellburn Street, Lochee
Takes its name from Wellburn house, where the Little Sisters of the Poor did so much dedicated work.

Wellcome Trust biocentre building

College of Life Sciences, Wellcome Trust, University of Dundee

A centre for medical research, the Wellcome Trust building is prominent inside Dundee University campus. The interior has a beautiful curved staircase and there is a three-floor-high stained-glass window by Julian Stocks with the title of Uses of Disorder.

The biocentre was established in Dundee in 1997, helped by a £10 million donation from the Wellcome Trust, which was believed to be the largest charitable donation to an institution in Scotland. A further £3 million came from other donors. The centre has an international reputation and employs over two hundred researchers and support staff in impressive surroundings.

Wellgate centre

Wellgate Centre

One of Dundee's central shopping areas, the Wellgate centre occupies the site of the old Well gait, or the road to the Lady Well. The lady in question was St Mary, the mother of Jesus Christ, who is the patron saint of Dundee, although the full Dundee title was 'the well of the Blessed Maria of Dundee', which is very colourful. There was once a Wellgait Port, a gate, here to provide access to the city but one which could be closed and locked to keep out these outsiders from Rotten Row – the Hilltown – who were reputed to cause trouble in Dundee. The Wellgate port was one of Dundee's ten ports or gates.

Originally, the well was outside the town boundary but in 1409 Sir James Scrymgeour of Dudhope allowed access. Until 1836 St Mary's well was Dundee's main water supply, where water caddies collected their water and sold it at a penny for ten gallons to the good people of the burgh.

Today the Wellgate centre contains a host of shops, restaurants and Dundee's central library. It is a bustling place, sheltered from the city's sometimes inclement weather.

Wellington Street
Commemorates the Duke of Wellington (1769–1852), the victor of Waterloo and other battles of the Napoleonic Wars. He was also prime minister from 1828–30. This street was named at the same time as Nelson Street.

West Ferry
At one time, West Ferry was one of the richest suburbs in the country as the jute barons built their mansions here. It was close enough to Dundee for an easy daily commute but far enough away to escape the bustle of the city. Time and dry rot have swept away many of the more elaborate mansions, but much of the atmosphere of quiet affluence survives, enhanced by high stone walls surmounted by the branches of mature trees. In the 1930s, when car ownership was nothing like as widespread as it is today, it was common to see Rolls Royce cars in West Ferry, which must have made the visitor believe that the area was incredibly wealthy. So much for appearances: a local taxi firm, owned by a man named Robertson, used Rolls Royces as taxis.

West Ferry begins at the prosaic Craigie Drive roundabout (or 'circle' as many Dundonians insist on calling it) and the name is pretty obvious: the western extension of Broughty Ferry. It is a major conservation area.

West Marketgate
Part of Dundee's inner ring road, this street has retained the historic name of Marketgate but has no connection to any market; it is well to the west of the original Marketgait. West Marketgate runs past Taymills and the police station. Opposite Taymills is a red-and-white sculpture of a water derrick to remind

people that the old Scouring burn is culverted under their feet. The sculpture is by Chris Kelly and Chris Biddlecombe, both of whom graduated from Duncan of Jordanstone College of Art.

West Park Road

Takes its name from the mansion of West Park, which was situated slightly to the east of the street. When Alexander Henderson lived there in the 1870s, his gardener, George Farquhar, was a frequent winner at local flower shows with his begonias and carnations. Henderson was the proprietor of South Dudhope mill and gave donations to charity including the DRI and the School of Art. In 1863 he financed a benefit concert at the Thistle hall in aid of an employee who was unfit to work. He was very active in the Free Church in Dundee and in organising a mission station in Africa in memory of David Livingstone. Mrs Henderson was involved in fundraising for the Free Church in Broadford, Skye.

West Port

The name comes from the western port, or gateway, into Dundee, which was situated at the end of the Overgait. The port was approximately where the West Port roundabout is now situated, but it was demolished in 1757. This port had some interesting history, for example when Mary, Queen of Scots visited Dundee in 1561, the provost and baillies of the town ceremonially handed her the keys at the West Port. There was also Dr Patrick Blair, he of elephant fame, who established a museum – called a Cabinet of Curiosities – and a botanical garden in this vicinity while the sloping ground around was filled with market gardens in pre- or early-industrial Dundee.

There is also a legend that after William Wallace killed the son of Governor Selbie, he made his exit from the West Port and escaped into the Carse of Gowrie.

Westcroft Place/Road

The name literally means the croft on the west, with a croft being a small parcel of land used as a farm, usually rented. It is a more common term in the Highlands, with the local name being a pendicle.

Westfield Lane/Place

Take their name from a small village that was here. The name speaks for itself, 'fields west of Dundee'.

Westfield Road, Broughty Ferry

Named after Westfield house. Mr McEwan of Westfield house gave money to the industrial school in 1852. Mr Pattullo of the same address donated greens to the soup kitchens in 1859.

Whaler's Lane

With the new development at the Riverside, there are a number of new streets. The public was asked for suggestions and a panel chose those considered most suitable. The new path beside the Tay road bridge will be known as Whaler's Lane, reflecting the whaling heritage of the city. Dundee sent whaling vessels to the Arctic from the 1750s to 1914 and at one time was the largest whaling port in Britain. Dundee also built the finest whaling ships in the world, with polar explorers actively seeking Dundee vessels for their voyages.

Whinny Brae, Broughty Ferry

A *whin* is an evergreen shrub and a *brae* is a hill slope so this was a slope covered in shrubs.

Whitefauld Road

A *fauld* was an enclosed area, a fold or pen, in which cattle were held for milking, or the part of an outfield in which cattle were held until they had manured the ground. The name suggests that the field could be unploughed land or land covered with bent or natural uncultivated grass; such fields were sometimes known as white fields.

Whitehall Street

Whitehall Street

Designed after the 1871 Improvement Act but not opened until 1883. It sits on top of what used to be mediaeval Dundee on a site once occupied by ancient closes and mansions. In August 1882 the paving committee decided that Whitehall Street and Whitehall Crescent should be named, 'in perpetuation of the name of one of the closes leading from the Nethergate to Fish Street'. One of the old mansions was built by Sir Patrick Lyon, a seventeenth-century royalist. When Charles II was restored to his throne in 1660, Lyon altered the name of his house to Whitehall in honour of the king, and adorned his doorway with the royal arms. The name remains.

There is a tradition that there was a mediaeval palace on this site from the days when King Malcolm Canmore married Princess, later Saint, Margaret in 1070. If true that would bring Dundee very much into the centre of mediaeval Scottish court life; alas there is no proof. However, David, Earl of Huntingdon, the brother of King William the Lion, was deeply involved with Dundee in the following century, so the royal connection was strong.

Whitehall theatre, 12 Bellfield Street

A busy theatre in the heart of the city that hosts a variety of acts from musicals to comedy. In 1890 a gentleman named John Young established this theatre as the Alhambra, which, at its peak, could hold 1,100 people. Young also operated the Tivoli theatre in Brown Street (which unfortunately burned down in 1924), and the Excelsior in the Exchange building in the 1880s.

Yorkshireman Arthur Henderson took over the Alhambra in the 1920s and converted it to a picture house and in the 1940s the name changed to the State cinema. When the council took ownership in 1969 it became a civic community theatre and today it is the Whitehall, operated by the Whitehall Theatre Trust, with seven-hundred seats.

Whitfield

A large peripheral housing scheme to the north of the city. The name simply means 'white field' or 'field of the bent grass'. Many of the streets in Whitfield have the prefix 'whit'. The estate was built in the 1960s, but, in common with many such developments of the period, ideas that appeared good at the time proved to be less than viable in the Scottish climate. There were two high-rise tower blocks that have since been demolished as the area was selected for a major development programme.

Arguably the most high-profile person to come from Whitfield is Elizabeth McColgan-Nuttall, better known as Liz McColgan, who was born Elizabeth Lynch and went to St Saviour's high school. McColgan's achievements are incredible. They include a silver medal for the 10,000 metres at the 1988 Seoul Olympics and a gold medal for same distance at the 1991 world championships in Tokyo. In perhaps her most emotionally charged race she took gold at the 1986 Commonwealth Games in Edinburgh in front of thousands of her adoring fellow Scots. She was the third woman in history to run the 10,000 in under thirty-one minutes. Whitfield, Dundee and Scotland should be proud.

William Barclay Square
Commemorates the Wick-born theologian William Barclay (1907–78). He was an author, lecturer at Glasgow university and a television presenter. He wrote the *Daily Study Bible*, published by the St Andrew Press. There are theologians who disagree with some of his teachings, but there is no doubt that he was an engaging writer.

William Fitzgerald Way
Dr Fitzgerald (1901–91) was Lord Provost of Dundee from 1970–3. He was also the Conservative candidate for Dundee in the 1973 by-election.

William Street, Maxwelltown
Around 1780, David Maxwell of Tealing, the Lord Dean of Guild, bought this land and had it laid out for streets. He insisted that each street was named after a member of his family, with William Street named for a male relative.

Willison Street
Remembers the Rev John Willison (1680–1750) who preached at the South church in Dundee from 1716 to his death in 1750. He campaigned against the system of patronage and was a vocal opponent of the Jacobite rising of 1745.

Wimberley Court, Broughty Ferry
Commemorates Major General Douglas 'Tartan Tam' Neil Wimberley MC (1896–1983). He won his Military Cross with the Cameron Highlanders at the Battle of Cambrai in 1917 and also served in Russia, Ireland and on the North-West Frontier. During the Second World War he led the 51st Highland division at the Battle of El Alamein in 1942 and thereafter in the advance across North Africa and into Sicily. Born in Inverness, he became principal of University College, Dundee and died in Coupar Angus. He was a very 'highland' Highland soldier.

Windmill Garden, Broughty Ferry
Named after a windmill that powered a joiner's workshop. In January 2015 a tribute to victims of the Holocaust was unveiled.

Windsor Street
Taking its name from the royal palace of Windsor, this street contains some fine architecture as it slopes down from Perth Road and invites admiring glances to the open vistas of the Tay and beyond to Fife. As the name suggests, this is a high-quality street.

There is also a Windsor Terrace that is part of Perth Road, west of Sinderins.

Windsor Street

Wishart's arch

Wishart's Arch

This was the East Port, the only town port, or gate, to survive to the present day, along with a tiny fragment of the old City Wall. It gets its name from the story that the Protestant minister, George Wishart (1513–46), preached here. The tale states that Wishart remained inside the city and preached to an audience who had plague and had to stay on the other side of the wall. Unfortunately for this account, Wishart was burned as a heretic in 1546 and these town walls date from the 1590s. The remainder of the walls were taken down in 1746.

Wishart memorial church, King Street
Mary Slessor the missionary taught at the Sunday School here. The area was known as Heaven and Hell, with the church above and a pub, the John o' Groats, situated below.

Wishart Street
This also commemorates the Protestant reformer and martyr, George Wishart, who was born in Angus, north of Dundee, in 1513. He became a schoolteacher in Montrose but when he was accused of heresy for teaching the New Testament he moved to England and then to Germany and Switzerland, where he studied with the Calvinists. Returning to Scotland in 1543, and assisted by John Knox, he proselytised for the growing religion of Protestantism. When Wishart preached the Protestant faith in Dundee and other places, Cardinal Beaton had him tried and then burned at the stake in St Andrews in 1546.

Wolseley Street
The works commission of the council sanctioned this street in July 1874. It was to be a 'new street, fifty feet wide on the Clepington Estate, and running from the north side of Dundonald Street'. It is most likely the street was named after Field Marshal Sir Garnet Wolseley, one of Britain's most successful Victorian generals, who had recently emerged victorious from the Ashanti campaign in west Africa. Wolseley took an army inland from the coast, capturing the Ashanti capital of Kumasi on 4 February 1874. He oversaw the battle from a hammock carried by four soldiers, puffing nonchalantly on a cigar as enemy bullets whizzed past. He was more fortunate than a previous British general, Charles McCarthy, whom the Ashantis decapitated, before decorating his skull for use as a drinking cup.

Wolseley was a national hero renowned for his meticulous planning. So much so that the saying 'all Sir Garnet' was the late-nineteenth-century equivalent of 'okay' or 'everything is perfect'. The Black Watch, Dundee's own regiment, took part in that Ashanti war and was commemorated with a song, one version of which contains the following lines:

March past, the forty-second,
March past, the forty-twa'
March past, the bare-arsed buggers
Comin' frae the Ashanti war

Garnet Wolseley's passion for innovation led him to press continually for military reform. Such was his persistence that he became the inspiration for Gilbert and Sullivan's 'very model of a modern major-general', in the operetta, *The Pirates of Penzance*.

Woodlands Gardens, Broughty Ferry
Takes its name from the Woodlands hotel in whose grounds the street was built.

Woodside
A small residential area in the north of Dundee with mainly four-in-a-block housing built in the 1920s.

Wurzburg Court/Lane
Named after Dundee's twin city in Germany. Wurzburg is over a thousand years old and was the home of prince-bishops at a time when Germany was divided into hundreds of small states. Wurzburg was the capital of the duchy of Franconia but is now part of Bavaria. The city boasts a UNESCO world-heritage site in the palace of the prince-bishops.

Wyvis Place
At 1,046 metres, Ben Wyvis is the tallest mountain in the northeast of Scotland. The name is said to mean Hill of Terror.

Yeaman Shore

Yeaman Shore

Once a very important thoroughfare from Nethergate to the harbour. The shore part is obvious as it was by the Tay, while the Yeamans were a local family with property at Dryburgh near Lochee. A. H. Millar believed they had a house here. George Yeaman was provost of Dundee from 1706 until 1708 and then from 1710 until 1712. The howff has a seventeenth-century sandstone memorial to the Yeaman (spelled Zeaman) family.

Now firmly inland, Yeaman Shore was once lapped by the Tay. Dundee theatre was also here and by the end of the eighteenth century there were busy shipbuilding yards stretching along Dundee's shoreline to Dock Street. For example, in the first week of May 1848, Calman and Martin's yard at Marine Parade launched two full-rigged brigs, John Calman's yard launched a schooner, Adamson's Yard launched two barges and Brown's yard at the back of the custom house launched a brig. There was also boatbuilding. Livies of Dundee is arguably the best-remembered boatbuilder, but, in 1884, Pearce Brothers built fifty boats for the Nile expedition to rescue General Gordon from Khartoum and John Brown built a further four.

Yewbank Avenue, Broughty Ferry
Built on the site of the mansion of Yewbank, home to the corn dealer George Harrower. When Harrower went bankrupt his house was sequestered and his wife left him. Obviously she had misread the 'for better or worse' part of the marriage contract.

L'Envoi
So there we have Dundee. A city with a history of merchant princes and close communities, of great fleets of jute ships and bearded whaling men, of sieges and beheadings, battles and marmalade, journalism and engineers, patronage and politics, penguins, dragons and elephants. It is a city of great personalities from the fictional Desperate Dan and James Bond to the brave Admiral Duncan and Mary Slessor. It was in Dundee that Churchill faced the Suffragettes, Kinloch argued for electoral reform and one of Scotland's first railways chugged its way northward to Newtyle. The academics and inventors made their name here: Patrick Geddes and Watson Watt to name but two.

There were vocal mill girls and aeronautical pioneers, medical pioneers and a legend that Jack the Ripper ended his life at the end of a Dundee rope. This is the spiritual home of the Black Watch, that most Scottish of regiments and a city in which immigrants from Ireland made their home. This is a city whose sporting legacy includes cricket and curling, racing and yachting, boxing, wrestling and the ubiquitous football.

There were riots and meetings, striking workers and a bridge that collapsed but overall Dundee has a light that reflects from the Tay on one of the most fascinating cities anywhere in Europe. Always and everywhere, the character of the people made and makes Dundee what it is. Where else are there such warm-hearted people who accept strangers with an open hand and a smile? Dundee accepts all and treats visitors with friendliness and hospitality. That is something that far larger and outwardly grander cities often lack; it is a sign of inner strength.

And what of the future? What does the twenty-first and succeeding centuries hold for Dundee? That is yet to be seen, but one thing is certain: given this city's reputation for innovation and adaptability, Dundee will embrace what comes and react with dynamism. More than that, Dundee will forge her own future as she has created her own past. It is a city of which her citizens should be proud and one that others should treat with respect.

In December 2014 Dundee was named a Unesco City of Design, one of only thirteen in the world; a major coup for a city once renowned for post-industrial decline. The last word should go to the Scottish Government Secretary for Culture, Europe and External Affairs, Fiona Hyslop, who said:

> Warm congratulations must go to everyone who has played a part in bringing this prestigious UNESCO City of Design accolade to Dundee, and indeed Scotland.
>
> This is a richly deserved accolade and further strengthens the city's growing reputation as a hub of cultural and creative excellence and an international centre for the creative industries. She sits by the waters of the Tay and under the shelter of the Law, facing south and extending her arms in welcome. She is waiting; she is ready; she is Dundee

Select Bibliography

Anson, Peter *Fishing Boats and Fisher Folk on the East Coast of Scotland* (J. M. Dent and Sons Ltd, 1930, 1971)

Archibald, Malcolm *Ardler: a thriving community* (Ardler Village Trust, 2008)

Archibald, Malcolm, *A Sink of Atrocity: Crime in Nineteenth Century Dundee*, (Black & White Publishing, 2012)

Archibald, Malcolm *The Dundee Whaling Fleet: Ships, Masters and Men* (Dundee University Press, 2013)

Archibald, Malcolm, *Whalehunters*, (Mercat Press, 2004)

Barrow, G. W. S. *Robert Bruce and the Community of the Realm of Scotland* (Edinburgh University Press, 1976)

Beatts, J. M. *Reminiscences of a Dundonian*, (J. M. Beatts, 1883)

Caledonian Mercury

Cameron, David Kerr *The Ballad and the Plough*, (Victor Gollancz, 1978)

Cockburn, Lord *Circuit Journeys*, (Byway Books, 1983)

Cruden, Stewart *The Scottish Castle*, (Spurbooks, 1981)

Dorward, David *Dundee: Names, People and Places* (Mercat Press, 1998)

Dorward, David *The Glens of Angus: Names, Places, People* (Pinkfoot Press, 2001)

Dorward, David *The Sidlaw Hills* (Pinkfoot Press, 2004)

Duncan, Neil *Duncan of Camperdown* (Craig-Niven Books, 1995)

Dundee Directory, the various dates

Dundee Courier and Advertiser

Glendinning, Miles (editor) *Rebuilding Scotland, the Postwar Vision 1945–1975* (Tuckwell Press, 1997)

Glendinning, Miles, MacInnes, Ranald & MacKechnie, Aonghus, *A History of Scottish Architecture* (Edinburgh University Press, 1996)

Kidd, William *The Dundee Market Crosses & Tollbooths*, (William Kidd, 1901)

King, Brian *Dundee Through Time* (Amberley Publishing, 2014)

Knox, William *Lives of Scottish Women: Women and Scottish Society 1800–1980* (Edinburgh University Press, 2006)

Linklater, Magnus and Hesketh, Christian *John Graham of Claverhouse, Bonnie Dundee: For King and Conscience*, (Canongate, 1992)

Maan, Bashir *The New Scots: The Story of Asians in Scotland* (John Donald, 1992)

MacDougall, Norman *An Antidote to the English* (Tuckwell, 2001)

McCraw, Iain *The Fairs of Dundee*, (Abertay Historical Society, Dundee, 1994)

McKean, Charles *Battle for the North: the Tay and Forth Bridges and the Nineteenth-Century Railway Wars*, (Granta books, 2006)

McKean, Charles, Whatley, Patricia and Baxter, Kenneth *Lost Dundee: Dundee's Lost Architectural Heritage* (Birlinn, 2008)

McKean, Charles, Harris, Bob and Whatley, Christopher A. *Dundee: Renaissance to Enlightenment* (Dundee University Press, 2009)

McKean, Charles and Walker, David *Dundee an Illustrated Introduction*, (Royal Corporation of Architects/Scottish Academic Press, 1984)

McKean, Charles *The Scottish Chateau*, (Sutton, 2001)

Millar, A. H. *Glimpses of Old and New Dundee* (Malcolm Macleod, 1925)

Miller, James *Salt in the Blood: Scotland's Fishing Communities Past and Present* (Canongate, 1999)

Miskell, L., Whatley, C., and Harris, R. *Victorian Dundee: Image and Reality*, (Tuckwell Press, 2000)

Nicoll, Andrew Strachan and Walker, Stuart Francis *Dundee Closes Study*, (Dundee Civic Trust, 2003)

Nicolaisen, W. F. H. 'Place Names of the Dundee Region' in Jones, S. J.(ed.), *Dundee and District*, (Dundee Local Executive Committee, 1968)

Parker, John *Black Watch* (Headline Books, London, 2005)

Paterson, Raymond Campbell *For the Lion* (John Donald, 1996)

Pennant, Thomas *A Tour in Scotland and Voyage to the Hebrides 1772* (Birlinn, 1998)

Robertson, Hamish *Mariners of Dundee: Their City, Their River, Their Fraternity*, (PDQ Print Services, 2006)

Robinson, Mairi, (ed.) *The Concise Scots Dictionary* (Aberdeen University Press, 1985)

Roe, M. 'George Mealmaker, the Forgotten Martyr', *Journal and Proceedings* (Royal Australian Historical Society), vol 43, part 6, 1957, pp 284–98

Scott, Andrew Murray *Modern Dundee: Life in the City Since World War Two*, (Breedon Books, 2002)

Shafe, Michael, *University Education in Dundee 1881–1981*: a Pictorial History (University of Dundee, 1982)

Small, Gordon, *The Lengs: Dundee's Other Publishing Dynasty* (Tay Valley Family History Society, n.d.)

Smout, T. C. *A History of the Scottish People 1560–1830* (Collins, 1969)

Stevenson, David, *Revolution and Counter Revolution in Scotland 1644–1651* (John Donald, 2003)

Stewart, Bob, *Breaking the Fetters* (Lawrence & Wishart, 1967)

Szasz, Ferenc Morton, *Scots in the North American West 1790–1917* (University of Oklahoma Press, 2000)

The Scotsman

Torry, Elizabeth P. D. *Mediaeval Dundee: A town and its people* (Abertay Historical Society, 1990)

Watson, Mark *Tayside and Deeside Tour Notes compiled for the 40th conference for the Association of Industrial Archaeology, held at Dundee in August 2013*

Webster, Callum, *What's in a Name: a Street History of Broughty Ferry*, (Dundee Civic Trust, 2014)

Whatley, Christopher A. Swinfen, David B., Smith, Annette M. *The Life and Times of Dundee*, (John Donald, 1993)

Whatley, Christopher A. *The Remaking of Juteopolis: Dundee circa 1891–1991*, (Abertay Historical Society, 1992)

Whatley, Christopher A *Diary of John Sturrock; Millwright Dundee 1864–65* (Tuckwell Press, 1996)

Primary Sources

Dundee Archives

Agriculture and Fishery Records

Custom and Excise Records: Dundee, Letter Book, Collector to Board

Dundee Police Commissioners Minute Book 1877–1879

Dundee Paving Committee

The Dundee Police and Improvement Act 1871: Dundee city archives TC/LAP/48

Dundee University Archives

John P. Ingram Papers (MS 73/26)

Lennox, Dr David *Working Class Life in Dundee for 25 Years* (MS 15/28/2)

Selected Websites:

www.broughtyferrycommunitycouncil.org

http://www.leisureandculturedundee.com/library/localhistory: various dates

www.downfieldgolf.co.uk

http://maps.nls.uk/view/74400021

http://www.fdca.org.uk/index.html: various dates

http://www.fdca.org.uk/Staple_Trade.html: various dates

http://ninetradesofdundee.co.uk/maltmen/

http://highmillproject.com/project/gallery-1/Accessed 01/06/2015 06.45

http://www.archidarchitects.co.uk/development-highmill-court.html: Accessed 31 May 2015

https://banneroftruth.org/uk/resources/articles/2008/robert-annan-a-trophy-of-grace/

accessed 19 July 2015